Congress, the President, and Public Policy

TRANSFORMING AMERICAN POLITICS SERIES
Lawrence C. Dodd, Series Editor

Dramatic changes in political institutions and behavior over the past two decades have underscored the dynamic nature of American politics, confronting political scientists with a new and pressing intellectual agenda.

Transforming American Politics is dedicated to documenting these changes, reinterpreting conventional wisdoms, tracing historical patterns of change, and asserting new theories to clarify the direction of contemporary politics.

TITLES IN THIS SERIES

Congress, the President, and Public Policy

Michael L. Mezey
DePaul University

Westview Press
BOULDER, SAN FRANCISCO, & LONDON

Transforming American Politics Series

Portions of Chapters 1 and 5 originally appeared in "The Legislature, the Executive, and Public Policy: The Futile Quest for Congressional Power," *Congress and the Presidency: A Journal of Capital Studies* 13, no. 1 (Spring 1986). Reprinted here by agreement with *Congress and the Presidency: A Journal of Capital Studies*.

Published in 1989 in the United States of America by Westview Press, Inc., 5500 Central Avenue, Boulder, Colorado 80301, and in the United Kingdom by Westview Press, Inc., 13 Brunswick Centre, London WC1N 1AF, England

Library of Congress Cataloging-in-Publication Data
Mezey, Michael L.
  Congress, the President, and public policy / Michael L. Mezey.
    p. cm.—(Transforming American politics series)
  Bibliography: p.
  Includes index.
  ISBN 0-8133-0493-8. ISBN 0-8133-0494-6 (pbk.)
  1. Presidents—United States. 2. United States. Congress.
I. Title. II. Series.
JK585.M49 1989
353.03′23—dc20   89-32834
                                                              CIP

Printed and bound in the United States of America

The paper used in this publication meets the requirements of the American National Standard for Permanence of Paper for Printed Library Materials Z39.48-1984.

10   9   8   7   6   5   4   3   2   1

For Susan

Contents

Tables

xi

Preface

The relationship between the president and the Congress has been under discussion as long as the U.S. Constitution has existed. It has been a discussion in which presidents, congressional leaders, Supreme Court justices, scholars from many disciplines, political pundits of all stripes, and ordinary citizens of every sort have participated. For many of the participants, the point of the discussion has been to understand who governs or who should govern, the president or the Congress, and what techniques and resources each of these institutions has at its disposal to work its will upon the other. Although I will touch upon certain of these topics, they are not the point of the discussion to be found in this book. My concern is not who governs but rather how we are governed, how good or bad our public policies are, and how the quality of those policies is affected by the manner in which the president and the Congress share political power.

The argument of this book is that the current relationship between the president and the Congress has adversely affected the capacity of the U.S. political system to produce good public policy. More often than not, the president and the Congress find themselves in a stalemate about what should be done, or else the solutions that they are able to agree to or that they allow to go into effect without their agreement fail to meet either managerial or democratic criteria for good public policy. And whereas it is clear that these twin tendencies toward stalemate or poor public policy have become more pronounced in recent decades, it is equally clear that this state of affairs cannot be attributed, as it often is, simply to the bad presidents, or the self-seeking legislators, or the more intractable policy problems that many believe we have experienced over the past thirty years or so. Rather, our inability to produce good public policy is rooted in our constitutional arrangement of separate political institutions sharing power and in our political culture, which is inclined to view government more in malevolent than in benevolent terms. Although it would be fine to have better presidents, more public-spirited legislators, and easier policy problems, even if we had, stalemate and poor public policy would still characterize our political system. The

United States will not have a government capable of achieving good public policy until the American people change the way in which they think about government and, based on that rethinking, make changes in their political institutions.

My "first draft" of the argument of this book was presented in an article entitled "The Legislature, the Executive, and Public Policy: The Futile Quest for Congressional Power," which Susan Webb Hammond of American University agreed to print in the fine journal that she coedits with Jeff Fishel, *Congress and the Presidency*. The frankly critical and prescriptive tone of the article would have made it unacceptable to most scholarly journals, but Sukie recognized the need for scholars to address these systemic issues. Her only condition, to which I readily agreed, was that a response to my article be printed in the same issue. But after reading the highly critical response, by Joseph Cooper of Rice University, I wasn't at all certain that I had made a particularly good deal. Nonetheless, Joe's comments, for all their acerbity, alerted me to several problems in my initial analysis, and what I say in the pages that follow is stronger because Joe's critique was as scathing as it was.

During the two years that this book has been in the writing, my friends and colleagues at DePaul University have been a continuing source of personal and intellectual support for me. Dick Meister, dean of the College of Liberal Arts and Sciences, more than anyone else, made this book possible by agreeing to an arrangement of my time that allowed me to write while at the same time functioning as his associate dean. I am more grateful than I can say for his support. Although they do not share my somewhat old-fashioned concern for political institutions, Harry Wray, Jim Block, and Larry Bennett have always been willing to share their knowledge of U.S. politics with me and to hear my ideas as well. I am also pleased to acknowledge a grant from DePaul's University Research Council, which enabled me to hire Carissa Scanlan, then an undergraduate student at DePaul, to track down some of the information contained in Chapter 6. The Senior Honors thesis of one of my students, Paul De Bella, also helped with part of Chapter 6 and is more fully acknowledged in the notes to that chapter.

Shortly after the *Congress and the Presidency* article came out, I developed a proposal for this book, which I sent to a number of publishers, and several of them expressed interest. But Miriam Gilbert and Holly Arrow at Westview Press were unique in telling me to write the book that I had in mind, rather than the book that they might have had in mind, and once contracting with me to do just that, they left me alone to do my work. Holly, who believed in this book before anyone else did (including me), left Westview early on in this project, but her replacement, Jennifer Knerr, was also unfailingly encouraging and upbeat (presumably a job requirement at Westview). Jennifer also efficiently attended to the various tasks of arranging for scholars to read the manuscript, collecting their advice, channeling all of that back to me, leaning on me to make the manuscript shorter (and it took a great deal of leaning), and seeing the whole package off to Westview's editorial production staff. Fortunately, upon its arrival there, my manuscript fell into the gentle hands of Marian Safran, an extraordinarily capable copy editor. Marian's skills and attention to detail saved me from countless errors in content and syntax, and for that I am very grateful. I am grateful as well for the suggestions that I received from Larry Dodd, Richard Fleischer, and Paul Brace, all of whom read and commented on my first draft. Naturally, all four of these good people are absolved from blame for any errors and misinterpretations that remain.

Those who live with people who write understand all too well Emily Dickinson's assertion that she hated to write but loved having written. As Dickinson could have predicted, my mood fluctuated with the progress of the book, but through it all my family proved to be consistently inspiring and supportive. Whereas some spouses make one feel guilty for taking time to write, my wife, Susan, a perpetually active scholar, made me feel guilty for not writing, and after a prolonged period in which I always seemed able to find other things to do, it was at her urging that I undertook this project. My daughter, Jennifer, a college sophomore and journalist, with genuine political convictions upon which she frequently speaks, writes, and acts, convinced me by her example that there were students who would care about my theme of good government. My son, Jason, a high school senior and accomplished writer, with a highly developed sense of the absurd, provided the comic relief. No matter how I was feeling about the book, Jason always could make me laugh and, by that simple service, remind me of what is truly important.

Michael L. Mezey
Chicago, Illinois

1

Political Institutions and Public Policy

On the day that George Bush was inaugurated as the forty-first president of the United States, he called for a "new engagement" between the president and the Congress, which would put an end to the political bickering that had come to characterize the relationship between the two institutions. Working together, Bush suggested, he and the Congress could meet the complex policy problems that the nation faced. The congressional leadership responded warmly to the president's inaugural address. "Bush is extending the hand of friendship," said Senate Majority Leader George Mitchell, "and we intend to extend ours in return."

Did the optimistic tone of inauguration day really signal the beginning of a new and more productive relationship between the president and the Congress, a relationship characterized by cooperation rather than by continuous conflict and stalemate? By the time that you read these words, the Bush administration will be well through its first year, so you will be in a somewhat better position than I am now, at the very beginning of Bush's presidency, to answer this question. But at the risk of sounding like a pessimist (or worse yet, being wrong), I must say that everything that I know about the relationship between the Congress and the presidency tells me that there will be no new relationship of the sort that Bush seemed to have in mind.

On the contrary, my guess is that despite the friendly words of inauguration day, the president and his people are today either in conflict with the Congress or very close to it. Although the president may have had some significant policy victories during his first year in office, as he moves toward the middle of his first term, he will have accomplished only a small percentage of the goals that he laid out for himself during his successful campaign and those hopeful early weeks of his presidency. On many of the most important issues of the day, he and the Congress will have reached a stalemate. On many other issues, there will have been adopted halfway measures whose singular virtue is their capacity to evoke the grudging agreement of both the president and the Congress,

1

but whose singular failing is that they do not deal effectively with the policy problems at hand.

As Bush's first term draws to an end, major problems will still be with the country. For his part, the president will probably lay most of the blame at the doorstep of the Congress; more, much more, would have been achieved but for the collective ignorance, hostility, indifference, or self-seeking behavior of the legislature, he will argue. Naturally, congressional leaders will view the situation and distribute the blame quite differently. The American people probably will not know who is really at fault. They will likely conclude that although their own representatives and senators are doing a pretty good job, the Congress as a whole is doing poorly. As for the president, the voters will have that gnawing sense that they could be doing better, that once again they have elected a chief executive who is not quite good enough. Their sense of disappointment may be so strong that they will deny the president reelection. More likely, despite their misgivings, they will decide to give him a second term (he may, after all, turn out to be as likable a fellow as his predecessor), but major goals that have not been accomplished in the first four years are unlikely to be achieved in the next four. Then it will be 1996 and the cycle of hope, accomplishment, stalemate, failure, recrimination, and disappointment will play itself out once again.

Overly cynical, you say. Academic nihilism at its worst. Well, hear me out first before you put me down as just another professional pessimist, curse the instructor who made you buy this book, and head for the used book store to see if you can cut your losses. Consider, if you will, the political past upon which my less than optimistic speculations are based. Remember the presidencies of Lyndon Johnson and Richard Nixon, each with early policy achievements (especially Johnson), but each in the end driven from office by congressional and public pressures. Remember the brief tenure of Gerald Ford, who vetoed more legislation and had more vetoes overridden in his two years in office than John Kennedy, Johnson, and Nixon had in their combined fourteen. Remember the beating that Jimmy Carter's proposals took in a Congress controlled by his fellow Democrats. Remember his charge, in the twilight of his presidency, that the Congress was the captive of special interests, unwilling and unable to act in the public interest. And remember Ronald Reagan's eight years in office, the first of which one scholar called a time of "unprecedented policy breakthroughs, unchecked by the normal restraints of separated institutions and intergovernmental division."[1] But Reagan's relationship with the Congress during his next seven years, the same scholar suggested, went through successive phases of "avoidance of hard policy choices, assertiveness by Congress, and survival efforts by the

President."[2] As he left the presidency, Reagan noted with regret the huge budget deficit that he was bequeathing to his successor, but, he explained, the Congress, not his administration, was to blame for this state of affairs.

Certainly there were special circumstances surrounding each of these administrations—war, scandal, economic distress, hostage taking by foreign governments, different parties in control of the legislature and the executive—special reasons why each of these presidents in the end went away mad, with a view of the Congress as an adversary that had, in many respects, gotten the best of him. But this span of twenty-five years and five presidencies suggests that there is more to the story than special circumstances and more to my predictions than academic cynicism. It is reasonable to believe that conflict, tension, and policy stalemate between the president and the Congress are now permanent features of the U.S. political landscape. In the chapters that follow, this assertion will be supported and its causes and consequences analyzed.

THE LEGISLATURE AND THE EXECUTIVE

Those who wrote the U.S. Constitution were in large measure responsible for this conflictual state of presidential-congressional relations. The creation of two independent political institutions—the presidency and the Congress—and the mandate that they share policy-making power, made persistent institutional conflict all but inevitable. But it would be a mistake to attribute the nature of the presidential-congressional relationship entirely to the Constitution, for there has been conflict between legislatures and executives for as long as these political institutions have coexisted.

Executive institutions predate legislatures. In most political systems for most of recorded history, all governing power was exercised by a single sovereign agency, such as a monarch or an emperor. Legislative bodies developed in response to demands for limiting the power exercised by these executives; these demands came from the newly autonomous centers of social and economic power that emerged as these formerly monolithic states modernized.[3] Thus, compared with the executive, the legislature is a relatively new institution, the creation of which is associated with the relatively modern view that unlimited governmental power in the hands of a small number of people is a bad idea.

Initially, legislatures acted primarily as advisory bodies to those who held executive power, but eventually they participated more fully in the making of policy decisions. The justification of the legislature's policy-making role was that its membership was representative of important interests abroad in the land, interests whose support executive leaders wished to have. Thus, when King John met with his barons at the field at Runnymede to sign the Magna Charta establishing the legal basis for Parliament, he conceded that the barons had the right to be consulted on policy decisions in return for their support, largely financial, of these decisions. Legislative power thus was originally founded on the principle that if executives wanted key societal interests to support their policies, they had to be willing to share policy-making power with those who represented these interests.

Later, when the practices of mass suffrage, popular elections, and political parties combined to make the legislature representative of broader publics, legislative bodies came to be viewed as the means for achieving popular control of political decisionmaking, or democracy. At this point, questions of the functions and powers of the legislature relative to the executive came to the fore. If the legislature represented the people, democrats argued, then it should control the policy-making process. If this was so, however, what were to be the residual functions of the formally sovereign executive?

This was a difficult question. The Whig philosopher John Locke, writing in celebration of parliamentary independence established by the Glorious Revolution of 1688, suggested that because government could proceed only on the basis of the consent of the governed and because the legislature represented the governed, the legislature should hold the supreme power "to make laws for all parts and for every member of the society, prescribing rules to their actions." The executive, in contrast, "should see to the execution of the laws that are made" by the legislature.[4] However, Locke also argued that the executive retained the "prerogative" to "act according to discretion for the public good, without the prescription of the law and sometimes even against it." Such executive discretion was necessary because the legislature "is not always in being, and is usually too numerous and so too slow for the dispatch requisite to execution . . . and because also it is impossible to foresee, and so by laws to provide for all accidents and necessities that may concern the public."[5]

Locke's discussion anticipated the problem encountered, but only partially resolved, by generations of political thinkers: that of differentiating legislative from executive power and deciding how much authority should be in the hands of each. Defining legislatures purely in terms of lawmaking functions and executives purely in terms of implementation functions was, as Locke foresaw, inadequate. Modern legislatures, by overseeing the bureaucracy and by the wording of the legislation that they enact, influence how laws are executed. Executives, in turn, are very much involved in deciding which laws will be considered, which approved, and what they will say, as well as in their application to specific cases. And in areas such as foreign policy, or in crisis situations, or in situations where the law is ambiguous, executives often make public policy with little if any participation by the legislature.

The boundaries, therefore, between the legislature's and the executive's realms have been drawn differently and with varying degrees of precision from nation to nation; because it has never been possible to distinguish clearly where legislative power ends and executive power begins, "territorial" conflict between the two institutions has been inevitable. In the United States, the question about this legislative-executive conflict that has been most frequently asked by political scientists and political pundits alike is whether the president or the Congress has dominated. Although this is certainly an important question, a more crucial and more difficult question, and the question that animates this book, is whether presidential rather than congressional control of the policy-making process means better or worse public policies and, by extension, whether the current arrangement of institutional power sharing in the United States makes for good or bad public policy. The question is crucial because achieving good rather than bad public policy should be the goal of any political system. The question is difficult because, among other things, it presupposes the existence of broadly accepted standards by which the quality of public policy can be judged.

EVALUATING INSTITUTIONAL PERFORMANCE

People expect more from their political institutions than that they simply act. People expect that their government will act wisely, that their leaders will do "the right thing," that they will make *good* public policy. Using the term "good" in this manner opens a whole range of complex philosophical questions for which there are no easy and certainly no brief answers. The term implies a generally accepted standard against which policy options can be assessed, with the disparity between the policy and the standard constituting a measure of the goodness of the policy. Aside from the measurement problems that such an assessment process would encounter, a prior issue is how to define the standard. What one person views as good, another, using a different standard, views as bad. So before we can deal with the implications of various institutional arrangements for the quality of public policy, we must address the question of standards. There are at least three categories of standards: contextual, democratic, and managerial.

Contextual Standards

At one level, judgments about what is good or bad policy will depend upon the ideology, history, and culture of the nation in question. From that perspective, definitions of good and bad public policy are country specific rather than generalized because a unique set of beliefs arise from the experiences and circumstances of each nation.

For example, a resident of Moscow, the capital of the Soviet Union, may view a government program that provides free, high quality health care for all citizens as good public policy, whereas a resident of Moscow, Idaho, may view a similar program as bad public policy. In contrast, both Muscovites may view government-funded research on agricultural problems as good public policy. What explains these different evaluations? The answer, in part, is that each person's evaluation takes place in a different political context. The citizen of the Soviet Union lives in a system where the expenditure of public funds to serve all of the health needs of all citizens is a legitimate, accepted, and even expected category of government action. It is viewed as both just and essential and therefore "good." Our Idahoan, however, lives in a system where such policies are generally viewed as unwarranted government intrusions on what should be the responsibility of individual citizens and therefore an inappropriate or "bad" course of action for the government to pursue. Good health, in the view of the Idahoan, is something that individuals should ensure through their own efforts, and justice, at least in this sense, is not a particularly salient criterion by which to evaluate public policy. These differences then between the two Muscovites are explained by different beliefs concerning the appropriate scope of government. Despite their beliefs' differing in regard to health policies, they are likely to come to similar conclusions in regard to agricultural research, with the Russian viewing such activity as simply one among a vast number of legitimate and desirable governmental undertakings and the American viewing this as one of the few areas where government involvement is justified.

Thus, evaluations of public policy always vary across nations because what seems to be good policy in one national context may be bad in another. But contexts are not uniform within a nation, particularly nations as diverse as either the Soviet Union or the United States. Judgments about what constitutes good or bad public policy may be made on the basis of regional or socioeconomic criteria that will vary within as well as between nations.

Consider, for example, two Americans, one a citizen of Albany, New York, and the other a citizen of Albany, Georgia. The New Yorker is a middle-aged, middle-income, black Democrat, working as an employee of the New York state government, while the Georgian is a middle-aged, middle-income, white Republican, who runs a peach farm. The two will likely agree that a number of public policies are good—for example, the Social Security system, student loan programs for higher education, and environmental protection legislation. Both know that they will need an income when they retire, both are struggling to send children through college, and both like to vacation at unpolluted lakes. However, the two Albanians are likely to disagree on a number of policies—for example, price supports for peaches, affirmative action for minorities, and child care legislation. The New Yorker views price supports for peaches as a waste of government money and as increasing the cost of the fruit that she buys. Her ethnic background and her gender have led her to support affirmative action programs and her experience of trying to work while her children were young has convinced her that day care is a good and worthwhile expenditure of government funds. The Georgian, in contrast, is generally skeptical about government spending, although he views the farm price support system as an important exception, one that serves as an economic safety net for him and his family. However, he thinks that government spending on "social" programs is bad public policy. Parents should take care of their own children, and because his wife and children work with him on the farm, the lack of affordable child care does not bother him at all. And affirmative action is another example of the federal government's meddling in areas where it doesn't belong.

The obvious point made by the example of the two Albanians is that in any nation citizens will often disagree about what constitutes good public policy because of who they are, their social circumstances, and their beliefs. Given such diversity, how then can one ever reach judgments about the quality of public policy? One person's good policy always will be someone else's disaster and it would be naive to think that even extended discussion will convince one or the other that his or her position is erroneous. It is at this point that discussions of what distinguishes good from bad public policy usually come to a halt.

Democratic Criteria

One way of sidestepping this problem in evaluating public policy is to use procedural rather than substantive standards. That is, we can ask how the differences that arise within a nation concerning the content of public policy are resolved. In some countries, differences of opinion about what governments should do are resolved by reference to an overriding ideology. In other nations, differences are resolved by the arbitrary decisions of a small elite. However, in countries such as the United States, different opinions about what policies governments should pursue are supposed to be resolved through democratic procedures. From this perspective, it can be argued that a policy is good if the process through which it is developed adheres to democratic standards.

What this approach does, in effect, is to substitute procedural for substantive criteria in order to reach judgments about the quality of public policy. It is based on the premise that even though citizens may not be able to agree on the value of competing policy proposals, they can agree upon certain procedures for deciding among these different proposals. Public policy then is good if it is developed according to these procedures.

To meet democratic standards, the content of public policies needs to be controlled either by the people directly or by their elected representatives. To the extent that public policy is made by elites acting beyond the control of mass publics, the policies are less democratic and therefore less acceptable by these standards. If public policy is to be made by elected representatives rather than by the people themselves—the ordinary situation in modern nations that call themselves democracies—then there is a double corollary to the principle of control by elected officials: These officials must be both responsive and accountable to those who elect them.

Responsiveness means that political leaders must take into account the wishes of those whom they represent when they make policy decisions. They do not always have to do what the people want, but they must always act in the interests of the people. According to Hanna Pitkin's formulation, responsiveness means that elected leaders "must not be found persistently at odds with the wishes of the represented without good reason in terms of their interests, without a good explanation of why their views are not in accord with their interests."[6] To ensure "a good explanation" when the actions of leaders conflict with the views of the led one needs accountability. **Accountability** means that citizens must be able to know who is responsible for policies that are enacted so that they can decide from whom to elicit explanations for policies with which they disagree and should they find these explanations unacceptable, so that they can register their disapproval by removing those responsible from office. To the extent that the responsibility for public policy is hidden or obscured, the capacity of the people to control policy outcomes is reduced.

Finally, it is axiomatic to democratic beliefs that majority preferences should prevail over minority preferences. However, majorities also need to respect the limits of their power, particularly as it affects the political liberties of minorities. That is, majorities must allow minorities to have their say before policies are enacted and to dissent, both before and after enactment, from those policies with which they disagree. Majorities must also refrain from enacting public policies that have the effect of reducing or eliminating the capacity of today's minority to become tomorrow's majority.

Managerial Criteria

Contextual criteria generate standards for evaluating the **goals** of public policy. Democratic criteria provide standards for evaluating the **procedures** by which policy goals and policy options are selected. Managerial criteria provide a third set of standards against which public policies may be evaluated, no matter what their goals are or by what procedures they have been adopted. Managerially, good public policy should be informed, timely, coherent, effective, and responsible. **Informed** means that policy should be based on the best information. **Timely** means that policy should not be delayed to the point where the problem to which the policy speaks is exacerbated. **Coherent** means that policy should fit with the extant body of relevant policies currently in force and that internally it should not seek contradictory goals. **Effective** means that policy should be designed to accomplish the ends or goals for which it is created. **Responsible** means that policy decisions should take into account the collective public interest, rather than simply the private interests of government decisionmakers or the narrow and short-term interests of small groups.[7]

There are few tensions between managerial criteria and contextual criteria. That is, policy that is uninformed, too late, incoherent, ineffective, and irresponsible can never achieve the overarching goals associated with any set of contextual criteria—social justice, economic development, or any other formulation of national policy goals. It can produce neither good public health policies in the Soviet Union nor good agricultural research policies in Idaho. Nor can it produce good farm policy in Georgia or good child care programs in New York. However, managerial criteria may well conflict with democratic criteria. That is, a policy-making process controlled by the people or their representatives in which governmental majorities make policy decisions in a manner responsive to the wishes of mass publics may well produce policy options that are uninformed, too late, incoherent, ineffective and irresponsible. Reconciling or, alternatively, deciding between democratic and managerial criteria is therefore one of the key problems in policy evaluation.

POLITICAL INSTITUTIONS AND GOOD PUBLIC POLICY

The extent to which a political system can achieve public policy that can be judged as good according to managerial or democratic criteria is influenced by the role of the legislature relative to that of the executive in the policy-making process. This occurs because the generic characteristics of each institution affect both its democratic character and its ability to achieve public policy that is informed, timely, coherent, effective and responsible. Legislatures tend to be collegial, representative, open, and nonspecialized, whereas executives tend to be more hierarchical, less representative, closed, and specialized.

Legislatures are **collegial** because they are collective bodies; their members are formally equal in voting power and their decisions are reached through majority votes. Executive structures, in contrast, are usually characterized by a formal and usable hierarchy, with the result that decisions are seldom taken through a voting process.

Legislatures are **representative** because they are elected by a larger public to which they are formally responsible and in whose interests they act. As multimember bodies, legislatures are also broadly representative of the different interests—geographical, ethnic, and ideological—that the nation comprises. Although certain executive leaders, such as prime ministers and presidents, typically are elected and are to that extent, representative, their singularity means that they are incapable of the broad national representation that characterizes the legislature. Those who serve with chief executives in cabinet or other high administrative posts often are not elected, and the members of the more permanent bureaucracy who constitute the bulk of executive personnel are never elected.

Legislatures are **open** because they meet publicly and keep records of their deliberations. Executives, in contrast, usually operate in a closed policy-making environment. Neither high-level cabinet and staff meetings nor lower-level meetings of civil servants are open to the public, and many important documents produced within the executive branch are not made public in the normal course of events.

Legislatures are **non-specialized** because membership in them requires no special training or expertise in public policy matters. Similarly, elected members of the executive, although often selected from among the most experienced politicians, are not required to have any special policy expertise. However, special qualifications are usually required of those who hold appointive positions and of all who hold positions within the permanent bureaucracy. Therefore, the executive is more specialized than the legislature.

MEETING DEMOCRATIC CRITERIA

These contrasting characteristics of legislatures and executives strongly suggest that the legislature must be central to the policy-making process if democratic criteria are to be met. As a broadly representative and collegial body, the legislature provides an arena within which the various interests that the society comprises can participate in the policy-making process. Because all of the members of the legislature are elected and because their reelection depends upon their ability to maintain the confidence of their constituents, legislators are likely to be quite sensitive and responsive to popular wishes. Because the legislature is an open institution that meets, deliberates, and decides in public sessions and because its actions are a matter of public record, when it makes public policy, citizens have the information that they need in order to decide whom to hold responsible for what is done.

The capacity of the executive branch to generate public policy through a process that meets democratic criteria is more problematic. In many political systems, those who head the executive branch are popularly elected, but in many others they are not. In all countries, however, the bureaucracy is composed of nonelected people with an indefinite tenure in office. Because most members of the executive do not rely upon popular election in order to stay in office, their responsiveness to public opinion and majority wishes is reduced. Although bureaucracies are supposed to be controlled by elected executives who in turn are supposed to be responsive to majority wishes, in practice such control is usually weak or absent because elected executives cannot possibly know or oversee all that is done within the bureaucracy. Finally, the fact that most executive-branch policymaking takes place privately further diminishes the capacity of citizens either to influence and control these decisions or to determine who is responsible for the decisions that are taken. Although the popular majorities that elect presidents may think of them as responsible for all that their subordinates within the executive branch do, the size and complexity of modern bureaucracies renders such responsibility largely illusory.

MEETING MANAGERIAL CRITERIA

Informed Public Policy

In all nations, the data upon which informed public policy is based are, for the most part, collected by the executive.[8] This occurs because public policymaking is largely an incremental process, with new policy building upon existing policy, reacting to its deficiencies, and expanding upon its strengths. Those in the executive who implement existing public policy, because they work on the same problems over a long period and because their background and experience encourage a great deal of policy expertise, usually have more sophisticated and complete information than nonspecialized legislators.

Even when the legislature has a large professional staff of its own, it usually does not have the ability to gather information completely independently of the executive. The most that can be hoped for is that the staff can provide the legislature with an independent evaluation of the executive's data. And in most legislatures, staff resources are insufficient to provide even this type of service.

However, because of its open and representative nature, there is a wider spectrum of views articulated in the legislature than in the less representative bureaucracy. Although this diversity may not produce expertise, it can provide the perspectives and arguments that help identify the best policy alternatives when the experts disagree or signal when expert policy advice should be ignored or at least tempered by political considerations. As Arthur Maass has noted, "the collective, nontechnical mind" of the legislature can bring to bear "insights and sensitivities that are likely to go beyond the perception and ken of any group of experts."[9]

On balance, then, the legislature is less likely than the bureaucracy to contribute to the generation of the technical and expert information upon which public policy should rest, but it can, by virtue of the breadth of views expressed within it, broaden the information base upon which policy alternatives are generated and selected.

Timely Public Policy

Legislatures always act more slowly than the executive. In any setting, the larger the number of people from whom agreement is required, the longer it takes to arrive at an agreement. Because it is a collegial body, with each legislator formally equal in power, a relatively large number of members must want to act before the legislature can proceed. Hierarchically organized bodies, such as executive agencies and cabinets, need agreement from a relatively small number of participants in order to act.

Simply providing a hearing for the multiplicity of interests represented in the legislature is time consuming, and reaching positions that a majority of members can support takes even longer. And on occasion, a great deal of time is consumed with no agreement reached. Delays are further fostered by the openness of the legislature. Representatives acting on behalf of particular interests may find it difficult publicly to concede or compromise those interests; therefore, the openness of the legislature can put a premium on posturing rather than on policymaking, and sometimes legislators may prefer having no policy at all to one that those whom they represent find unacceptable. In more closed, more homogeneously composed, and less representative executive arenas, it is easier for agreements to be reached and for policy to proceed.

However, the shared expertise in the executive and the absence of direct links between it and broader populations may encourage a certain conservatism—not an inability but rather a reluctance to act. In that case, the greater diversity of opinion in the open legislative arena may mean that the legislature can prod the executive into action. Policy needs that may not be so apparent or seem so pressing to those who do not, as a condition for retaining their positions, have to respond to public pressures may be articulated in the legislature, may thereby generate publicity and pressure, and may compel more expeditious action than the executive, left to its own devices, would be willing to undertake. In sum, while legislatures themselves cannot act in so timely a fashion as the executive, they sometimes can encourage executives to act in a more expeditious manner.

Coherent Public Policy

Legislative action often appears to be incoherent. Policies approved on one day may be inconsistent with those approved the day before. Calls for lower budget deficits may be followed by appropriation and revenue legislation that makes large deficits inevitable. A policy to discourage citizens from smoking may coexist with a policy of price supports for tobacco growers.

Although such incoherence can characterize public policy from any source, the nonspecialized, collegial, and representative nature of the legislature seems to make such policies more likely to emerge from that body. Those who are not experts in a policy area will be less likely than those who are to see how a particular proposal fits, or fails to fit, with the existing body of public policy. Moreover, an institution that is representative of diverse interests and that operates largely through compromise may view an incoherent yet consensual policy as more desirable than a coherent policy for which support sufficient for approval cannot be generated.

The executive branch is vulnerable to similar pressures. Presidents and prime ministers are also surrounded by people with diverse views that need to be conciliated, and as bureaucracies grow and become more complex, negotiation and compromise prove to be as much a part of their policy-making process as that of the legislature. Nonetheless, the legislature is less receptive than the executive to the systematic analysis that coherent public policy requires.

Effective Public Policy

Producing policy that achieves the goals that it is designed to achieve is in part dependent upon the quality of the information that the policymaker has and in part on the timeliness of the policy; therefore, lack of good information and of timeliness in the legislature adversely affect its capacity to produce effective public policy. In addition, the compromise or process-oriented nature of legislative activity may work against policy effectiveness: There may be a conflict between the policy that will achieve the widest agreement and the one most likely to solve the policy problem at hand. To the extent that legislatures seek policy alternatives that reconcile widely disparate views, they run the risk of producing policy that although broadly supported, simply does not work.

The executive too may be tempted toward consensual as opposed to effective policies. Even bureaucrats must seek support for their policy initiatives; moreover, a consensual policy, by virtue of that characteristic, sometimes can be effective simply because supported policies may be more likely to succeed than those that are unsupported. However, policies also must be judged by their capacity to accomplish goals, and executives usually seem more willing than legislatures to make that evaluation.

Responsible Public Policy

Given their representative nature, legislatures are subject to pressures for **responsive** policymaking that often come at the expense of **responsible** policymaking. As the legislature seeks to respond to the short-term interests of popular majorities or intense minorities, its members may lose sight of the long-term issues involved. Thus, a policy that defers maintenance on public facilities so that tax increases can be avoided or so that the money can be diverted toward more immediate ends may be responsive to popular wishes right up until the time that bridges and highways collapse and the population suffers the consequences of such deferred maintenance decisions. The public expects their political system to be run responsibly, and meeting that expectation may require a degree of nonresponsiveness to more immediate demands.

Because legislative terms are short and because constituents may want visible indications of their representatives' effectiveness, legislatures may be more oriented toward short-term responsiveness than long-term responsibility. Similarly, legislators may be encouraged to respond to the narrow interests of their constituencies rather than to a more general public interest because the former is what they think that their constituents expect from them. Those in executive positions, because they are not subject to the same intense representational pressures as are legislators, are ordinarily in a position to advocate more general rather than more narrow interests and to resist demands for policies that might be responsive to immediate concerns but that will do damage to long-term interests.

THE CHALLENGE

This discussion of the comparative capacities of legislative and executive institutions to produce good public policy leads to different conclusions depending upon which standards are used to assess the quality of public policy. If democratic criteria are used, the analysis points toward a prominent role for the legislature, based upon that institution's broad electoral base, its openness, and its responsiveness to public demands. However, if managerial criteria are used, the analysis leads away from the legislature and toward the executive. The generic characteristics of the legislature suggest that ignorance, delay, incoherence, ineffectiveness, and irresponsibility are more likely to characterize its policy-making activities than those of the executive.

There is an obvious dilemma here, a contradiction between a desire for public policy arrived at through processes that meet democratic criteria and a preference for public policies that are informed, timely, coherent, effective, and responsible. Put simply, a strong legislative role is an essential component of democracy and a strong executive role is an essential prerequisite to public policies that are good according to managerial criteria. That is the reason why the manner in which the legislative-executive relationship is organized affects the quality of a nation's public policies. A brief description of four models of legislative-executive relations currently in operation around the world, each distinguished by a different balance of policy-making power between its legislative and executive institutions, suggests the range of alternatives.[10]

In **balanced systems,** exemplified by that of the United States, the legislature and the executive share political power on a more or less equal basis. Thus, the U.S. Congress regularly initiates policy proposals, deliberates among alternatives, and decides upon the course of action that the nation will pursue. The president and the bureaucracy are policy-making partners of the legislature, with significant prerogatives of their own in regard to policy initiation and deliberation. Both the Congress and the president can act independently of each other, and conversely, each has the capacity to stop the other from acting. The United States government represents the most obvious example of a balanced model, but the individual states are examples also, and, at one time, the legislatures of the Philippines, Chile, and Costa Rica also belonged in this category.

Representational systems are characterized by a more dominant policy-making role for an executive operating through a political party or a coalition of political parties that commands a dependable majority in the legislature. In these systems, exemplified by the government of Great Britain, the primary policy-making role lies with the executive, composed of the prime minister, her cabinet, and the bureaucracy. Parliament affects policy primarily through the vigorous performance of its representational activities—articulating constituency and group demands, seeking solutions to the problems of individual constituents, and otherwise serving as a conduit between popular views and those who make public policy. Whereas the executive dominates the policy-making process, Parliament, through discussion and debate, sets the parameters within which the executive operates: Parliament modifies executive initiatives, holds the executive publicly accountable for its actions, and oversees the implementation of policy decisions. Representational systems operate in nations influenced by the British parliamentary model, in other European parliamentary systems, and in more open Third World political systems such as India and Sri Lanka.

In **bureaucratic systems,** policy-making power is concentrated in the hands of a small group of military and civilian bureaucrats. Although the legislature is clearly subordinate to these bureaucratic elites, its members have some degree of independence and often engage in the activities typical of legislatures in balanced and representational political systems. However, such activities have a relatively limited impact on those in the executive who make the major policy decisions, and individual legislators who seek to test these limits are vulnerable to personal and political intimidation by those who wield executive power. The legislature as a whole is equally vulnerable; bureaucratic systems have a record of political instability, with the result that legislatures are often suspended or abolished by military coups. Bureaucratic systems are found most frequently in Latin America, Asia, and Africa, with countries such as South Korea, Taiwan, Brazil, Pakistan, and Liberia standing as examples.

In **authoritarian systems,** the executive can, if it wishes, exercise virtually unlimited policy-making power. Written constitutions often provide theoretical checks on the power of the executive, but in practice the policy control of executive leaders in authoritarian systems extends as far as they wish to push it. Such systems have quite weak legislative institutions whose primary functions are to mobilize support for policies developed by the executive, to provide a channel for communication between the rulers and the ruled, and to deal with policy grievances from individuals and groups. These minimal legislatures have virtually no role in determining the major features of public policies and at most a marginal role in developing the specifics and in overseeing the implementation of policies that have been decided by the executive. Marxist political systems stand as the most prominent examples of authoritarian systems in operation; other nations, however, such as Paraguay and Libya, also can be placed in this category.

In bureaucratic and authoritarian systems, where democratic commitments are at best tenuous, the tension between democratic and managerially sound public policy is easily resolved in favor of the latter because dominant power is vested in the executive. However, in balanced and representational systems, normally characterized by a stronger commitment to democratic principles, resolving this tension has proven to be a good deal more difficult.

In the twentieth century, the democratic state has been repeatedly challenged by those who have been all too willing to eliminate democratic practices ostensibly to maximize managerial values. In Italy, Benito Mussolini and his Brown Shirts smashed the republic, promising a system that would make the trains run on time. In Germany, the collapse of the Weimar Republic and the Nazi takeover was heralded by many as a move toward more stable and effective government. During the post–World War II era, Brazil, Argentina, Greece, and the Philippines were among the many nations where military juntas have abolished legislative institutions in the name of more efficient and effective government. And although the methods and rationale are somewhat different, the argument in Marxist political systems for a concentration of power in the hands of the party and for a limited role for democratic institutions such as elections and legislatures is that policy decisions taken by executive leaders will achieve public policy that meets managerial criteria.

In the West, the reconciling of democratic institutions with managerially good public policy has been complicated by the expanding scope of government authority and the concomitant growth of bureaucratic power. Gradually, and usually without constitutional changes, a good deal of policy-making control in Western democratic systems has shifted from legislative chambers to bureaucratic board rooms. In theory, this administrative apparatus operates under the direct control of either popularly elected presidents or, in parliamentary systems, prime ministers and their cabinets, with oversight of the entire executive system exercised by the legislature. In practice, political executives have not proven to be consistently effective in controlling the bureaucracy, and legislative oversight has generally been a hit-or-miss operation. Therefore, although these polities continue to be publicly committed to democratic principles and have assumed few of the repressive characteristics of bureaucratic or authoritarian systems, there is a danger that the democratic practices of balanced and representational systems will become little more than facades behind which a nonresponsive administrative state operates, beyond the control of the public or their elected legislators and chief executives.

This course of events will be applauded by many who are disturbed by the apparent failure of legislative institutions to produce managerially sound public policies. Although the weakening of democratic institutions will be noted, perhaps even with regret, at least, it will be argued, the administrative state will produce better public policies. But others will not give in so easily. To find a way to reconcile the democratic principles of popular government guaranteed by strong legislatures with the executive's capacity to produce more informed, timely, coherent, effective, and responsible public policy is one of the primary challenges confronting societies that aspire to be democratic in more than just name. Meeting this challenge requires a frank acknowledgment of the endemic weaknesses of legislative institutions as bodies capable of making managerially good public policy and an equally frank appreciation of the dangers to a democratic society inherent in unbridled executive authority. It is insufficient to say that public policy poor from a managerial standpoint is the price that one must pay for a democratic society or, at the other extreme, simply to place one's faith in executive power and hope that those who hold it will continue to adhere to democratic principles. Escapism of either sort simply will not do.

As we shall see in Chapter 2, those who wrote the U.S. Constitution some two hundred years ago were keenly aware of this challenge. The system of balanced power sharing between legislative and executive institutions that they created was an attempt to combine safeguards against governmental tyranny with managerial concern for good public policy. However, because ultimately they proved to be more concerned with too much rather than too little government, their design, rather than reconciling democratic with managerial principles, produced a constitution against government, a system incapable of policy actions meeting either set of criteria. During the two centuries that have passed since that constitution was written, U.S. political institutions have undergone significant changes, the presidency more so than the Congress, but this structural bias against governmental action has remained. Chapter 3 traces the evolution of the Congress and the parallel transformation of the presidency.

As the presidency moved to a position of greatly increased prominence, it seemed to embody for many the possibility of a reconciliation of democratic and managerial criteria. An elected chief executive with strong and direct ties to the people and in control of both the Congress and the administrative state, it was hoped, would guarantee both democracy and effective government. In Chapter 4, the practices associated with such a presidential-primacy model are described, and the strategies employed by presidents as they have sought to control the Congress are explored. In Chapter 5, these strategies are assessed from the perspective of managerially good public policy, and the conclusion is reached that either policy stalemate or poor public policy has been the typical result.

Chapter 6 describes, through a series of case studies, the development and use of new techniques to produce policy action in a political system designed for stalemate. Although such techniques often succeed in either breaking stalemates or in allowing government to function without the need for institutional action, the policy results of such techniques seldom comport with either democratic or managerial criteria for good public policy. Chapter 7 suggests better ways to reconcile the demand for public policy that adheres to democratic process criteria with the demand for public policy that is managerially sound.

2

The U.S. Constitutional Framework

Those who wrote the U.S. Constitution did not use terms such as "managerial," and when they used the term "democracy," they attached to it a meaning somewhat different from its current one. Nonetheless, when the Founders gathered in Philadelphia in the summer of 1787 to design a new system of government, managerial and democratic standards for good government were very much on their minds. Their primary goal was managerial—to create a government that would be able to act wisely and effectively. However, they also wanted to make certain that their new government would pose no threat to individual liberty and could be fairly said to be based on the consent of the governed. The Founders recognized (as we did in Chapter 1) contradictions between these goals: They knew that a government strong enough to take decisive public actions might also move in the direction of tyranny. Just as important, they were convinced that if government was too dependent on the people, its capacity to act effectively would be diminished.

The document that they produced represented their attempt to reconcile and thereby satisfy these contradictory goals. Their concern for effective government was apparent in their most significant decision: to create a national government that in certain important policy areas would be superior to the existing state governments and therefore capable of acting on behalf of all the people of the several states. Their decision to include an independent and potentially powerful executive in their plan for a new national government was also motivated by their commitment to effective government. However, their fear that concentrated government power could be detrimental to liberty was reflected in their decision to specify and thereby limit the powers of the new national government. What is more important, they constructed an elaborate system by which a president, a legislature of two chambers, and a Supreme Court, each structurally independent of the other, would share this power. Finally, by providing for the direct election of the House of Representatives, indirect election of the Senate and the president, and an appointed Supreme Court, the Founders thought that they had allowed for a degree of representation sufficient to imply popular consent but limited enough to avoid the dangers that they associated with unbridled democracy.

The question that underlies this chapter is whether or not the Founders succeeded in designing a political system that optimized both their managerial and their democratic standards for good government. To answer this question, one needs to understand the decisions that they made about how governmental power should be organized, decisions that were a product of the beliefs that they carried with them to Philadelphia and of the events that they perceived taking place around them. Thus, they drew in part from the writings of philosophers such as David Hume, Locke, and Montesquieu, in part from their own knowledge of governmental practices in ancient as well as more contemporary societies, and in part from their own experiences with American governments as they had operated both before and after the Revolution of 1776.

GOOD GOVERNMENT

In the first paragraph of the very first *Federalist* paper, Alexander Hamilton said that the debate on the Constitution was to be about "whether societies of men are really capable or not of establishing good government from reflection and choice."[1] Exactly what Hamilton and his colleagues meant by "good government" has been the subject of some disagreement among scholars. One view depicts the Founders as descendants and exponents of the liberal philosophy of John Locke and the British Whigs, a philosophy that emerged in seventeenth- and eighteenth-century England during the epic struggle between the monarch's claimed divine right to govern absolutely and the Enlightenment notion that because man was endowed with natural rights, he had to consent to being governed. A government based on popular consent, British Whigs argued, would have as its first object the preservation of life, liberty, and property against the forces of despotism. Whig philosophy so conceived had a strong antigovernment bias to it in the sense that its goal seemed to be to allow individuals to pursue their own private ends with as little interference from government as possible.[2]

An alternative view, articulated most convincingly by historian Gordon Wood, is that although the Founders were undoubtedly influenced by Whig thought, they developed a somewhat different, more radical version of it with a more sophisticated conception of good government. This version began too with government premised on popular consent. In the words of John Adams, "good government is republican government."[3] But in the radical Whig view, republican government meant more than simply government based on popular consent; it also meant government in the public interest. According to Adams, citizens of a republic must exhibit "a positive Passion for the public good, the public Interest." Without that passion, "there can be no republican government, nor any real liberty."[4] Such a passion for the public good derived from a public virtue that encouraged individuals to sacrifice their personal interests to the greater good of the whole.

Public virtue so defined, Wood argued, formed the essence of American republicanism.[5] Without virtue, republics became corrupt because citizens placed their private interests ahead of the public interest. Ironically, the more prosperous a republic became, the more likely such corruption was to take place because prosperity produced greed and self-interested behavior, which led inevitably to instability and disorder. The radical Whig's position was that when public liberty was unconstrained by civic virtue, by a sense of the public good, it degenerated into "licentiousness," which in turn "degenerated into anarchy and anarchy inevitably led to tyranny."[6]

Although the view that classical republicanism rather than Lockean principles guided the early Americans may well be exaggerated, it still can be said that the Framers' support for a government founded on popular consent was based at least in part on their belief that such a government could operate in a qualitatively better way than did the all too familiar despotic alternatives. For the Framers, republican government was good government not only because it protected liberty but also because it guarded against the dangers of liberty. It did the latter by creating the conditions for public virtue by which individuals would subordinate their private interests to the general collective interests of the people as a whole. In this sense, true republican government represented for the Founders a way to reconcile the tension between government based on popular consent and government that produced good public policies or, in other words, between democratic and managerial standards for good public policy.

The Founders were concerned thus not simply with the structure of government but also with what government did. The question they confronted was how best to organize a republic so that it would produce good public policy. By the time of the American Revolution the experience of colonial history had led them to the conviction that the republican virtue that they sought depended upon a strong legislature. However, the experience of the new nation during the period between the Declaration of Independence and the establishment of the Constitution convinced them that their initial disposition toward a strong legislature was a mistake. The story of the U.S. Constitution and the arrangement of legislative-executive power that it provides is the story of this change of heart.

IN THE BEGINNING THERE WERE LEGISLATURES

The Founders' favorable attitude toward legislative power can be traced to the ideology and experience of the British Whigs and their demand for parliamentary supremacy. Their view was that the right of the rulers to govern was contingent upon the people retaining the right to choose a body of people to represent them and, through such a body, to have a voice in the making of all laws. Liberty, in their view, was connected with this principle of representation.

The structural embodiment of this principle of representation was the legislature, an institution that had long been in existence in colonial America. In 1619, the Virginia Company, by authorizing its governor to call together representatives of the plantations to make laws for their own government, created the House of Burgesses. This first legislative body in the New World soon claimed the sole right to impose taxes, and in short order the Virginia model was adopted in the other colonies. When colonial control by chartered companies ended, the executive power in each colony remained in the hands of royal governors appointed by and responsible to the Crown. These governors were in nearly constant conflict with the colonial assemblies and with the privy councils, composed of wealthy colonists, with whose advice they governed. As tensions between the colonists and the Crown increased, the colonial assemblies came to be more than simply lawmaking institutions. In the words of James Wilson of Pennsylvania, the assemblies "were the guardians of our rights, the objects of our confidence and the anchors of our political hopes."[7]

This commitment to assemblies as representative institutions and the explicit hostility to executive power represented locally by the governor and at a distance by the king, was a cornerstone of the political faith of colonial America. The legislature would discover "the common sense of the people"[8] and thereby evince the civic virtue that was at the heart of American republican theory. This faith in legislative institutions was apparent in the decision to have the Continental Congress direct the revolutionary war. And despite the problems encountered in that enterprise, after the victory over the British was secured, the forms of government instituted in the newly independent states and in their national confederation continued to concentrate virtually all power in legislative bodies

In the states, the legislatures were supreme. They not only retained their prerevolutionary powers in regard to the purse, but they also became the ultimate lawmaking authority and "the heirs to most of the prerogative powers taken away from the governors by the Revolution."[9] Many of the state constitutions gave the legislature the power to appoint and control the governor and often the judiciary as well, and in most cases the larger more democratic assemblies dominated the smaller, more aristocratic senates.

At the national level, the Articles of Confederation united legislative, executive, and judicial powers in the Congress. The executive power under the articles was in the hands of an executive Committee of the States that would operate only during congressional recesses and over which one member, serving no more than one year, would "preside." All powers exercised by the committee had to be explicitly vested in it by a vote of nine states in the Congress; the Congress also established and appointed other committees and officers to manage the general affairs of the nation. Finally, the Congress served as the court of last appeal for all issues arising between and among the states.

Dominant legislatures of this sort were viewed as consonant with the theory of separation of powers to which the leaders of the new nation claimed to adhere. At the time of the Revolution the theory was viewed solely as an injunction to protect the legislature from executive manipulation. The prevailing view was that the British king had corrupted Parliament through bribes and appointments. Similar activities had been observed in the colonial governments; there was particular contempt directed toward the councils, which although ostensibly part of the legislature, served at the pleasure and therefore under the influence of the governor. By placing the executive firmly under the control of the legislature, the designers of the postrevolutionary constitutions asserted that they were protecting the notion of separation of powers by eliminating the possibility of executive intimidation and manipulation of the legislature.

THE TROUBLE WITH LEGISLATURES

It was at this point, with legislative bodies firmly in control of the states and the new nation, that the deficiencies of such an arrangement became apparent. One of the problems had been foreseen by Locke himself who noted that even though the supreme power was in the hands of the legislature, legislatures were not always in session. The laws that they made, however, were always in force and were not self-executing. Therefore, "it was absolutely necessary that the executive power" always be available because there is "always need for the execution of the laws that are made."[10] A very weak executive would not be able to execute the law. In Massachusetts, for example, the first postrevolutionary constitution had placed executive power in the hands of a twenty-eight-member council. Samuel Otis's view of this arrangement was that "if there is any [executive power] you would be puzzled to find it."[11]

A second objection to legislative control, also anticipated by Locke, was that the legislature was too large and therefore did not operate with sufficient dispatch. During the revolutionary war, this state of affairs had become painfully apparent to George Washington as he sought to lead the Continental Army while waiting for the Congress to supply him with the wherewithal to do the job. Washington "experienced on a daily basis the inability of Congress to organize itself for the war effort. It was his lot to conduct a campaign with troops who were poorly trained, underfed, and ill-clothed, as well as badly supplied with weapons and ammunition."[12] In vain Washington urged the Congress to appoint responsible executives to handle these tasks with an efficiency that could not be mustered by the congressional committees that had been designated to do these jobs.

Locke's argument that laws had to be carried out and his and Washington's plea for efficiency and dispatch might well have been answered by an executive institution with very little strength or independence, an administrator that would simply execute the laws that the Congress enacted and make certain that things got done on time. But other arguments developed that laid the groundwork not simply for the creation of an executive but for the establishment of a **strong executive.** For the Founders also had come to see the strong legislatures of the postrevolutionary period as sources of disorder and as actually destructive of the concept of good government in the public interest. These second thoughts about legislatures and their connection with good government emerged primarily from the Founders' experiences with state legislatures under the Articles of Confederation. The original Whig idea that representatives of the people would discover the public interest and act virtuously in favor of it as against individual interests had worked well enough during the prerevolutionary period, when the public interest was easily identified as opposition to the Crown and its prerogatives. However, once the Revolution had been won, this consensus broke down and factionalism, largely along economic lines, emerged.

In the view of many people of substance, the state legislatures had developed the habit in these economic conflicts of favoring those who had less rather than those who had more. Among other things, the legislatures had authorized the issuing of paper money and had passed laws suspending the rights of creditors to recover from debtors.[13] The writer Noah Webster lamented these "public invasions of private property" and "wanton abuses of legislative power."[14] James Madison charged that the state legislatures were "much more disposed to sacrifice the aggregate interest, and even authority, to the local views of their constituents" and that "measures are too often decided not according to the rules of justice and the rights of the minor party, but by the superior force of an interested and overbearing minority."[15]

Often the legislatures were moved in these apparently unjust directions by the power of public opinion and the threat and actuality of civil disobedience. Benjamin Franklin came to the conclusion that "we have been guarding against an end that old states are most liable to, excess of power in the rulers, but our present danger seems to be a defect of obedience in the subjects."[16] Early in the proceedings of the Constitutional Convention, Elbridge Gerry asserted that the "evils we experience flow from an excess of democracy."[17] The situation was not helped by the low quality of state legislators. Gerry's view was that in his native Massachusetts "the worst men get into the legislature—men of indigence, ignorance, and baseness."[18] And with all power in the hands of these legislators, there was no recourse against unwise or imprudent actions. The legislature, according to Madison, was "extending the sphere of its activity and drawing all powers into its impetuous vortex."[19]

The views of the Founders about how and where power should be vested to assure republican virtue had shifted completely. "Where once the magistracy had served as the sole source of tyranny, now the legislatures . . . had become the institution to be most feared."[20] This shift represented more than simply a loss of faith in legislative institutions but rather a loss of faith in the classical republican assumption that citizens of a republic would behave virtuously. As historian Forest McDonald concluded, the postrevolutionary experience taught the Founders that "there were threats to liberty and property that were peculiar to republics, if the people did not have an adequate measure of virtue; and they had become convinced that the American people did not have it."[21]

A NEW CONSTITUTIONAL DESIGN

It was in this context, therefore, that the Founders assembled in summer 1787 to write a constitution. Their goal was to create a national government stronger than that existing under the Articles of Confederation, one that would be able to exercise responsibly powers currently being exercised irresponsibly by the state legislatures. And to guarantee that the new national government would not simply replicate the evils of the state governments on an even larger and more dangerous scale, a strong executive branch had to be a central part of the new plan.

Although this goal was not incompatible with the Founders' altered views on the requisites and structure of good government, it was, to say the least, fundamentally subversive of the general public's notions on these issues. The ends that the Founders were seeking, particularly in regard to the executive power, could easily be depicted as a plot to resuscitate the dreaded executive power against which the Revolution had been fought and as a nullification of the powers of the legislature, the institutional core of Whig philosophy and the institutional means to achieve government by popular consent.

The job of the reformers was made somewhat easier by the absence from the convention of any strong supporters of the current governmental arrangements, but there were present several who although committed to change, remained deeply suspicious of executive power. George Mason of Virginia, for example, conceded that secrecy, dispatch, and energy were indeed executive rather than legislative qualities but argued that these executive characteristics were contrary to the "pervading principle of republican government."[22] Edmund Randolph of Virginia, who agreed with Gerry that "the evils under which the United States currently laboured" were due to "the turbulence and follies of democracy," also warned that a strong and unified executive was the "foetus of monarchy,"[23] a sentiment echoed by Hugh Williamson of North Carolina, who predicted that such an officer would "spare no pains to keep himself in for life, and then lay a train for the succession of his children."[24]

At the Constitutional Convention, these suspicions were met first by the creation of a strong and popularly elected House of Representatives along with an equally strong executive and second by the construction of a complex system of relationships among the House, the president, and an indirectly elected Senate. This system would limit the likelihood of abuses by either the legislature or the executive. The entire package, Hamilton concluded, ensured that "the excellence of republican government may be retained and its imperfections lessened or avoided."[25]

A POPULARLY ELECTED
HOUSE OF REPRESENTATIVES

Despite the concerns that the Founders had about legislatures, once it was decided that a national government with significant policy-making authority would be established, there was never any question that the national legislature would play a central role in exercising that authority. The Founders' Lockean principles, although shaken by their postrevolutionary experience, still survived, as Madison's terse affirmation in *Federalist No. 51* makes clear: "in republican government, the legislative authority necessarily predominates."[26] The Constitution that the Founders produced began by describing the legislative branch of government and by declaring that "all legislative powers herein granted" were vested in the Congress. These powers were far from trivial: They included the power to tax, to regulate commerce, to declare war, and to raise and support armies. The issue for the Founders thus was not whether or not power should be given to the legislative branch. Rather, they argued over whether the legislature should be connected with the state governments or with the people of the states and to what extent the legislature should have the final say on matters of public policy.

Debate on the first issue focused on the method for selecting members of the House of Representatives. The initial Randolph plan before the convention called for two legislative chambers, with the members of the first "elected by the people of the several states" and the members of the second elected by the members of the first. Roger Sherman of Connecticut, among others, opposed this scheme, arguing that the people "should have as little to do as may be about the Government. They want information and are constantly liable to be misled."[27] George Mason disagreed with Sherman, arguing that the House of Representatives should be "the grand depository of the democratic principles of Government" and that direct election was "the only security for the rights of the people."[28] James Wilson asserted that popular election was essential if the people were to have confidence in their government, confidence without which "no government could long subsist."[29] Madison agreed, calling the election by the people of at least one branch of the legislature "a clear principle of free Government."[30]

Similar support for the democratic nature of the House was apparent in the debate over the frequency with which the members should be elected. There was strong support for the notion of annual elections. Sherman, by now reconciled to an elected House, thought that annual elections would be a means of keeping the legislators close to the people. "By remaining at the seat of government, they would acquire the habits of the place which might differ from those of their constituents."[31] But others thought that annual elections would make the legislators too dependent upon the people. Randolph supported biennial elections because he "was sensible that annual elections were a source of great mischiefs in the States,"[32] whereas Hamilton supported a three-year term on the grounds that it would promote "neither too much nor too little dependence" on the people and because frequent elections "tended to make the people listless to them."[33] Madison, ever the diplomat, persuaded his colleagues that the worst aspect of annual elections would be the inconvenience for legislators, forcing them to travel constantly between the seat of government and their constituencies, thereby taking away from the time that they would need to "acquire that knowledge of the affairs of state in general without which their trust could not be usefully discharged."[34] He supported Randolph's position for biennial elections and that carried the day.

It should be noted that although the views of those advocating election by the people and relatively short terms in office were certainly a product of republican principles, they also reflected distaste for the only apparent alternative—selection of representatives by the state legislatures. That option would have substantially weakened the concept of a national government because, in the words of Rufus King, the state legislatures "would constantly choose men subservient to their own views as contrasted to the general interest."[35]

Others recognized that a strong and democratic House was necessary if the new Constitution was to be approved. This was apparent in the debate over the power to originate money bills. Randolph thought that giving this power to the House would "prevent popular objections to the plan,"[36] and Gerry agreed, predicting that if the Senate were to share this power with the House, "the acceptance of the plan will inevitably fail."[37]

Thus it was that republican and nationalist forces came together at the convention to support a House of Representatives that would be elected once every two years by the people and would exercise the full legislative power of the national government, particularly the crucial power of the purse, which had always been the foundation of legislative authority. These forces turned next to the task of guaranteeing that such a body would not replicate on a grander scale the abuses of the similarly constituted state legislatures.

A STRONG AND SEPARATE EXECUTIVE

The argument of the Founders for a strong executive was rooted in their view of the requisites of a good government. Far from being dangerous to the notions of republican government, a strong executive, argued Hamilton, was essential: "Energy in the executive is a leading character in the definition of good government." Such an executive was necessary to protect the country against foreign attacks, to provide a "steady administration" of the laws, to protect property against unjust attack, and to protect "liberty against the enterprises and assaults of ambition, of faction and of anarchy."[38] These latter traits, it should be recalled, were the enemies of the civic virtue upon which republican government was predicated.

The convention's intention to create a strong executive was clear at the outset when, at James Wilson's urging, it vested the as-yet-to-be-defined executive power in a single person rather than in a council, as Randolph and others favored. A single executive would, Wilson said, give the "most energy, dispatch and responsibility to the office."[39] Just as crucial as its singularity, perhaps more so, to the strength of the executive was its independence from the Congress. The Founders were convinced that the legislature was the most likely source of the evils that the executive was designed to protect against; therefore, if they made the executive dependent on the Congress, they would defeat one of the main purposes of the executive. As John Adams put it, "the people's rights and liberties, and the democratical mixture in a constitution, can never be preserved without a strong executive, or, other words, without separating the executive from the legislative power."[40] Thus the separation of powers, invoked earlier to protect the legislature from the executive, was now transformed and made reciprocal to justify "strengthening the magisterial parts of the government at the expense of the legislature."[41]

The institutional independence of the presidency turned upon the design of the presidential-selection process. The key decision here was the almost last moment abandonment of a provision that would have had the president elected by the House of Representatives. Such a procedure was similar to the manner in which the majority of states selected their governors and was certainly preferable to the most obvious alternative—direct election by the people—which many of the Founders thought would invite demagoguery and decrease the likelihood of a reputable person's being chosen.[42] Roger Sherman thought that the people "will never be sufficiently informed of characters,"[43] and George Mason joked that transferring the choice of a president to the people would be analogous to referring "a trial of colors to a blind man."[44]

However, although there were deficiencies in popular selection, there also were deficiencies in election by the House. Gouverneur Morris thought that placing this power in the hands of the legislature would produce less desirable results than even popular election. The people "will never fail to prefer some man of distinguished character or services," but a legislative selection would "be the work of intrigue, of cabal, and of factions."[45] Madison reminded his colleagues that one of the reasons that a strong presidency was necessary was "to control the National Legislature," which, like the state legislatures, could be expected to have a "strong propensity to a variety of pernicious measures."[46] If the president's election and especially his reelection were in the hands of the legislature, it would be a virtual certainty that he would slavishly adhere to the instructions and wishes of the majority of that body, a result, Morris said, that would inevitably lead to legislative "usurpation and tyranny."[47]

As the convention neared the end of its business, the issue of how the president would be selected had not been resolved to the satisfaction of the delegates. The option of direct election of the president had been rejected for the last time on August 24, receiving the votes of only two state delegations. Although the plan calling for selection of the president by the House of Representatives had been approved on several occasions, many continued to worry that such a selection mechanism might be vulnerable to corruption and that it would render the president subordinate to the House. This dilemma was resolved when, two weeks before the convention adjourned, the Committee of Eleven advanced a third alternative—a group of electors chosen for the specific and sole task of electing the president and the vice president.

A similar plan had been suggested by Hamilton early in the convention but had not been seriously considered. According to Gouverneur Morris, a member of the committee, the plan spoke to "the indispensable necessity of making the Executive independent of the Legislature." Because the electors would meet only in state groups in their own state capitals rather than assembling together at one place, the danger of corruption in the selection of the president would be obviated.[48] The major objection to the plan was its provision that in case no candidate received a majority of the electoral votes—in the view of some delegates the most likely occurrence—the choice of the president would revert to the indirectly elected Senate. The suggestion that the backup selection process be moved to the House of Representatives was opposed by representatives of the smaller states, who knew that the larger ones would dominate that body. This impasse was broken by Hugh Williamson, who suggested that if the House should be called upon to select a president, each state delegation in the House would cast a single vote. With this provision in place, the new election process was approved, with only Delaware dissenting.

Before the Electoral College compromise was approved and when it was thought that the selection of the president was going to be entirely in the hands of the legislature, advocates of a strong presidency looked to a long term of office—Hamilton had suggested a lifetime appointment— as the guarantor of executive independence from the legislature. Once it had been decided that the Congress would play a secondary role in the selection process, the partisans of a strong presidency were willing to accept a shorter term, thus allaying the fears that a president serving a long term might turn toward despotic modes of behavior. With the endorsement by the convention of the president's perpetual eligibility for reelection, the barring of his cabinet members from simultaneous service in the Congress, and the acceptance of a provision prohibiting increases or decreases in the president's compensation during his term, advocates of a strong presidency were satisfied that they had accomplished their goals. The package as a whole clearly established the executive's independence of the legislature to a much greater degree than the state and national models that had operated during the postrevolutionary period.[49]

SEPARATION OF POWERS
VERSUS CHECKS AND BALANCES

After the separation of the president from the Congress, primarily to assure the strength of the former against the dangers of the latter, had been established, the question of how the two institutions would jointly exercise policy-making power had to be resolved. The intellectual obstacle was the doctrine of **separation of powers,** upon which the Founders had rested much of their argument for the institutional independence of the executive. Under a "pure" version of the doctrine, the legislature would have certain distinct powers given to it and the executive certain powers of its own, with each branch restricted to the exercise of just those powers allotted to it.[50]

There were two problems with the pure version. Practically, it was clear that policymaking required institutional cooperation that would be hampered by strict separation and that, just as important, separation would open the door to abuses of power, for if there was a clear separation of powers, nothing would prevent one branch of government from abusing those powers given exclusively to it. For example, if the president had the sole power to make governmental appointments, what would prevent him from appointing political cronies or people of low quality as the British king had done? And if the Congress had the sole power to legislate, what would protect against the national legislature's falling into the same pattern of abuses that had characterized the activities of state legislatures?

The Founders were thus in the interesting position of having to argue that the separation of powers that they had so forcefully advocated to justify the creation of an independent presidency did not mean complete separation between the various branches of government. The task of making this argument fell to Madison. He began by saying that according to the theory of separation of powers as handed down by "the oracle" Montesquieu, the "accumulation of all power, legislative, executive and judiciary in the same hands, whether of one, or few, or many, and whether hereditary, self-appointed or elective, may justly be pronounced the very definition of tyranny."[51] Madison was satisfied that the Constitution protected against such a concentration of power by separating the institutions through distinct selection processes and by preventing anyone from holding office simultaneously in more than one branch of government. And such a clear separation of institutions was not incompatible with an overlapping of powers; in fact, some degree of shared powers was inevitable and indeed essential to the maintenance of institutional independence.

Although general distinctions among the functions of each branch of government could be made, "no skill in the science of government has yet been able to discriminate and define with sufficient certainty its three great provinces—the legislative, executive, and judiciary."[52] In the constitutions of the several states, Madison noted, although the separation principle was recognized, "there is not a single instance in which the several departments of power have been kept absolutely separate and distinct."[53]

But an absolute separation also had to be avoided so as to forestall the very tyranny against which the separation doctrine was designed to protect. For unless the executive had a voice in the process of legislation, the legislature would inexorably increase its power and encroach on those powers properly in the hands of other branches. Against such encroachments, the "parchment barriers" of a constitutional enumeration of prerogatives would not prevail.[54] Nor would appeals to the people stop such encroachments; in such conflicts the people would prefer the legislature to the executive or the judiciary because its members "are numerous. They are distributed and dwell among the people at large" and they enjoy "a personal influence among the people."[55] Thus, the protection against tyranny could not be accomplished by a complete separation of powers.

So, in the end, Madison argued, an independent executive alone would not provide sufficient protection against the tyranny of the legislature. It was ironic that for institutional independence to survive, a system of "mutual relations" among institutions was required, one that would prevent the "gradual concentration of powers in the same department" by "giving to those who administer each department the necessary constitutional means and personal motives to resist encroachments of the others."[56] This strategy of "reciprocal distrust"[57] provided the Founders with a safeguard against the legislative tyranny that they feared and at the same time provided reassurance to those whose primary fear was executive despotism.

This approach constituted a retreat from the idea that good government depended upon "moral principles or rhetorical persuasion." Only by "placing a series of obstructions in its path" could a republican government be saved from the forces that would otherwise corrupt it.[58] The Founders thus reverted to the views of John Locke who, though committed to legislative authority, "had that distrust both of Kings and of legislatures which made him unwilling to see power concentrated in either of them."[59]

THE NECESSARY CONSTITUTIONAL MEANS

Even though the Framers often spoke about their desire to prevent abuses of power by either the legislature or the executive, it is clear that their major concern was legislative abuses. The "series of obstructions" that they placed in the Constitution were, for the most part, aimed at the corruption, the misinformation, and the propensity to injustice that, in their view, typified legislative institutions.

The Veto

Pursuant to the plan for a partial rather than a pure separation of powers, the Constitution did not vest legislative powers exclusively in the Congress. In order to complete the process of legislation, bills had to be presented to the president for his signature. If he failed to sign a bill, Congress had the opportunity to enact it over the president's veto provided that the support of two-thirds of each chamber could be secured. Earlier, Hamilton had advocated an absolute presidential veto, and the convention agreed initially to a veto that could be overridden only by a three-fourths vote. However, the more easily obtained two-thirds was accepted in compensation for the decisions to move from legislative selection of the president to the Electoral College scheme and to allow the president unlimited eligibility for reelection.

The veto, in Madison's view, would "restrain the Legislature from encroaching on the other coordinate Departments, or on the rights of the people at large; or from passing laws unwise in their principle, or incorrect in their form."[60] George Mason was more blunt: The danger from the Congress was unwise legislation and the aim of the veto was to "discourage demagogues" in the legislature from attempting to pass such "unjust and pernicious laws."[61] Gouverneur Morris was quite specific about what those laws might be: "emissions of paper money, largesses to the people, a remission of debts," evils against which "a strong check will be necessary."[62]

Appointments

Under most postrevolutionary state constitutions, appointments of judges and high administrative officials were controlled by the legislature. This practice was a product of the Whig view that the royal control of appointments had allowed the king to bestow favors and through that process exercise a corrupting power on the legislature. However, by 1788, concern had shifted from executive to legislative corruption. According to Madison, legislative appointment had eliminated "all responsibility" and created "a perpetual source of faction and corruption."[63]

The fear was that members of the new Congress would either appoint themselves to administrative positions or involve themselves in unsavory patronage schemes. In any event, no one could be held responsible for the appointments, given the collective nature of the legislature.

It is understandable that most of the convention's discussion of the appointment process focused on the judiciary. Madison opposed a plan for the legislative appointment of judges, citing the danger of "intrigue and partiality" and observing that the members could not be competent "judges of the requisite qualifications."[64] A week later he suggested, and the Convention agreed, that judges be appointed by the Senate, "which as a less numerous and more select body would be more competent judges, and which was sufficiently numerous to justify such a confidence in them."[65] Later, Gouverneur Morris moved for presidential appointment of judges, but this was defeated. When the Committee on Detail reported in early August, the president had the power to appoint executive officers, whereas the Senate retained the power to appoint judges as well as ambassadors.

Morris, however, continued his assault on senatorial appointment. He considered the body as "too numerous for the purpose; as subject to cabal; and as devoid of responsibility."[66] There the matter stood until the closing weeks of the Convention when the same special committee (upon which, as already noted, Morris sat) that had produced the Electoral College compromise, also produced a new version of the appointment power in which the president would appoint all officers, judges, and ambassadors with the advice and consent of the Senate. Morris defended the plan as an ideal compromise: "As the President was to nominate there would be responsibility, and as the Senate was to concur there would be security."[67] Although opposed by Wilson as weakening the executive and by Gerry as giving the president too much power, the proposal was accepted.

Once again, the separation-of-powers approach yielded to the checks-and-balances strategy. Prior to the Revolution, state governors had abused the appointment power, and in the postrevolutionary period, legislatures had been the culprits. The plan for sharing the appointment power between the president and the Senate would protect against abuses by either institution.

War and Peace

On the question of control of foreign affairs, the convention dealt rather quickly with the issue of war but struggled long and hard on the issue of treaties. The Committee on Detail's simple recommendation was that the Congress be given the power "to make war." Charles

Pinckney of South Carolina led the attack on this provision, arguing that the proceedings of the Congress would be "too slow" and that the House would be "too numerous for such deliberations." Pierce Butler suggested that given Pinckney's argument, the power to make war should be vested with the president, "who will have all the requisite qualities, and will not make war but when the nation will support it." Mason opposed both Butler and Pinckney, arguing that the president "could not be safely trusted" with the power to make war and that the Senate also was an inappropriate body to hold the power. Madison suggested, and the convention agreed, that the word "make" be struck from the provision and that the word "declare" be substituted, "leaving the Executive the power to repel sudden attack."[68]

A strong congressional role in decisions to go to war was thus ensured. The president's war-making role was to be limited to that of responding to an immediate attack and once the country was at war, to assuming the "supreme command and direction of the military and naval forces as first general and admiral of the Confederacy."[69] The convention was much more sharply divided on the issue of treaty making. In the debate over the war-making power, Oliver Ellsworth of Connecticut, supporting a strong congressional role, argued that "it should be more easy to get out of war than into it. War is also a simple and overt declaration. Peace [is] attended [to] with intricate and secret negotiations."[70] This distinction was reflected in the Committee on Detail's proposal placing the treaty-making power in the hand of the Senate rather than the House, on the theory that the former could move with greater dispatch and secrecy than the latter. Indicative of the lingering distrust for the executive was the absence from this version of any role for the president in the treaty-making process.

Opposition to this proposal came from two quarters. Friends of the presidency, such as John Mercer of Maryland, thought that the treaty-making power "belonged to the Executive department."[71] Madison agreed, arguing that because the Senate represented the states, the president, as a representative of the nation as a whole, should be an agent in treaties.[72] Representatives of the large states, noting that treaties would be the law of the land, were particularly concerned that a bare majority of the Senate, representing only a small percentage of the population, could, through the treaty-making power, take significant actions. As an example, James Wilson pointed out that a previously approved provision barred Congress from taxing exports, but "the Senate alone can make a treaty requiring all the rice of South Carolina to be sent to some particular port."[73]

The Committee of Eleven, in reporting its various compromises to the convention early in September, responded to the advocates of a strong presidency and those who feared abuses of senatorial power: The power to make treaties was moved to the president, acting "by and with the advice and consent of the Senate." Treaties, in order to go into effect, would need to be approved by a two-thirds vote of the Senate. Wilson, who had been generally displeased about the additional powers conferred upon the Senate by the committee (including at that point the power to select the president if the Electoral College failed in that mission), decried "the dangerous tendency toward aristocracy"[74] and renewed his proposal that the consent of the House as well as the Senate be required for treaties. Roger Sherman disagreed, arguing that "the necessity of secrecy in the case of treaties forbade a reference of them to the whole Legislature."[75] This view prevailed, and Wilson's proposal to add the House to the process received only the one vote of his own Pennsylvania.

The discussion then turned to the requirement that two-thirds of the Senate approve a treaty, an issue that was tied up with sectional concerns. One of the great fears among the southern states was that the northern states would, in a treaty, negotiate away the right to free navigation on the Mississippi. The two-thirds provision, designed to assuage these fears,[76] prevailed over Wilson's argument that "the minority might perpetuate war against the sense of the majority."[77] During this discussion, Madison offered a compromise that would have allowed peace treaties to be approved by a majority and that would have even allowed two-thirds of the Senate to make peace treaties without the agreement of the president. Madison defended the latter provision with the interesting argument that the president "would necessarily derive so much power and importance from a state of war that he might be tempted, if authorized, to impede a treaty of peace."[78] This view was seconded by Pierce Butler, who thought it "a necessary security against ambitious and corrupt Presidents."[79] But Gouverneur Morris, ever the friend of a strong presidency, thought "that no peace ought to be made without the concurrence of the President, who was the general guardian of the national interest."[80] In the end, both proposals failed in the face of sectional concerns that any provision making it easier for the Senate to control treaties might harm particular areas of the country.

In summary, the convention, following Ellsworth's suggestion, increased the difficulty of declaring war by giving this power entirely to the Congress but, in their view, made it easier to achieve peace by removing the legislative power of the House from the treaty-making process in favor of another power-sharing arrangement between the indirectly elected Senate and the president. Moreover, the specific words of the constitutional provision indicate that the convention viewed the treaty-making power as truly shared. As Edward Corwin noted in his study of the presidency, the phraseology allowing the president to make treaties "by and with the advice and consent of the Senate," rather than confining the Senate to the limited role of ratifying treaties arrived at independently by the President, clearly "associates the president and the Senate throughout the entire process of treaty-making."[81] John Jay observed that the proposed arrangement would draw upon the particular strengths of both the Senate and the president: "Our negotiations for treaties shall have every advantage which can be derived from the talents, information, integrity and deliberate investigations, on the one hand, and from secrecy and dispatch on the other."[82]

The Senate

The most prominent check on legislative power was the creation of a second independent legislative chamber. As Wilson put it, "a division of power in the legislative body is the most useful restraint upon the legislature because it operates constantly."[83] After the convention had ended, Madison cited the Senate as the saving grace of a republican system in which "the legislative authority necessarily predominates. The remedy for this inconvenience is to divide the legislature into different branches."[84]

The Senate's genealogy can be traced back to the privy councils that existed under the prerevolutionary state constitutions. After the Revolution, the functions of the councils typically were turned over to second chambers, which usually were elected by the people, but from larger constituencies than the colonial assemblies, thereby yielding a smaller legislative body, often composed of people of somewhat higher status than members of the more numerous assemblies. However, in the view of the Founders, these bodies too had fallen prey to the vices of legislatures. Writing in 1785, Madison lamented "the inability of the senates to give wisdom and steadiness to legislation."[85]

Edmund Randolph's Virginia plan, the starting point for the convention's deliberations, provided for a bicameral national legislature; that such an arrangement would find its way into the final document was never seriously in question. Nor was the function of a second chamber in doubt. Early in the convention, when Randolph was asked what the functions of such a chamber would be, he responded that the Senate was to provide a cure for the "evils" that arose from "the turbulence and follies of democracy."[86] Gouverneur Morris sounded the same theme, suggesting that the object of the second chamber was "to check the precipitation, changeableness, and excesses of the first branch."[87] George Mason was even more explicit, saying that "one important object in constituting the Senate was to secure the rights of property."[88] Morris proposed that senators serve for life so that the Senate would not exhibit "a servile complaisance" to the House and so that its members would "have great personal property" and "aristocratic pride."[89]

Whereas the existence and purpose of the Senate were clear from the outset, the questions of how the Senate would be selected, how the states would be represented in it, and what its powers would be were more continually at issue. Randolph had suggested election of the Senate by the House; others advocated direct election by the people as practiced in the states; still others suggested election by the state legislatures. The first two options were rejected as defeating the purpose of the Senate. Selection by the House would not achieve an independent Senate and selection by the people would leave the Senate as vulnerable to the "turbulence" of democracy as the House. As the convention progressed, the notion of the Senate as the keystone of the federal arrangement began to emerge. The ultimate solution was that the Senate would be selected by the state legislatures and that each state would be represented equally within it. The term of six years (lifetime appointments, as Morris had suggested, would have been unacceptable) would guard against "the mutability of public councils arising from a rapid succession of new members."[90]

Save for the right to originate revenue bills, which would be reserved for the House, the Senate would have an equal voice with the House in all legislation. In Madison's view this would "double the security of the people" against "schemes of usurpation or perfidy where the ambition or corruption of one would otherwise be sufficient."[91] However, the convention seemed to be worried most about the "ambition and corruption" of the House, for, as we have seen, the Senate was given significant powers in regard to treaty making and the appointment of administrative and judicial officers.

It is important to remember today that two hundred years ago the Senate, though designated by the Framers as a legislative body, was viewed by them as more akin to a privy council. Throughout the debates at the convention, when delegates used the term "legislature," they were almost always referring to the House of Representatives. It is far from certain that the Founders would have been willing to confer substantial powers in regard to foreign policy and governmental appointments on the modern democratized Senate described in the next chapter.

Presidential Power

Whereas the members of the convention argued at length about the power of the president in regard to the veto, appointments, and war and peace, other provisions of the Constitution dealing with presidential power seem to have been adopted virtually without debate. These include the president's responsibility "to take care that the laws be faithfully executed," role as commander in chief, and responsibilities to give information to the Congress on the state of the Union, to recommend measures to the Congress that he judged "necessary and expedient," to convene special sessions of the Congress, and to make appointments to fill vacancies that occurred when the Congress was in recess.[92]

The Constitution's phrasing of the president's major powers seems rife with ambiguities. How was the president to "make" treaties? What is implied by the statement that he shall faithfully execute the laws? Must all laws be executed, or does he have any discretionary power in this respect? Are there other, broader powers in foreign affairs implied in his treaty-making and commander-in-chief roles? There are a number of plausible explanations for the vagueness of the Constitution and the virtual silence of the convention on so many of these key aspects of presidential power. Whereas the Founders were quite familiar with legislative institutions, their main experience with executive institutions had been with the British Crown, the royal governors, the weak governors of the postrevolutionary states, and the collective executive at the national level under the Articles of Confederation. Because they knew that they wanted a strong executive that would still be compatible with republican liberty, none of these existing models was, in their view, worthy of emulation. Thus, their vagueness might mean that they really did not know exactly what they wanted this office to look like. They must have known that they were leaving a good deal unspecified, but perhaps they were comforted by their certain knowledge that Washington would be the first president and that his necessarily precedent-setting inter- pretations of presidential power were likely to be appropriate and generally accepted.

Finally, it is also possible that their vagueness about the presidency bespoke their desire for a much stronger presidency than the country at large probably would have been prepared to accept. The Founders may have assumed that presidents could interpret the general terms of Article II in an expansive way when that was necessary, whereas the more specific terms that the Founders used in their enumeration of congressional powers in Article I would restrict similar attempts by the legislature to expand its power. Intended or not, as we shall see in Chapter 3, presidential power did, in fact, expand primarily through this mechanism of interpretations by incumbent presidents, which in turn set precedents for their successors.

A CONSTITUTION AGAINST GOVERNMENT

In Chapter 1, the need to reconcile the responsiveness and liberty guaranteed by strong legislatures with the executive's capacity to act effectively and responsibly was described as the fundamental challenge confronting political systems that maintain a commitment to popular government. Those who wrote the Constitution at the Philadelphia convention attempted to meet this challenge with a constitutional design that established a national government composed of separate institutions sharing power.

What the Founders were seeking was good government, but they also recognized two standards of good government between which there existed a substantial tension. The first was republicanism, which Madison defined in *Federalist No. 39* as

> a government which derives all of its powers directly or indirectly from the great body of the people, and is administered by people holding their offices during pleasure for a limited period or during good behavior. It is *essential* to such a government that it be derived from the great body of the society. . . . It is *sufficient* for such a government that the persons administering it be appointed either directly or indirectly by the people.

In Madison's view, no other form of government "would be reconcilable with the genius of the people of America; with the fundamental principles of the Revolution; or with that honorable determination which animates every votary of freedom to rest all our political institutions on the capacity of mankind for self-government."[93]

Their second standard for good government was that it be effective. In Madison's terms: "Energy in government is essential to that security against external and internal danger and to that prompt and salutary execution of the laws which enter into the very definition of good government." Madison described once again the "irregular and mutable legislation" and "the vicissitudes and uncertainties which characterize the state administrations." He argued that "stability in government is essential to national character and to the advantages annexed to it, as well as to that repose and confidence in the minds of the people, which are among the chief blessings of civil society."[94]

Madison then explained the difficulties involved in reconciling the two standards of good government, "in combining the requisite stability and energy in government with the inviolable attention due to liberty and to the republican form," in "mingling" the two elements of liberty and stability "in their due proportions." He encapsulated the problem in the following passage:

The genius of republican liberty seems to demand on one side not only that all power should be derived from the people but that those intrusted with it should be kept in dependence on the people by a short duration of their appointments; and that even during this short period the trust should be placed not in a few but a number of hands. Stability, on the contrary, requires that the hands in which power is lodged should continue for a length of time the same. A frequent change of men will result from a frequent return of elections; and a frequent change of measures. from a frequent change of men; whilst energy in government requires not only a certain duration of power, but the execution by a single hand.[95]

Madison's words provide us with an understanding of the ambivalence with which he and his colleagues approached the task of designing the Constitution. By their words and deeds they manifested profound doubts about the perfectability of people and of political institutions based upon the people. Nonetheless, true to their republican principles, they began by consigning the bulk of governmental powers to a strong legislature, with one house elected directly by the people and the other indirectly through the state legislatures. The Framers did so, even though they knew that they would be paying a price in terms of effective public policy, that the members of the popularly elected House might well be of low quality and therefore uninformed, that given its large size, it would be slow to act, and given its connection with the people, it might be too responsive to their self-interested demands and therefore too disposed toward unwise policies. "In all very numerous assemblies," Madison wrote, "passion never fails to wrest the scepter from reason."[96]

Their remedy for these failings was to create a series of checks upon legislative power. If a majority of the House acted unwisely, it would still need to convince a majority of the indirectly elected Senate. If majorities of both chambers acted unwisely, the president could still veto their actions, in which case the support of two-thirds of each chamber would be necessary in order to proceed. If the Congress appointed judges and other officers of government, it might do so in a corrupt manner, so it was left to the president to nominate such officials and to the Senate to confirm the nominations. If the Senate were to negotiate treaties, the parochial interests of individual states might distort the process, so the president and the Senate were given this power to exercise jointly.

The problem was that the remedy for the failings of legislatures did little to increase the likelihood of effective public policy. What the Founders created was not simply a constitution against the legislature. They were also suspicious of the executive, as witnessed by the checks imposed upon the president in regard to appointments and the making and approval of treaties and his dependence upon the legislature for money, for declarations of war, and for action to raise and support military forces. Thus, even though the primary goal of the Founders may have been to protect against legislative abuses by installing various obstructions to legislative actions, these obstructions also acted reciprocally, to impede executive as well as legislative action.

In this sense, the plan that they produced is more properly viewed as a **constitution against government** in its entirety rather than simply a set of safeguards against legislative dominance. The system of mutual checks, in John Dickinson's view, would protect against "errors and frauds in government," not simply against legislative errors.[97] Madison saw it as a system that recognized the imperfectibility of man. "If angels were to govern men, neither external nor internal controls on government would be necessary." But men clearly were not angels, so there was "the necessity of auxiliary precautions." The best strategy was "to divide and arrange the several offices in such a manner that each may be a check on the other."[98]

The Founders' attempt to achieve republican government while at the same time avoiding its dangers resulted then in a government whose policy-making procedures could adhere to neither managerial nor democratic standards. From a managerial standpoint, policy actions of any sort would be difficult to take because the government was beyond the control of majorities in any single institution. Instead, action required the support of majorities in both chambers of the Congress, support from the president, and, it may be argued, support from a majority of the Supreme Court. What would emerge from such a complex process was anyone's guess, but it was unlikely to be policy that was informed, timely, coherent, effective, and responsible.

The system also failed to conform to democratic criteria because all the institutions involved in the policy-making process, save the House of Representatives, were either significantly distanced or removed entirely from the influence of popular majorities. The system was designed that way for a number of reasons: the Founders' fears that too much power in the hands of the people would produce anarchy, their desire to guarantee the independence of the various institutions by creating a different method for selecting the personnel of each, and their desire to protect minorities, particularly wealthy economic minorities, from the tyranny of majorities.

The Founders probably would not have been upset by their failure to develop a system that would conform to democratic standards, for that was never their goal. But they were intent on creating a system that would have the capacity to act and to act effectively, and Hamilton at least was aware that they might have failed to do so. During the ratification debates, Hamilton put the relationship between checks and balances and action this way: "When you have divided government and nicely balanced the departments of government; when you have strongly connected the virtue of your rulers with their interests; when, in short, you have rendered your system as perfect as human forms can be; you must place confidence; you must give power."[99] Similarly, in *Federalist No. 26* he said, "Confidence must be placed somewhere . . . it is better to hazard the abuse of that confidence than to embarrass that government and endanger the public safety by impolitic restrictions on legislative authority."[100]

Perhaps the Founders simply overestimated the capacity of the system to avoid deadlock and to allow appropriate governmental action to occur. Jeffrey Tulis suggested that the Founders knew that by creating a legislature characterized by deliberation and an executive characterized by energy, conflict between the two branches would ensue, but they hoped that such conflict would produce effective governmental decisions rather than stalemate or deadlock.[101] They probably hoped as well that the system of checks and balances, by slowing down the decisionmaking process, would create conditions under which the public good or the public interest would be more likely to emerge. Once that happened, they assumed that those holding the levers of power in the separated institutions would act cooperatively and the system would work.

However, it is at least equally plausible that after the experience of postrevolutionary America, the Founders were much more willing to run the risk of government inaction than face the dangers of unwise government action. As Henry Adams summarized the Founders' views, including those of his great grandfather John: "The great object of terror and suspicion to the people of the thirteen provinces was power; not merely in the hands of a president or a prince, of one assembly or several, of many citizens or of few, but power in the abstract, wherever it existed and under whatever name it was known." Whereas other nations had decided that a supreme power needed to be vested somewhere, for the Founders, "no such supreme power need exist in government . . . because absolute power in any form was inconsistent with freedom, and . . . the new government should start from the idea that the public liberties depend upon denying uncontrolled authority in the political system in its parts or its whole."[102]

AN INVITATION TO STRUGGLE

Thus, despite Hamilton's concern for placing confidence, despite the Founders' fears of governmental weakness, despite their passionate desire for good government with the strength to act wisely and effectively, in the end they constructed a "Newtonian relationship"[103] between the executive and the legislature, one in which any attempt by one branch to act forcefully or to change the relationship would provoke an equal and probably opposite reaction from the other. In this sense, Corwin's view that the system of checks and balances provided "an invitation to struggle for the privilege of directing American foreign policy"[104] can be extended to the entire operation of the federal government as it was designed by the Framers.

Struggle has indeed been the hallmark of legislative-executive relations in the United States. Tension between the president and the Congress would have occurred even under a different constitutional format, but the roots and the rules of presidential-congressional relations are also very much a product of the principles and compromises articulated and entered into by those who participated at the Philadelphia convention. It was there, at the very founding of the republic, that the challenge of reconciling managerially good public policy with what they viewed as minimal democratic procedures was taken up. Unfortunately, the complex system of joint presidential-congressional government that they designed created a policy-making process that failed to meet democratic standards and because of its strong bias toward inaction, would also fail to produce policies that would meet managerial standards.

Much, of course, has happened between 1787 and now. As we will see in Chapter 3, the context within which U.S. political institutions operate has changed dramatically, particularly in regard to the scope of the government, its involvement with foreign countries, and its relationship with the American people. These changes have meant that the president and the Congress today differ in many important respects from the way in which they were envisioned by the Founders. As generations of presidents, representatives, senators, and Supreme Court justices have read the words of the Constitution and turned those abstract phrases to the real task of governing, they have clarified the ambiguities of the document and found new meanings and interpretations of the powers that it confers. This in turn has meant new attempts to deal with the challenge of reconciling democracy with good public policy.

3

The Transformed Presidency
and the Evolved Congress

It probably would not surprise the Founders to know that the presidency and the Congress of today are quite different from the institutions that they created two centuries ago. Although they certainly could not have foreseen the magnitude of the economic, social, political, and geographical changes that would take place, they knew that the nation's future would be different from its past and that the Constitution would have to be designed with that in mind. As Hamilton advised the readers of *Federalist No. 34*, constitutions "are not to be framed upon a calculation of existing exigencies but upon a combination of these with the probable exigencies of the ages."[1]

The Founders thus drew up the Constitution in such a manner that it could accommodate the many changes that they knew would take place. Such, perhaps, was the reason for the studied ambiguities in the phrasing of the executive power noted in Chapter 2 or the reason for empowering the Congress in the last paragraph of Article I, Section 8, "to make all laws which shall be necessary and proper for carrying into execution" the powers "vested by the Constitution in the Government of the United States." It is clear that the Founders decided that theirs would be a "living Constitution," one whose terms could be interpreted and altered to meet the real tasks of governing.

Thus, the most significant modifications in the policy-making roles of the Congress and the presidency and in the relationship between the two institutions occurred, not through the formal process of constitutional amendment, but through a more informal process typically set in motion by circumstances in which the words of the Constitution proved inadequate to the governmental problems at hand. In such instances, presidents usually asserted power and Congress, often after some initial resistance, ultimately acquiesced. Only rarely did the Congress or, when called upon, the Supreme Court reject such presidentially initiated redefinitions of executive power. In fact, during the twentieth century, Congress took the lead by conferring new powers on the president. And once a new power was exercised by a president, the only thing that his successors needed to do when they wanted to exercise that power was to cite the earlier action as a justifying precedent. In any case, the result, whether through new laws, judicial decisions, or a president's precedent-setting action, was an expanded understanding of executive power.

Nonetheless, it would be a gross but not uncommon oversimplification to reduce the history of U.S. political institutions to presidential ascendency and congressional decline. In fact, as the prominence of the national government increased, both the president and the Congress became more powerful. What did happen, however, was that the cumulative impact of all that took place from 1787 on was to transform the presidency into an institution radically different from the one described in the Constitution, an institution that would be barely recognizable to those who designed it. The Congress, in contrast, although also a very different and more prominent institution today than it was two hundred years ago, remains in its essential aspects what it was then: a legislature, with the basic structure and format that have always characterized such institutions.

So there are two separate courses of institutional development to describe: the transformation of the presidency and the evolution of the Congress. But first let us turn to a description of the changes that took place in the larger society, changes to which the president and the Congress needed to adapt.

CONTEXTS

Quite obviously, America today is different from the America of 1888, which in turn was different from the America that the Founders knew. Recounting the changes that have taken place in U.S. politics, society, and culture over the years since the Philadelphia convention is an enterprise that has filled library shelves. Only three such contextual changes, selected because of their special significance for the Congress and the presidency, are discussed here: the increase in the size of government, the internationalizing of the environment within which that government operates, and the democratization of the U.S. political system.

Size of Government

When the Constitution was written, the population of the United States consisted of fewer than 870,000 people, of whom most were living along the eastern seaboard. Although there were centers of commerce in Boston, New York, and Philadelphia and nascent industries as well, the economy of the new nation was primarily agrarian. A nation of this sort required certain minimal services from its government. Probably the most essential were to provide for defense against attacks from foreign and Indian nations, to protect against domestic disorder, and to establish and operate courts of law. Government's role in the economic life of the country was to provide an environment that would enable individuals to operate within a free market, and to that end, the new national government was responsible for establishing a stable monetary system, enforcing the obligations of contracts, protecting patents, and seeing to it that the mail was delivered. To pay for all these tasks, the government was authorized to collect taxes and to borrow money. The government established to perform these functions did not have to be very large: In the beginning, it had 50 employees (9 in the State Department, 2 in the War Department, and 39 in Hamilton's Treasury Department). As departments were added, these numbers grew, but by 1821, there were still fewer than 7,000 people employed by the federal government.[2]

Today, the United States is a continental nation with a population of about 250 million. It is an industrial, and even a postindustrial society, with agriculture an ever-decreasing part of the economy and with most of its population working in either manufacturing or service jobs. The responsibilities of governments at all levels have expanded, but those of the national government have increased geometrically from the few essentials identified earlier. The contemporary federal government, among other things, builds roads and airports, owns and operates certain railroads and power companies, partially regulates the environment as well as the food and drugs that are consumed, oversees the production of farm products and energy, has a role in educating children and in protecting the public health, finances academic research in both the sciences and the humanities, and although adhering to the basic tenets of market capitalism, nonetheless provides a wide array of economic goods and services to various categories of people, including the elderly, the disabled, army veterans, the unemployed, the poor, college students, bankers, fishermen, and owners of small businesses, to name but a few recipients of federal assistance.

To do all that it does, the national government is organized into no fewer than 400 bureaus and agencies employing approximately 2.8 million civilians and 2 million members of the armed forces. Among the civilians are accountants, attorneys, statisticians, doctors, biologists, engineers, librarians and countless other professionals—the experts required to deliver the expanded services to which the national government is now committed.

As the number of governing tasks and the number of people necessary to perform them expanded, policy-making became, for both the president and the Congress, a considerably more demanding task than the Framers of the Constitution could have possibly envisioned. For the president, the extraordinary increase in the number of people and agencies ultimately responsible to him as chief executive and as commander in chief had the effect of expanding both the power and the organizational complexity of his office. The Congress needed to find ways to legislate in policy areas about which its members knew very little while at the same time exercising some degree of control over the rapidly expanding executive branch. In short, the Framers' Constitution against government needed to adapt to the nation's continuously rising expectations for a more active governmental role in the life of the country.

Internationalization

Concerns about U.S. relations with foreign countries and with the possibility of war were not far from the minds of those who wrote the Constitution. "To provide for the common defense" are among the first words in the document, and the responsibility to raise and support an army and a navy figures prominently among the duties of the Congress. The Framers' belief that strong leadership was especially important at times of national danger was one of their major justifications for creating an independent president and for conferring the role of commander in chief upon him. Nonetheless, although the United States fought a war with Britain in 1812 and several local wars in Latin America during the nineteenth century, and although relations with European powers always occupied the attention of U.S. leaders, for its first one hundred years or more international relations were less important to the United States than they were to the countries of Europe.

This was so for a number of reasons: the geographical isolation of the United States from militarily strong powers, its proximity to militarily weak neighbors in its own hemisphere, its capacity to expand its territory through the internal conquest of Native Americans and Mexicans rather than through more risky overseas expansionism, and, finally, the nation's relatively high degree of economic self-sufficiency.[3] But all of this came to an abrupt end in the twentieth century. With respect to economics, the new century saw the end of U.S. self-sufficiency as the United States, like every other industrial nation, came to rely upon natural resources located in other countries. Wars and alliances designed to protect access to foreign resources and markets became as much a part of U.S. policy as they had always been for Europe. And today, a truly international economic system, in which trade and monetary matters often are the most important dimension of U.S. relations with other nations, has emerged.

The United States has, since the turn of the century, fought in two world wars and two major regional wars in Asia. It has been instrumental in the development and deployment of weapons capable of destroying large portions of humankind and has been involved since 1946 in a prolonged cold war with an adversary capable of using such weapons against it. Most important of all, the United States has become a world power with a huge standing army, a mammoth military establishment, and a self-defined role as the policeman and protector of the free world. Pursuant to that role and contrary to Washington's advice against entangling alliances, the United States now has bilateral and multilateral military arrangements around the world. Contrary to the isolationist slogans of the nineteenth century, the United States now concerns itself with the internal and external politics of nations in every corner of the earth and has regularly intervened, diplomatically and militarily, in the affairs of other countries.

The internationalizing of U.S. politics has had a dramatic impact on the power of the presidency and on the president's relationship with the Congress. Presidential power expanded on the assumption that the executive had both a special responsibility and an ability to act in foreign and military policy. Because of the need for quick and decisive actions during international crises and a growing presumption that the president had more information on these issues than anyone else, the Congress and the American people—each in their own way seeking the psychological comfort of knowing that someone was in charge in the dangerous and unpredictable world of international relations—were more willing to accept broader presidential powers in this area than in the context of more normal domestic politics.[4] And as more issues acquired this international dimension, it became increasingly difficult to draw clear lines between U.S. military and foreign policy concerns on the one hand and U.S. domestic policy concerns on the other, thereby further enhancing the power of the presidency.

Democratization

Those who wrote the Constitution, as we have seen, were suspicious of rule by the people and frightened by an "excess of democracy." Therefore, the House of Representatives was the only part of the national government to be elected directly by the people. The Senate was to be selected by the state legislatures, members of the Supreme Court were to be appointed by the president with the advice and consent of the Senate, and the president was to be selected by electors who in turn were to be selected by state legislatures, thereby removing that office by at least two steps from the direct influence of the people. Finally, when the Founders referred to the "people" who would elect only the House and indirectly elect the president and the Senate, they meant white males, and several of the Founders meant only white males who held property.

The rapidity with which this very limited commitment to democracy would expand testifies to the difficulty of restraining the forces of popular government. The first barrier to fall was the Founders' elaborate plan for the president to be chosen through the independent and considered judgment of a small group of knowledgeable electors or failing that, by the House of Representatives. By the time of the presidential election of 1800, the Electoral College plan had been subverted by the emergence of national political parties. The parties organized slates of electors pledged in advance to the party's candidates for president and vice president, thereby eliminating the possibility of the electors' acting independently. And by 1828, with the election of Andrew Jackson, nearly all state constitutions had been changed so that the voters rather than the state legislatures would choose among these competing slates of electors. This, combined with the virtual disappearance of property qualifications for voting, enabled Jackson to claim that he was the first president elected by the people, although "the people" would not include the majority of women until 1920 and most southern blacks until the late 1960s.

Jackson's claim was further bolstered by the democratization of the process by which the parties decided which candidate their slates of electors would support. In the period immediately after parties emerged, the power to nominate presidential candidates was exercised by the party's members of Congress. In the 1820s, this "congressional caucus" system began to yield to national party conventions that included a broader, more representative group of party members from all over the nation, rather than the small party elite that happened to be serving in the Congress. During the Progressive Era at the beginning of the twentieth century, the process of democratizing the convention itself began with the introduction of presidential-preference primaries. Primaries gave citizen-members of the party the opportunity to express their wishes to the convention delegates about who the party's nominee should be, and in some states the delegates themselves were actually selected in party primaries. Finally, the post-1968 reform era established the current system, in which practically all delegates to the national convention are selected on the basis of the presidential candidate whom they favor, with the selection taking place either at local caucuses open to all party members residing in a particular locale or in primaries. Now the convention formally confers the party's nomination on a candidate who in effect has been selected by a broader democratic process that takes place prior to the convention. This, combined with the democratization of the Electoral College, has produced what the Founders feared the most: a president in fact, though not in law, popularly elected by the people.

As for the Congress, the major effect of democratization was felt in the Senate where the constitutional plan for state legislators to select senators began to erode as early as the 1830s. During that decade, the practice of the public canvass came into being. Candidates for the Senate would campaign for the election of state legislators who, once in office, would in turn vote for them for the Senate. A few decades later, the practice of parties' endorsing slates of state legislative candidates pledged to a particular senatorial candidate emerged, followed at the end of the century by a direct primary method for selecting the senatorial candidate to whom the legislative candidates would be pledged. In some states, constitutions were amended to require state legislators to select the candidate who won the primary and in other states the legislators were to be further advised in November by a popular vote between the winners of the party primaries. Thus, by 1913, when the Seventeenth Amendment, requiring popular election of senators was approved, about half the states already had procedures of one sort or another that provided the functional equivalent of direct election.[5]

With direct election of senators and the adoption of presidential-preference primaries, the democratization process took a decidedly antiparty turn. This was ironic in light of the crucial role that the parties had played in democratizing the Constitution during the first decades of the republic. In the early years, their activities had democratized the Electoral College and expanded the suffrage. Later Andrew Jackson's Democratic party, with the slogan of "equal rights for all, special privileges for none," declared war on monopolies, opened the door of public service to the common man, encouraged the rapid distribution of public lands, and introduced the mass election campaigns in which "stump speaking developed into an art and cajolery a profession, while whisky flowed freely at the hustings."[6] Moreover, during the nineteenth century, urban political parties were instrumental in integrating newly arrived immigrants into the political system.

However, by the end of the nineteenth century, a segment of the U.S. population, with the Progressive movement in the forefront, had come to view the parties as undemocratic organizations run by a small and corrupt oligarchy of political bosses. The key to the power of this oligarchy was their capacity to decide who the party's nominees would be for every state and local office, from town council to the U.S. Senate. And because many parts of the nation were at that time dominated by a single political party, nomination in those one-party states was tantamount to election. The combination of boss domination of the nomination process and one-partyism, the Progressives argued, effectively removed the people from the process of electing their political leaders. At the national level, things were not much better. Although citizens could select between the nominees of the parties in relatively competitive presidential elections, the nominees themselves were picked in the proverbial smoke-filled rooms of national conventions dominated by party bosses from around the country.

The primary system, the Progressives felt, was the key to wresting control of the party's nomination process from these leaders and returning it to the people. Primaries would allow the rank-and-file members of the party to decide who the party's nominees would be for state and local offices and for seats in the House and the Senate. At the presidential level, party members would either elect delegates to the national convention in primaries or at least cast presidential-preference votes that presumably would influence the nomination decisions that the party leaders would make at the convention. The success of the Progressive movement was quite striking. By 1910, forty-four of the forty-six states had some form of a primary law, and by 1916, more than half the delegates to each national party convention were directly elected in primaries.[7]

As the influence of party leaders on the nomination process declined, candidates for office became to that same degree independent of the party organization. Rather than to ingratiate themselves with party leaders, prospective candidates had to campaign among and establish their own relationship with the voters, a relationship increasingly unmediated by party organizations. And because they were no longer beholden to party leaders for their nomination, officeholders were no longer obliged to heed the advice of these leaders about the positions that they should take on the issues of the day. Thus, the strength of party organizations in the Congress began to decline, and, as we shall see, presidential candidates also came to be increasingly independent of their political parties.

Factors other than the primary system also contributed to the decline of U.S. political parties. During their heyday, local and state parties had flourished by providing patronage jobs and various social services to the party faithful. With the advent of civil service reform at the national level and its more gradual implementation in the states, patronage positions became scarcer. As the scope of government expanded with the New Deal, citizens began to receive services as a matter of public policy rather than as political favors from party workers. Thus, while the primary system weakened the connection between party leaders and elected officials, these other changes weakened the connection between party organizations and individual citizens. And so it was that the parties lost their role as the focal point of a system of popular government, as the crucial link between citizens and their political leaders.

As political parties began to move to the periphery of U.S. politics, the electronic media emerged to provide a new, direct, and continuous link between citizens and politicians. The effect was most apparent in regard to the presidency. First on radio, with Franklin Roosevelt's fireside chats, and now on television, presidents have spoken directly to the American people. Today, the process begins with the media focus on the presidential nomination and election cycle and continues after the election with constant news coverage of the president and his doings as well as televised addresses and news conferences. Whereas formerly the president's election and popular support after the election depended heavily upon the work of party leaders inside and outside of Washington, presidents today rely instead upon television and their own personal coalition of friends and supporters to get them elected and upon their media connection with the people to maintain their support once they are in office.

The cumulative effect of the democratization of the presidential-selection process and of the emergence of the "prime time" presidency[8] has been to make the presidency the object of popular expectations for strong and effective government and for solutions to nearly every national problem. In Bruce Miroff's words, "for most Americans the presidency has come to be nearly all there is to democratic politics."[9] Theodore Lowi called this phenomenon the "personal presidency." Americans identify directly with the presidency and the office becomes one of "tremendous personal power drawn from the people." This, Lowi said, is the equivalent of a "new democratic theory that the presidency with all powers is the necessary condition for governing a large democratic nation."[10]

The steady disintegration of political parties also forced members of Congress into a more direct relationship with their constituents. As local party organizations atrophied, legislators had to rely on their personal contacts and their own fund-raising capacities in order to get reelected. As a result, they became more attentive to their constituents; visits home became more frequent, and they worked harder to ensure that their constituencies got their fair share of the programs and services supplied by the federal government.

Legislators even discovered the utility of television. As early as 1956, the Congress had its own recording studios for its members, many of whom now use these facilities to videotape their own programs for distribution to television stations in their districts or states.[11] House and Senate sessions as well as committee meetings are televised, and some of the most vivid public images of the Congress in action have come from such events. The Senate Foreign Relations Committee hearings on the Vietnam War gripped the nation during 1971, as the Watergate hearings did in 1973 and 1974, and as the Iran-Contra hearings did in summer 1987.

The twentieth-century member of Congress, then, like the twentieth-century president, has sought and to some extent achieved a more or less direct relationship with the people. The political leaders' close dependence on the people, which the Founders feared as a mortal danger to the political system, is now a reality. In addition, "the people" now include virtually everyone, rich and poor, white and black, male and female, all directly connected with their leaders. Because the Founders looked to different modes of selection as a means of maintaining institutional independence, this common dependence on the people might suggest a firmer ground for cooperation between the two houses of the Congress and between them and the president. But this has not been the case. Instead, the still distinct constituencies and electoral cycles for each office, combined with institutional power sharing and weakened political parties at both the local and the national level, have meant even higher levels of tension and conflict.

INSTITUTIONAL CHANGE

Political institutions and what they do are shaped by the larger political and social environment within which they operate. Therefore, changes in that environment lead to institutional change. First, an altered environment causes the functions and responsibilities of the institution to change. An agrarian society expects different things from its political institutions than does an industrialized society. As the former yields to the latter, institutional functions change accordingly, and this in turn precipitates change within the institutions. An internal structure designed to discharge one set of responsibilities must change if it is to discharge new ones.

In the United States, the forces of growth, internationalization, and democratization increased the power and prominence of the national government and therefore of both the president and the Congress well beyond what those who designed the Constitution could have reasonably expected. However, these forces also had distinct effects on the presidency and the Congress. In the case of the presidency, the power and prominence of the office increased to such an extent that the institution was in effect transformed. This transformation reflects the institution's completely changed relationship with its external environment.

The relationship of the Congress with its external environment also changed, but the most significant changes were internal: in the way the Congress went about its business, in the way it distributed power, and in the behavior of its members. These internal changes were produced in part by the contextual forces to which both the Congress and the president were responding and in part by the changes that the presidency was undergoing. For the Congress then, the story of its evolution focuses for the most part on internal change.

THE TRANSFORMATION OF THE PRESIDENCY

The transformation of the presidency from the office defined so ambiguously in the Constitution to the dominant institution of the national government resulted from a process with several components: the assumption of presidential responsibility in regard to foreign policy, the discovery and expansion of "inherent" executive powers, the aggressive use of the veto power, a shift in the original understanding of the appointment power, the emergence of a significant presidential role in policy initiation, the delegation by the Congress to the executive branch of broad discretionary authority, and the creation of the institutional presidency.

Foreign Policy

As early as George Washington's administration, it became accepted that the presidency was the nation's sole office for dealing with other countries and that the president alone, by virtue of his constitutional power to receive foreign ambassadors, could recognize and establish relations between the United States and foreign governments. Moreover, the notion of joint presidential and senatorial responsibility for foreign policy implied by the words of the treaty-making clause ("by and with the advice and consent of the Senate") quickly disappeared after Washington's one attempt, in 1789, to consult the Senate in person on an Indian treaty ended in embarrassment for both sides. Neither Washington nor his successors tried again to consult personally with the entire Senate as part of the treaty-making process, although written communication as well as informal consultation has regularly occurred.[12] The Senate's formal role has evolved into the more exclusively legislative one of deciding whether or not a treaty should be approved, rather than the quasi-executive consultative role suggested by the constitutional wording.

When controversies have arisen over the extent of presidential power in the area of foreign policy, they have, in most instances, been decided in favor of the president. As the foreign commitments of the United States became more complex and as the country moved in the mid-twentieth century to the near permanent war status symbolized by a large standing army, the claim of presidential prerogatives in international issues came to be more widely accepted. A constitutional foundation for such a claim was articulated by the Supreme Court in its 1936 *Curtiss-Wright* decision, recognizing, in Justice George Sutherland's words, "the very delicate, plenary, and exclusive power of the President as the sole organ of the federal government in the field of international relations."[13] Although this widely quoted passage from the Court's decision was dicta in the sense that it was not relevant to the case at hand, its suggestion that the president had special powers in international matters that he did not have in domestic matters has nonetheless been the starting point for current discussions of presidential prerogatives on issues of war and peace.[14]

As for Congress's war power, the president's capacity to say what the foreign policy of the United States is, as well as his capacity as commander in chief to position U.S. forces around the world, has enabled him to create situations in which war becomes almost unavoidable. Wars are now begun de facto under presidential leadership rather than declared de jure by the Congress, and as the Korean and Vietnam conflicts demonstrated, such presidential wars can continue for several years without a formal congressional declaration of war.

To be sure, the foreign policy relationship between the president and the Congress has not developed in an entirely one-sided manner. In the post-Vietnam period, for example, Congress tried to define a new role for itself in such decisions by passing the War Powers Resolution and by taking a greater interest in arms sales agreements and intelligence matters. Whereas these efforts have proven to be at most a partial restraint on presidential war-making prerogatives, Congress has been somewhat more successful on issues that involve the financing of U.S. foreign policy. In matters such as foreign aid and weapons systems, the Congress has frequently forced presidents to settle for less than they wanted, and occasionally it has denied presidential requests outright. During the Reagan years, the administration battled continuously with the Congress for funds to finance its Strategic Defense Initiative, and, as we shall see in Chapter 6, the Congress used its power of the purse as a lever to influence Reagan administration policies aimed at overthrowing the government of Nicaragua.

On occasion, the Senate has rejected treaties that have been negotiated by the president. Every schoolchild should know of the Senate's refusal after World War I to ratify the treaty negotiated by President Woodrow Wilson that created the League of Nations. More recently, Senate opposition and ultimate refusal to ratify the Strategic Arms Limitation Treaty (SALT II), negotiated by President Carter, changed the course of events in regard to disarmament policy. And even after treaties have been approved, the Senate has sometimes asserted a right to, in essence, cointerpret their provisions with the president. Thus, in 1987, under the leadership of Sam Nunn, chair of the Armed Services Committee, the Senate advocated and attempted to enforce an interpretation of the 1972 antiballistic missile (ABM) treaty that was at odds with the view of the Reagan administration.[15]

Finally, and more informally, the Congress has always provided a forum for dissenting voices, and through these activities has had probably its most telling impact on how presidents have chosen to conduct foreign policy. In the late 1960s, the intensifying criticism from the Congress helped to create the domestic pressures that ultimately led to U.S. withdrawal from Vietnam. Again, in 1985, congressional dissent caused the Reagan administration to alter its policy of "constructive engagement" with South Africa and to move reluctantly toward economic sanctions. Finally, in 1986, the Congress took control of that issue, enacting sweeping sanctions over the president's veto.[16]

Despite these signs of a continuing congressional role in foreign-policy making, presidential power in such matters has steadily increased. Although the Congress has often resisted and occasionally blocked the president, such actions usually require extraordinary assertions of congressional will. The rules governing the struggle between the president and the Congress in the area of foreign policy, simply put, are the principle of presidential initiation, the presumption of presidential prerogatives, and the practice of congressional reaction. Congressional consultation and involvement in foreign policy decisions as they are taken, despite the intentions of the Founders, has been the exception rather than the rule.

Discretionary Power

The argument for inherent presidential prerogatives in foreign policy can be generalized into a case for broad discretionary authority for the president as he exercises his regular administrative responsibilities. The issue has really been whether presidential power is restricted to simple execution of the laws or whether a broader range of unspecified powers "comes with the territory." This issue was first raised in regard to foreign policy as part of a debate between Hamilton and Madison on the constitutionality of Washington's decision in 1793 to declare U.S. neutrality in the then current war between the British and the French—a presidential action apparently without specific constitutional authorization. Hamilton argued that when one compared the general terms in which the Constitution phrased presidential power with its specific enumeration of legislative powers, it was reasonable to impute certain unspecified inherent powers to the presidency. In brief, if the Constitution did not prohibit the president from doing something, Hamilton's view was that he could do it. Madison disagreed, arguing that Hamilton was grafting the royal prerogatives of the British Crown onto the new presidency, a step that, in Madison's view, fatally combined legislative with executive powers and invited presidential tyranny.[17]

U.S. presidents appear to have sided with Hamilton on this question, frequently acting on the basis of what they viewed as inherent powers. For example, Abraham Lincoln asserted that there were "emergency powers" implied in the Constitution that the president could exercise even when to do so would be directly contrary to specific constitutional provisions. Citing such powers, Lincoln raised the size of the army beyond the number that Congress had authorized, even though the Constitution explicitly conferred the power to determine the army's size upon the Congress. In addition, he spent funds without congressional authorization, issued the Emancipation Proclamation, and suspended the writ of habeas corpus. All of these measures either were without constitutional authorization or were contrary to the words of the Constitution, but were justified, according to Lincoln, because "measures otherwise unconstitutional might become lawful by becoming indispensable to the preservation of the Constitution through the preservation of the nation."[18]

Following Lincoln's precedent, several of his successors have claimed the right to go outside the law or the Constitution, particularly in the interests of national security. In 1942, after the attack on Pearl Harbor, Franklin Roosevelt ordered the removal of Japanese-Americans from the West Coast and their detention for the duration of World War II. Richard Nixon justified his Watergate activities with the statement that when the president acts unlawfully in the interests of national security, "that means it is not illegal."[19] And during the Iran-Contra affair, Ronald Reagan maintained that congressional restrictions on aid to the Nicaraguan rebels did not bind the president, and that in the arms-for-hostages component, he could ignore the statutory requirement that he inform the Congress of a covert operation. All of these presidential actions rely upon the Hamilton-Lincoln position that presidential discretionary powers, though not mentioned in the Constitution, nonetheless exist.

The Veto

Although struggles between the president and the Congress in the area of foreign policy have been episodic, the struggle over the control of domestic policy has been continuous. One issue from the outset was the proper use of the presidential veto. It seems clear from the constitutional discussions that the Founders anticipated a variety of legitimate uses of the veto power; however, some argue that the veto's primary purpose was to protect the independence of the presidency from possible attack by the legislature.[20] But this position is dubious because, as Corwin noted, during the first twenty-eight years of the republic only one of the seven vetoes cast involved the protection of presidential prerogatives. As for the viewpoint that the president should exercise the veto power only when he thinks that the Congress has acted unconstitutionally, Corwin concluded that since the Civil War, vetoes on constitutional grounds have been almost unknown.[21] Washington's very first veto (of a bill dealing with the apportionment of seats in the House of Representatives) was clearly based on his concerns about the constitutionality of the act, but his second (and last) raised no constitutional issue: It simply involved his disagreement with the Congress on the wisdom of a bill dealing with military personnel. Given the presence of several of the Founders in the Congress at the time as well as the proximity of these events to the Constitutional Convention, it is noteworthy that neither Washington's first nor even his second veto raised any concerns in Congress about misuse of the power. Both vetoes were easily sustained and in both instances the acts in question were revised to meet Washington's objections.[22] Thus, whatever the "real" intent of the Framers, the fact is that nearly every president, beginning with Washington, has used the veto on a completely discretionary basis.

What the Founders probably did not anticipate was the dramatic increase in the number of presidential vetoes and the infrequency of congressional overrides. Their assumption may have been that the veto would be used sparingly because the elected House would be working with an indirectly elected Senate and therefore would seldom make unwise legislation; confrontations between the president and the Congress would therefore be rare. The way things turned out, the veto has been used more frequently simply because the number of bills passed by the Congress each year has increased. Through 1988, presidents used the veto 2,469 times; 1,050 of these were "pocket vetoes," not subject to congressional override. Of those vetoes that the Congress had the opportunity to override, it did so in 103 instances, or just over 7 percent of the time.[23] This virtual finality of presidential vetoes has increased their utility to the president because it has allowed him to use the threat of a veto as a bargaining tool to discourage the Congress from acting contrary to his wishes.

Even though the veto, when either used or threatened, has become a more powerful weapon in the president's arsenal than originally anticipated, presidents have continued to seek an even stronger veto power. Ronald Reagan was the most recent but certainly not the first president to propose an "item veto," which would enable him to reject a part of a bill while accepting the rest. Congress has been understandably reluctant to agree to such a change because it would diminish the Congress's ability to get the president to accept legislative provisions that he does not like by tying them to provisions that he favors. The application of the item veto to appropriations bills, members of Congress fear, would in effect cede budgetary power to the president, who could selectively approve those expenditures that he favored while rejecting others.[24]

For its part, the Congress has sought to restrict the practice of presidential pocket vetoes. Ordinarily, bills unsigned by the president become law if he has not returned them to the Congress within ten days. A pocket veto occurs when the president fails to sign legislation, but because Congress has adjourned, he cannot return it. Originally intended to apply to adjournments at the end of a Congress, pocket vetoes in recent years have been used by presidents during the recesses that occur between the first and second sessions of a Congress, and occasionally during summer recesses. After the Supreme Court cast constitutional doubt on such a procedure, the Ford administration agreed not to use the pocket veto in that manner, an agreement honored by the Carter administration but violated by the Reagan administration, thereby putting the issue back into court.[25]

Appointments

The joint power of the Senate and the president over executive and judicial appointments also has been a source of conflict. The first issue that arose was whether those executive officials who were subject to Senate confirmation had a special continuing responsibility to the Congress that derived from their having undergone that confirmation process. During Washington's administration, this question was raised in regard to the secretary of the treasury, and although the issue was to flare up again during the presidency of Andrew Jackson, Hamilton, by his decision to act as Washington's minister rather than as a minister of Congress, resolved the question in favor of presidential responsibility.

The more controversial aspect of the issue was whether or not officers nominated by the president and approved by the Senate could be removed from office by the president without the consent of the Senate. Hamilton, writing in *Federalist No. 77*, suggested that the Senate did have such a role, asserting that "the consent of that body would be necessary to displace as well as to appoint."[26] Apparently, this was another area of disagreement between the two leading coauthors of *The Federalist Papers*, for Madison, in his role as speaker of the House during the First Congress, argued that once their appointment was approved, members of the executive were responsible only to the president. The power of removal, therefore, was an inherent element of both executive power and of the president's duty to see that the laws be faithfully executed.[27]

This issue finally came to a head when the Congress tried to protect its allies in Andrew Johnson's post–Civil War cabinet from presidential firing by passing the Tenure in Office Act of 1867. The act declared that cabinet members were "subject to removal by and with the advice and consent of the Senate." Johnson's decision to ignore this provision when he fired Secretary of War Edwin Stanton led to his impeachment and trial by the Senate. Johnson's acquittal, by one vote, seemed to vindicate the view that executive appointees were solely responsible to the president, and Congress finally conceded the point in 1887 by repealing the Tenure in Office Act.

Although the Congress today no longer contends that senatorial confirmation makes the officeholder formally responsible to the legislature, it still views such officers as accountable to the Congress in the sense that when called upon to testify before congressional committees, they are obliged to do so. Executive-branch officers who are not subject to confirmation (close presidential advisers as well as those who hold civil service positions) are not viewed as so obliged. On this reasoning, as the power and importance of the Executive Office of the President has grown, Congress has sought to extend the Senate's confirmation process to those precincts. Presidents have resisted, believing that their advisers should be accountable to them alone. In 1974, as part of its attempt to regain budgetary power, Congress passed legislation making the director and deputy director of the Office of Management and Budget (OMB) subject to confirmation by the Senate. The legislation was also motivated by congressional dislike of Roy Ash, Nixon's OMB director, and an earlier version of the bill would have forced Ash, as sitting director, to go through the confirmation process. Nixon vetoed that proposal, seeing it as an attempt to infringe upon the president's removal power. Congress then revised the bill to make it applicable to future OMB directors, and Nixon signed it.[28]

Congress continues to seek a broader role in the confirmation process in order to encourage a greater degree of accountability and also to be able to exercise some influence on the president's nomination decisions. On various occasions, presidents have avoided nominating people for executive positions who they knew would face harsh questioning in the Senate; on other occasions, nominations have been withdrawn after senatorial criticism. One of the few 1981 defeats suffered by the Reagan administration occurred when Ernest Lefever, a staunch anticommunist ideologue, was nominated to the State Department post of assistant secretary for human rights and humanitarian affairs. After prolonged deliberation, the Republican-controlled Senate Foreign Relations Committee rejected the nomination, and Lefever was persuaded to withdraw. Even if a nominee cannot be defeated, Senators can at least use the confirmation process as an opportunity to stake out their position on the issues that will be within the prospective appointee's purview. With the prospect then of some influence over the nomination process and some accountability after confirmation, the Congress has sought to increase the number of appointees subject to senatorial confirmation with its sights set at this writing on the president's national security adviser.

Legislative Leader

Although it seems clear that, in the words of one scholar, "neither Locke nor the Founding Fathers saw the executive as a legislative leader who would actively make laws,"[29] the Constitution allowed the president a policy-initiating role by providing that he could recommend for Congress's consideration "such measures as he shall judge necessary and expedient," and that "on extraordinary occasions" he might even convene a special legislative session. This constitutional opening was seized by Alexander Hamilton, who, on Washington's behalf, recommended and saw the Congress pass a major plan for organizing the new nation's financial affairs.

Modern presidents play a leading, proactive role in the legislative process rather than the solely reactive one implied by the veto power or the role of making occasional recommendations suggested by the "necessary and expedient" clause. Fred Greenstein noted that the modern (post-1932) presidency evolved from a situation in which "there was at best a somewhat grudging acceptance that the President would be 'interested' in the doings of Congress" to one in which "it has come to be taken for granted that he *should* regularly initiate and seek to win support for legislative actions as part of his continuing responsibilities."[30]

Ever since 1921, when the Congress gave the president broad initiating powers in regard to the annual budget, his proposals have established the parameters within which Congress has exercised its most important prerogative—the power of the purse. However, the importance of the Budget and Accounting Act of 1921 extends beyond the specifics of budget policy. Its passage signified congressional acceptance of the president's role as policy initiator, to the point where today Congress often refuses to move in a policy area until it has a specific proposal from the White House. Although political scientists argue about whether more legislation originates with the president or with the Congress, this dispute usually turns on the question of exactly where the legislative ideas were first conceived: with the president, a bureaucrat, or a member of Congress. What is no longer disputed by anyone is the key role of the president as the "catalyst to pull together all the supporting forces in Congress and the country for the most innovative actions."[31]

Delegated Power

Presidential power also has increased at the implementation stage of the policy process as a result of congressional decisions to delegate broad administrative powers to the president. Theodore Lowi identified this tendency as a legacy of Franklin Roosevelt's presidency. During the New Deal period, "Congress accompanied each program and each appropriation with a grant of authority and jurisdiction that left each agency pretty much to its own judgment as to what to do and how to do it."[32]

From a constitutional standpoint, the issue was whether the Congress, as it legislated, had to provide for all contingencies or whether it could draft legislation containing general guidelines and allow the president and his agencies sufficient discretion to fill in the specifics. From a practical standpoint, as public policy became more complex and as the sphere of government action expanded, the option of precise congressional specification became impossible. The Congress simply could not provide for all contingencies, and these practical considerations prevailed over constitutional niceties. The Supreme Court, while repeatedly warning the Congress that it must be careful when it delegates power, consistently upholds virtually all challenged delegations.[33]

Institutionalization of the Presidency

The increasing size of government and the increasing propensity of Congress to delegate power has meant a larger executive branch, which in turn has encouraged an expanded presidency. At one time the office of the president consisted of little more than the president, a secretary, and a messenger or two. It was not until 1857 that Congress even appropriated funds for the president's staff; as recently as 1934 there were still only 45 full-time employees in the White House.[34] Today there are more than 1,500 people employed in the White House and the Executive Office of the President. They include presidential advisers, counsels, special assistants, staff members of various presidential agencies, along with personnel "temporarily" assigned to the White House from other federal agencies.

The growth of the president's staff is intimately connected with the growth of the bureaucracy, for the Congress expects the president, as "chief executive," to coordinate and control the expanded government.

As Franklin Roosevelt's Committee on Administrative Management (commonly known as the Brownlow Committee) concluded in its 1937 report, the president needs help to do this job effectively. The Brownlow Committee report was cited as justification for a significant increase in the size of the White House operation. Particularly important were the new agencies that were established within the Executive Office of the President. The creation of the National Security Council moved the conduct of U.S. foreign policy more firmly under the control of the president and away from the State and Defense departments by providing him with the staff support, information, and advice that he needed to do that job effectively. The same services on economic matters were provided by the Bureau of the Budget and the Council of Economic Advisers.

The increase in the size of the presidency, from one man and a few aides to a large and highly complex organization, is referred to as the **institutionalization of the presidency.** This phenomenon as well as the bureaucratic expansion that produced it raised the public prominence of the executive relative to the Congress. As a result, it came to be expected that policy initiatives would come from the direction of the White House rather than from the Congress, and the president's enlarged staff enabled him to move on a number of different policy fronts at the same time. Although the president himself might be occupied with only a few specific issues, the institutionalized presidency can work on many policy issues simultaneously. Whereas in an earlier time presidents needed to leave many things to the Congress simply because they did not have the time or the staff to deal with them, today there seems to be no issue so small, no issue so marginal, that it cannot attract the attention of someone on the White House staff.

The institutionalized presidency also provides the president with more information on more issues than Congress or any other policy participants normally have available to them. In the area of foreign policy, this information has come to be an especially powerful weapon in the president's arsenal. His access to intelligence data and his capacity to declare so much of it confidential has created what Arthur Schlesinger has called "the secrecy system," a system that "overawed Congress and the nation" and produced the doctrine that "we must trust the President because only he knows the facts."[35]

Summary

From the sparse and ambiguous words of Article II of the Constitution, the modern presidency emerged, magnified far beyond its original design by the steadily expanding scope of government and the internationalizing of the environment within which that government operates. As the powers of the presidency increased, the office also became democratized. The link between the presidency and the American people became more direct, thereby anointing expanded presidential powers with democratic virtue. Presidents recognized early the powerful dynamic between the democratization of their office and their capacity to justify greater presidential power. Andrew Jackson, for example, justified his veto of the Bank Bill in terms of his responsibility to protect "the humble members of society."[36] Lincoln made no apologies to the Congress for his sweeping assertions of new powers, speaking of his "rightful masters, the American people" as the only ones to whom he need account.[37] And Theodore Roosevelt declared in his *Autobiography* that the course that he followed during his presidency was one "of regarding the executive as subject only to the people."[38] Although the Founders no doubt would have been appalled by a theory that based presidential power on democratic principles, today it is commonplace for presidents to justify the exercise of their undisputed powers as well as their attempts to expand their power in terms of a popular mandate conferred upon them by the people.

In short, the twentieth-century United States has become a presidential nation, with the president at the head of its government and at the center of the nation's political consciousness. Such a transformation appears to provide a simple solution to the challenge of reconciling democratic with managerial criteria for good public policy. With the president at once the democratic tribune of the people, popularly elected and popularly accountable, and also the head of the executive branch of government, the institution where the likelihood of managerially sound policy is maximized, increased presidential dominance of the policy-making process would presumably optimize both sets of criteria. As we will see, things have proven to be a bit more complicated.

THE EVOLUTION OF THE CONGRESS

While the presidency was transforming itself, the Congress was reorganizing itself. As the prominence of the federal government increased, so too did the work load of the Congress, thereby precipitating changes in internal structure, in congressional career patterns, and in the activities to which legislators devoted their attention. Moreover, as the political system became democratized, the relationship between the legislators and those whom they represented changed.

TABLE 3.1
Average Number of Public Bills Enacted by Each Congress, 1789–1986

1789–1808	93.9	1889–1908	514.2
1809–1828	145.9	1909–1928	626.0
1829–1848	148.1	1929–1948	803.2
1849–1868	249.7	1949–1968	806.1
1869–1888	406.6	1969–1986	616.1

Sources: For 1789–1948, George Galloway (1961), *History of the House of Representatives* (New York: Thomas Y. Crowell), pp. 303–305. For 1949–1986, Norman J. Ornstein, Thomas E. Mann, and Michael J. Malbin (1987), *Vital Statistics on Congress, 1987–1988* (Washington, D.C.: Congressional Quarterly Press), p. 110.

Work Load and Size

The Congress, like the presidency, has been affected by the growing scope of the national government. It now legislates in a variety of areas that could not have been anticipated by those who framed the Constitution. One index of this increased scope of congressional activity is the number of laws enacted during the two-year life of each Congress. The average number of public acts and resolutions passed by the Congress increased steadily from fewer than 100 every two years in the early Congresses to more than 800 every two years through the late 1960s (see Table 3.1).

The Congress, as its work load increased, became a full-time body. The early Congresses were part-time assemblies that "ordinarily worked only after the harvest season and before spring planting."[39] Even as late as the pre–World War II period, the average congressional session lasted perhaps six months. Now the Congress convenes in early January and frequently does not adjourn until just before Christmas, although it takes periodic recesses during the year.

As the country grew, the size of the Congress grew as well. The Senate began with 26 members and with the admission of each new state into the Union, increased its membership by 2, arriving at its current figure of 100 in 1959 after Alaska and Hawaii achieved statehood. The House began in 1789 with 65 members, and twenty years later, it had more than doubled to 141. Some sixty years later it had doubled again, reaching 293 at the end of the Civil War. From that point, the House grew more slowly, reaching its current size of 435 in 1913.

Committees and Seniority

The increase in the size of the Congress altered the character of the institution. Originally, the House was small enough to be a genuinely deliberative body, and the early Senates were so small that they were less like legislatures and more like the advisory councils to the president that some of the Founders had envisioned. In the early sessions of the House, most major issues were debated as they were at the Constitutional Convention, by the entire body acting as a "committee of the whole." After general agreements had been reached, the bills were referred to select committees for fine tuning. But as the House became larger and its work load increased, deliberating each question on the floor of the House became logistically impossible. As a result, early in the nineteenth century a system of standing committees gradually emerged. The committees provided smaller and therefore more efficient decisionmaking units, a way to divide and deal more expeditiously with the House's growing work load. Some congressional expertise also was encouraged, as at least a few members continued on each committee from one Congress to the next. By 1816 the Senate too had a committee system, one essentially compatible in numbers and structure with that of the House.[40]

From these beginnings, the committees eventually came to be the heart of the congressional policy-making process. As early as 1825, committees possessed, according to George Galloway, the leading historian of the U.S. Congress, essentially the same powers and responsibilities under congressional rules as they have today.[41] However, it was not until the end of the nineteenth century that the committees began to exhibit their modern characteristics of independence from party leaders and highly specialized subject area jurisdictions. By 1885, when Woodrow Wilson wrote that "Congress in its committee rooms is Congress at work,"[42] there was a good deal of membership continuity and therefore a greater degree of policy expertise on each committee. As the Congress moved through the twentieth century, the seniority system for selecting committee chairs became entrenched, the decisionmaking autonomy of the committees became more firmly established, and policy specialization was further encouraged by the creation of a large number of subcommittees, each with its own narrow jurisdiction within which it was essentially free to operate beyond the control of leaders outside the subcommittee. In the One Hundredth Congress (1987–1988), there were 22 standing committees and 140 subcommittees in the House and 16 standing committees and 85 subcommittees in the Senate.

The evolution of the congressional committee system is related to both the expanding scope of government and the rise of executive power. The origin of the committee system was part of an attempt by the post-Jefferson Congresses to retrieve some of the policy initiative that they sensed had already begun to move toward the executive. The committees were seen as a way for the Congress to reassert itself legislatively, as a way of "broadening the scope of the operation of the House and restricting the executive."[43] If Congress was to legislate, it needed to have strong committees, and as the legislative responsibilities of Congress became more complex, this need became more apparent. The powerful congressional committee system of the 1880s described so vividly by Wilson operated during a period characterized by relatively weak presidencies and a strong role for Congress in the national policy-making process. Congressional government, if that phrase aptly describes the period, was of necessity committee government.

During the twentieth century, the locus of national policymaking moved more decisively in the direction of an enlarged and more powerful executive branch. While Congress continued to need policy expertise to discharge its legislative responsibilities, it also needed a way to oversee and to control the rapidly expanding administrative state. Both of these needs were met by the committee system. The expertise resident in the committees was available not only to help Congress make public policy but also to provide it with the capacity to understand and to supervise a growing executive apparatus.

As the committee system moved to the center of the congressional policy-making process, political parties began to play a lesser role. Strong political parties and strong committees do not have to be incompatible; in fact, the two coexisted for much of the latter half of the nineteenth century. However, at the end of that century and the beginning of the twentieth, the forces of populism and progressivism that had attacked party organizations in general turned their attention to the task of dismantling many of the prerogatives of the congressional party leaders. Most important was the formalizing after 1911 of the seniority system, by which committee chairmanships were automatically awarded to the majority party member with the longest tenure on the committee. This development placed committee chairs completely beyond the reach of party leaders; if the chairs were reelected, they would retain their committee posts regardless of the wishes of the leadership. Thus, although policy specialization had created some degree of committee autonomy during the late nineteenth century, with the end of strong congressional party leadership, committee autonomy became the rule.

Finally, committee autonomy was further bolstered by enhanced staff support. In 1891, the fifty-eight House committees employed a total of 62 staff members, while the fifty Senate committees employed 41. By 1986, committee staff totaled 1,954 in the House and 1,075 in the Senate.[44] Thus, not only did legislators themselves develop expertise from continuous service on their committees, but also a more or less permanent and increasingly professional staff provided the committee members with information that in many cases could rival that possessed by the bureaucracy.

Autonomous committees and weak party leadership combined to decentralize policy-making power in the Congress. Power in the modern Congress is vested in its numerous committees and subcommittees, all with relatively permanent memberships, specific jurisdictions established and protected by formal rules, large operating budgets, and strong staff support. Although particularly skillful party leaders have sometimes been able to provide some degree of centralization to congressional policymaking and although new generations of reform-minded legislators have discussed and occasionally tried to restore the power of party leaders, the Congress continues to be characterized by what the most astute observer of its recent history and politics called a "void in centralizing institutions."[45]

Professionalism

As the committee system came to be more autonomous and as the seniority system took hold, the Congress began to become a more professionalized institution in the sense that people came to both the House and the Senate with the intention of staying for an extended period of time. This had not always been so. Congressional service, in the early years of the republic, was more an avocation than a profession. "Prior to the Civil War one just did not make a long-run career out of continuous Senate service, except perhaps as a fluke," according to Douglas Price. "Major political figures drifted in and out of the Senate as convenience dictated." During the early part of the nineteenth century, it was not uncommon for members of the Senate to resign partway through their terms, often to take positions in state government. However, by the second half of the century, the number who left began to drop, and in the twentieth century, continuity in Senate membership became the norm.[46]

The House of Representatives during the eighteenth and much of the nineteenth century also was characterized by generally high membership turnover at each election; fifteen elections, the last in 1882, produced turnover rates in excess of 50 percent.[47] But during the twentieth century, there has been a steady increase in the number of terms served by the average member of the House and a steady decrease in the number of new members entering after each election (see Table 3.2).

One of the forces driving the professionalization of the Congress was the increased scope of the federal government. As federal policies became more important, congressional service came to be more attractive than service in state government. A second driving force was the seniority

TABLE 3.2
Tenure of Members of the House of Representatives, 1903–1988

Congress	Average Tenure (Years)	First Termers (percent)	Ten or More Terms (Percent)
1903–1904	6.2	31.3	1.8
1923–1924	7.2	27.1	4.2
1943–1944	8.8	22.9	11.1
1963–1964	11.4	15.2	17.0
1983–1984	9.2	18.4	12.6
1987–1988	11.2	11.0	16.0

Sources: For data between 1903 and 1964, Nelson W. Polsby (1968), "The Institutionalization of the U.S. House of Representatives," *American Political Science Review* 62:1 (March):146. For data between 1983 and 1988, Norman J. Ornstein, Thomas E. Mann, and Michael J. Malbin (1987), *Vital Statistics on Congress, 1987–1988* (Washington, D.C.: Congressional Quarterly Press), p. 18.

system. The idea that longevity in the Congress and continuous service on a committee ultimately would be rewarded by a committee chairmanship provided a strong incentive for legislators to make a career of congressional service. The development of the seniority system from a norm into a practically unbreakable rule coincided exactly with the increase in average tenure and the decline in turnover in the House. And the increase in voluntary retirements among senior members, which caused the downswing in the average tenure figures for 1983–1984, has been attributed by some to the modifications in the seniority rule and the reduction in the power of committee chairs that occurred during the congressional reform era of the 1970s.[48]

Oversight

A more professionalized membership, a stronger committee system, and a larger, more expert staff constituted part of the congressional response to the increasing scope and complexity of the national government. Another response was the growing tendency to delegate power to the executive. This tendency produced an increasing congressional emphasis on the task of overseeing the executive in order to determine the effectiveness of public policies, to detect and prevent waste, dishonesty, and abuse of governmental power, and to ensure that the executive branch, as it exercised the power delegated to it by the Congress, was carrying out the latter's intent.

Legislative oversight of the executive branch is not an entirely new phenomenon. During the Second Congress, the House asserted this right by appointing a select committee to investigate General Arthur St. Clair's defeat by the Indians. George Galloway listed twenty-one major committee investigations focusing on the economy and efficiency of executive branch activities during the period from 1810 to 1826, another thirty-six such investigations between 1830 and 1860, and seventy more between the Civil War and the turn of the century.[49]

In more recent years, legislative oversight has become firmly institutionalized as a function of the standing committees. The Legislative Reorganization Act of 1946 required that each committee of the House and Senate "exercise continuous watchfulness" on the execution of laws by the agencies within their jurisdiction. To enable the committees to comply with this oversight mandate, the act also provided a large increase in committee staff personnel. In the years after the 1946 act, a dramatic increase in oversight activity on the part of congressional committees took place; all current commentaries on the Congress suggest that this task continues to be a crucial part of what committees, and therefore the Congress, do.[50]

Paradoxically, it is also the consensus of those who have studied congressional oversight that despite the organizational emphasis on it, Congress does a fairly poor job of oversight. Louis Fisher concluded that in regard to government expenditures, presidential discretionary powers have increased and congressional oversight efforts "have been sporadic and ad hoc rather than systematic and sustained."[51] Others have argued that the oversight task is too large and too complicated to be carried out effectively, that when it is undertaken, political and personal concerns of legislators rather than policy concerns are likely to be the motivating forces, and that legislators generally have few incentives to do the job well.[52]

Localism and Fragmentation of Power

One of the reasons for Congress's poor performance in regard to oversight may be the increasingly local orientation of its members, a phenomenon that seems to have accompanied increased tenure. Today, the virtual invulnerability of House incumbents to reelection defeat and the only slightly greater vulnerability of Senate incumbents are attributable to and in turn encourage the assiduous attention that legislators accord to the specific needs and more general policy concerns of their constituencies and those who finance their reelection campaigns. With political parties weakened and renomination and reelection dependent almost entirely on the legislator's own resources and record, legislative "careerism" requires that constituency concerns govern both the policy decisions of legislators and the manner in which they allocate their time and that of their staff.

Increasing legislative careerism also reinforces the extremely decentralized and in some respects fragmented distribution of power in the Congress.[53] When members were "amateurs" in the sense that they were not particularly concerned about continued reelection or when their electoral fortunes were in the hands of strong party organizations, they may have been more willing to develop a national view of policy questions, to enter into party-brokered compromises, and to perform necessary but thankless chores such as agency oversight. But as the influence of party leaders declined, power in the Congress became fragmented, not just among increasingly autonomous committees and subcommittees, but eventually among various ad hoc groups and informal caucuses. Today, the Congress is the province of the "policy entrepreneur," with each member in business for himself or herself and each using positions of power in committees or subcommittees to advance personal, policy, and reelection goals. In this way "committee government served the personal ambition of representatives and senators, providing each person an opportunity to share congressional power."[54] James Sundquist described the current situation this way: "The greater the freedom of the individual members from leadership pressure and coercion, the greater their leeway to behave in whatever manner is best calculated to enhance the probability of reelection."[55]

Summary

The One Hundredth Congress of 1987 is different from the First Congress of 1789. It has more than six times as many members, a more complex internal structure, a more professionalized and career-oriented membership, a much larger and more powerful executive with which to contend, and its members have a more direct relationship with their constituents. However, like the First Congress, it remains a legislature. Its members represent constituencies, meet at a central place, deliberate the issues of the day, and take legislative action. The early Congresses also exhibited the traits of localism and at least some of the tendencies toward decentralization of power that are characteristic of the modern Congress. As a legislature, the modern Congress remains the embodiment of the republican principle of government through the consent of the governed, perhaps even more today, given the wider electorate and the advent of direct election of senators. However, whereas the democratic aspects of the Congress have become more prominent, the modern Congress may be no more capable, and in some respects less capable, of producing effective policy than earlier Congresses were.

CONGRESSIONAL AND PRESIDENTIAL APPROACHES
TO PUBLIC POLICYMAKING

As the focus of American government shifted from the state to the national level and as the scope of national government activity widened, both the president and the Congress came to be increasingly active policy-making institutions. However, the perspectives that each brought to national policymaking, the attention that they devoted to such matters, the manner in which they organized themselves to deal with public policy, and the way in which the public perceived them came to be increasingly disparate. This disparity is in part attributable to the distinct generic characteristics of legislatures and executives and in part to the distinct development paths that the president and the Congress followed.

National or Local Perspectives

The president brings a national rather than a sectional or local perspective to public policy. This is attributable to his singular status as the only officeholder with a national constituency (the vice president's status, it should be noted, is completely dependent on that of the president) and to the nationwide interest and excitement that a presidential election generates. Once the president is in office, public evaluations of how well he is doing are to a large degree determined by how well the country seems to be doing economically, and these assessments are based more on national unemployment and inflation rates than on the economic condition of particular regions or demographic groups.[56] His special responsibilities for foreign policy further bolster this national perspective because such decisions are usually viewed as having an undifferentiated impact on the nation as a whole. In brief, presidents need to address policy questions on the basis of what's good for the country as a whole, not because they are wiser or more patriotic than legislators, but because, politically and practically, that is the only criterion that makes sense for them.

Members of Congress, in contrast, bring a decidedly local perspective to national policy questions because that is what makes sense for them. In the House, the frequency of elections, the marginal role of political parties in the election process, and the resulting reliance of legislators on their own fund-raising skills and on their own personal political organizations have, more than ever, encouraged representatives to adopt a local perspective. Whereas it would be wrong to suggest that all that legislators ask about a proposed public policy is how it will affect their constituencies and therefore their reelection chances, it seems clear that in most cases this is the threshold question—the first question that they ask before moving on to other considerations.[57]

Even though senators have a longer election cycle, they are not immune to the pressures of localism. First, all must seek renomination and reelection. Second, at any one time, one-third of the members are, like their colleagues in the House, two years or less from an election day. Third, senatorial elections have become so expensive (an average of just over $2.5 million per candidate in 1986) that incumbent senators raise campaign funds throughout their six-year terms. Finally, senators have become significantly more vulnerable to election defeat because they have been facing more visible and better financed challengers. Such close races may well be tipped against an incumbent by votes that appear contrary to constituency concerns. So although senators are certainly not under the continuous reelection pressure that representatives confront, they still must be attentive to constituency concerns and to the implications of policy proposals for their states.

Policy or Representational Activities

Members of Congress tend to be more interested in representational activities, whereas the president tends to focus more on policy or law-making activities. Few congressional reelection campaigns, particularly in the House of Representatives, turn on the incumbent's record and activities in regard to the great national issues of the day. Rather, the primary factors tend to be service to and visibility among constituents.[58]

It is an axiom that legislators who want to get reelected must spend time in the constituency between elections. In 1976, House members were in their districts on average for part of twenty-two weeks of the year, an allocation of time made easier by the fact that each member was allowed thirty-three trips home annually at government expense. Legislators also must be attentive to case mail—letters requesting their assistance with problems that constituents may be having with the federal government. Case mail can run anywhere from 10,000 to 50,000 pieces a year, depending upon the size of the legislator's constituency.[59] In 1987, House members had over 40 percent, and Senators 34 percent, of their staff assigned to their district offices, where they presumably dealt primarily with these constituency service requests.[60] When citizens think that their representative is working hard for the constituency and helping to secure a good slice of the federal pie for local interests, reelection tends to be easier. Nearly all representatives view such activities as an important part of their job,[61] and citizens view them, along with the legislator's personal characteristics, as the most important basis for their evaluations of incumbents.[62] Thus, for both representatives and senators, representational activities consume a significant amount of their time and that of their staff, resources that otherwise might be devoted to national public policy concerns.

Because of the Twenty-second Amendment, the president has only one reelection to worry about, four years after he gets into office. Although the outcome of that one campaign depends on many factors, it is unlikely to turn on how many times he has visited a particular part of the country, or how well he has handled requests for favors that find their way to the White House, or how federal resources are distributed among the various states. The most important factors that influence presidential elections tend to be the perceived state of the nation as a whole, calculated largely in economic terms. When international events figure in the outcome of presidential campaigns, the relevant factors are whether or not the nation is at war and how the strength and prestige of the nation is perceived abroad. Although reelection is important to first-term presidents—and as Watergate attested, it can be of consuming importance—the American people have in this century denied reelection to only two elected incumbents, Herbert Hoover and Jimmy Carter. The first instance occurred in the context of the greatest U.S. economic disaster and the second in the context of widespread economic discontent and the national humiliation inflicted by the Iranian capture of the U.S. Embassy and personnel in Tehran. For a president in his first term, therefore, being concerned primarily with national policy questions is probably the best reelection strategy. Of course, once reelected, presidents will never run again. At that point, they tend to start pondering their place in history, and although this may not be entirely healthy, it further intensifies the presidential focus on policy rather than representational activities.

Perceived Complexity or Perceived Simplicity

Both the presidency and the Congress have become more complex institutions over the years, but complexity has had disadvantages for the Congress that it has not had for the presidency. Lawrence Dodd and Richard Schott discussed the tendency of the press and the public "to view Congress as a mysterious, ineffectual relic of the nineteenth century. By closing its committee doors, creating a multiplicity of committees, and confusing jurisdictional lines, Congress isolated itself from the nation. Out of sight and often out of mind, Congress lost the country's attention and respect and often became an object of scorn and derision."[63] Simply put, the Congress responded to the growing complexity of national public policy, to its increased work load, and to its own internal growth by becoming a very complicated institution. Even in these days of open committee meetings and televised floor debates, it is well understood only by its senior members and by a relatively small coterie of Washington insiders. The institution remains quite opaque to even relatively informed citizens and certainly to the mass public. For most people, the Congress is their own legislator, a few visible leaders, and nothing else.

Although the presidency and the executive branch as a whole have come to be even larger and more complex than the Congress, this complexity is not especially visible to most citizens, and, what is more important, the people as a whole do not associate the complexity they do perceive with the president. What the public sees is something much simpler. For them, the presidency is a man, his family, and a few close aides. If they are at all aware of the National Security Council, the Council of Economic Advisers, OMB, and the huge Washington bureaucracy, they do not connect these institutions with the presidency. Ironically, the hostility toward Washington bureaucrats that so many people harbor is not transferred to the person in charge of the bureaucracy, the chief executive. On the contrary, as Ronald Reagan demonstrated, the public accepts, applauds, and apparently sees no irony in presidential attacks on the bureaucracy that he ostensibly controls.

While the Congress was losing the nation's attention as it responded to the increased complexity of its task, the president was attracting the nation's attention. First through radio and later through television, the president came to dominate the nation's political consciousness. Although not every president has been able to stir the emotions of the nation—positively or negatively—no president has been ignored. Congress has never stirred anyone's emotions (except perhaps the president's), and most of the time most people are at best indifferent toward it. It is, of course, not surprising to find the singular presidency more visible and more important in a psychological sense to the American people than the collective Congress. It is easier to identify with an individual than with a collective institution, such as the Congress, in which no one leader gets a great deal of attention. Also, because in most instances no one can speak for the Congress or even for a large part of it, there is no reason to pay a great deal of attention to the speaker or the majority leader. Even though the president cannot always speak for the entire executive branch, he has the formal right to do so, and more often than not, policy consequences will follow in a rather immediate and direct fashion. Thus, it pays to pay attention to the president.

These different public perceptions of the president and the Congress work to the president's advantage. His dominant public position and the sense of identification and support that he can engender from the mass public allows the president to take policy initiatives and to establish policy agendas for both the legislative and the executive branches, things that Congress usually cannot do.

Centralized or Decentralized Organization

The differential consequences of complexity for the Congress and the presidency extend beyond popular perceptions. The strong committee and subcommittee system that the Congress developed, abetted by weakened political parties, led to a system of broadly distributed power within both the House and the Senate. As power within the Congress became more decentralized, decisionmaking became more difficult because a larger number of people, each with some influence and a great deal of independence, needed to be satisfied before policy agreements could be reached. In addition, each chamber developed a large body of written and unwritten rules that although necessary in order to allow an increasingly complex institution to operate, also had the effect of reducing its capacity to act in an expeditious manner. For the Congress, then, a system of decentralized power reinforced by intricate rules of procedure accentuated the disinclination to act that at least to some extent characterizes all legislatures.

The presidency too had to cope with increased complexity but did so through an increased emphasis on centralization rather than decentralization of power. The growth in the size and importance of the White House staff during the twentieth century and its tendency to dominate the process for arriving at key policy decisions reflect the presidency's centralizing response to governmental complexity. Centralization served to enhance the capacity of the president to take policy actions. Whether or not he acted wisely or effectively or whether or not the enlarged White House staff created new problems is not important here. What is important is that the Congress, on the one hand, responded to complexity with structural arrangements that ultimately diminished its capacity to act, and the presidency, on the other, responded with structural changes that enhanced its capacity to act. These disparate organizational responses in turn reinforced the popular disposition to look toward the White House for initiatives and action.

CONCLUSION

As U.S. national political institutions have developed from the constitutional founding to the present, the transformed presidency has come to stand at the very center of the political system, expected to act and organized to do so; meanwhile, in regard to national policymaking, the Congress has evolved into a secondary institution, expected to react to presidential initiatives and poorly organized to act on its own. The contrasting courses of development that each institution has followed reinforce our earlier discussion of the differential capacities of executive and legislative institutions to produce managerially good public policy. However, although these factors all point to the desirability of executive rather than legislative control of the policy-making process, the president continues to be constrained to a significant degree by the constitutional design of shared power among independently elected political institutions, each endowed with the capacity to check the actions of the other.

Presidents have developed various strategies for dealing with this contradiction between the policy leadership that is expected of them and the constraints that the constitutional system places upon them. These strategies are supported and applauded by those who view the transformed presidency as the institution that holds out the best hope for national public policy that can be judged as good according to both democratic and managerial standards. What these strategies are and whether they can achieve good public policy by either set of standards will be explored in Chapters 4 and 5.

4

The Machinery of Presidential Domination

Over the past some two hundred years, forty men have come to the office of the presidency. Each has been expected to provide political and governmental leadership while at the same time operating within the constraints of a constitution that would inevitably frustrate his boldest attempts to lead. Sooner or later, each president has become aware of this gap between what is expected of him and his constitutional capacity to deliver on those expectations. And today, with more expected of the president than ever before, with the president at the very center of popular political consciousness, the gap between expectations and capacity to perform has widened.

The primary institutional obstacle to presidential dominance is the Congress. If a president is to control the policy-making process, legislators have to be persuaded to follow his lead or else the president needs to find ways to proceed without their assent—in other words, to expand the prerogatives of his office. Those presidents who have been able to do this, though often labeled as tyrants by their contemporaries, have been heroes in the eyes of historians. As James MacGregor Burns observed, "the classic test of greatness in the White House has been the chief executive's capacity to lead Congress."[1] Those presidents who have done the most to expand the power of the presidency relative to that of the Congress and those who, working within the current understanding of their power, have been most successful in leading the Congress have been ranked by scholars as among the great and near great presidents. Those at the middle and bottom ranks of the various "greatness" scales have been either passive presidents dominated by the Congresses with which they served or active presidents who tried but failed to get the Congress to do what they thought best.

Every president labors in the shadow of his great predecessors, concerned with how history will judge him and his achievements. Will he be remembered with Abraham Lincoln or Franklin Pierce? With Woodrow Wilson or Chester Arthur? With Franklin Roosevelt or Herbert

Hoover? One of Lyndon Johnson's aides said that he and his colleagues talked frequently about the "greatness" polls and what it would take to get their boss into the "top ten."[2] Most presidents are probably aware that the great and near great presidents are far outnumbered by those who have been judged as mediocre or failures. They even may be aware that the accomplishments of the great presidents have been given added luster both by the passage of time and by the popular mythology that has grown up around them. And if they look closely, they also may discover that no president, not even the greatest, succeeded in leading the Congress for his entire tenure in office, that few succeeded in doing so for more than a year or two, and that all went through periods of intense congressional resistance to their priorities and proposals.

"I've watched the Congress from either the inside or the outside, man and boy, for more than forty years," said Lyndon Johnson, "and I've never seen a Congress that didn't eventually take the measure of the President it was dealing with."[3] But this knowledge did not deter Johnson, nor would it have been likely to deter other presidents, from the quest for a presidency that would be remembered as among the few and the great. At least in the modern age, people modest about their capabilities and realistic about their frailities have not normally found their way to the White House. Thus, from the time that he is elected to the time that he leaves the White House, a president's tenure in office is marked by a search for strategies that will enable him to achieve that dominance of the policy-making process that so many of his predecessors have sought and so few have achieved.

PRESIDENTIAL-CONGRESSIONAL MODELS

Few presidents have been keen students of U.S. history in the sense of having read extensively about past presidencies. However, historians and political scientists who have studied the office have been able to define various types of presidencies, each characterized by a different approach to executive power and a different relationship with the Congress. These models of legislative-executive relations, although they may not be clearly defined in the minds of individual presidents, nonetheless provide a useful starting point for understanding the ideal types to which presidents aspire and, conversely, those that they try to avoid.

In his widely read book, *Presidential Government*, James MacGregor Burns identified three types of presidencies and connected each with one of the Founders: Alexander Hamilton, James Madison, and Thomas Jefferson. He associated the Hamiltonian model with strong, heroic presidencies and compliant Congresses, the Jeffersonian model with a strong presidency working cooperatively with a Congress bound to him by strong partisan loyalties, and the Madisonian model with the checked and balanced relationship between the legislature and the executive embodied in the design of the Constitution.

Presidential Primacy

Alexander Hamilton was George Washington's secretary of the treasury, his chief liaison with the Congress, and the architect of his administration's policy agenda. Although Hamilton was never president himself, his activities as Washington's "first minister" exemplified, in Burns's view, strong presidential government "in which the President would act vigorously and creatively, dominating the legislative process as well as the executive, upsetting the carefully contrived balance of power between . . . the President and other branches, and being curbed less by formal constitutional restrictions than by the pressures and exigencies of the political arena."[4] The Hamiltonian, or "presidential primacy,"[5] model stands then for a president who is firmly in control of the Congress and who has the full complement of inherent and discretionary powers first identified by Hamilton in his *Pacificus Letters* and expanded upon by subsequent "great" presidents.

Theodore Roosevelt's notion of "stewardship" constitutes the broadest modern interpretation of the Hamiltonian model. He argued that the president should not be seen "as the servant of the Congress." Rather, his power was "subject only to the people," whom he was bound to serve "affirmatively in cases where the Constitution does not explicitly forbid him to render the service." As president, Roosevelt believed "that it was not only his right but his duty to do anything that the needs of the nation demanded unless such action was forbidden by the Constitution or by the laws."[6]

Roosevelt's articulation of stewardship suggests a darker side to this **presidential-primacy** model, a potential to move beyond constitutional limits toward executive absolutism. This is captured by Arthur Schlesinger's concept of the "imperial presidency." Such a presidency, Schlesinger said, is characterized by "an unprecedented concentration of power in the White House and an unprecedented attempt to transform the Presidency of the Constitution into a plebiscitary Presidency," a presidency that "instead of being accountable every day to Congress and public opinion, would be accountable every four years to the electorate. Between elections, the President would be accountable only through impeachment and would govern, as much as he could, by decree."[7] As will be pointed out in Chapter 6, the possibility that a president's quest for primacy may lead him toward imperialism constitutes one of the very real risks to the U.S. political system and serves as a caution against the theory that broad presidential power is compatible with democratic criteria for good government.

Stalemate

The Madisonian model, in contrast to the presidential primacy model, closely adheres to the constitutional design of legislative and executive power sharing maintained by a system of mutual institutional checks. The model incorporates a less active presidency, a stronger and occasionally dominant role for the Congress, and therefore, a limited government disposed toward legislative-executive stalemate. Challenging the stewardship theory of his political nemesis Theodore Roosevelt, President William Howard Taft articulated the essence of the Madisonian model when he wrote

> that the president can exercise no power which cannot be fairly and reasonably traced to some specific grant of power or justly implied and included within such express grant as proper and necessary to its exercise. Such specific grant must be either in the federal Constitution or in an act of Congress in pursuance thereof. There is no undefined residuum of power which he can exercise because it seems to him to be in the public interest.[8]

Just as there were two variants of the presidential-primacy model, so there are two variants of the Madisonian model: a "whig" variant, in which the Congress dominates a submissive presidency, and an "adversarial" variant in which the "Congress and the presidency are coequal and competitive."[9] This is an important distinction. The whig variant suggests that the Congress is in control of public policymaking, whereas the adversarial variant implies public policy-making deadlock engendered by a mutual assertion by the president and the Congress of their own powers and the recurrent refusal of either to yield to the other. In this sense, the adversarial variant is more aptly described as a stalemate model.

The whig variant is largely a nineteenth-century phenomenon typical of the presidencies between Jackson and Lincoln as well as some of the post–Civil War presidencies. Given the transformed presidency, discussed in Chapter 3, it would be difficult to envision a modern manifestation of the whig variant. Instead, the argument of this book is that the **stalemate** variant—a balanced and often confrontational legislative-executive relationship—is now the typical arrangement of institutional power in the United States.

Cooperation

Burns's Jeffersonian model shares with the Hamiltonian model the idea of a strong presidency firmly in control of a vigorous national government and its policy agenda. However, whereas the Hamiltonian model emphasizes presidential force and when necessary, unilateral presidential action, the Jeffersonian model emphasizes a collegial and cooperative relationship between the president and a congressional majority, founded upon their shared membership in the same national political party. Although the president is the leader of his party, "he governs with at least the passive consent of his fellow party leaders who have some independent power," said Burns, "and ultimately he is governed by party purposes and limited, as well as supported, by the other national party leaders."[10]

The Jeffersonian model has been labeled the **party-government** theory, thus underlining its connection with the literature that has long called for reforms that would make national political parties in the United States more responsible, more unified, and more disciplined.[11] Given the steady erosion of party strength, discussed in Chapter 3, the party-government model has functioned only rarely in the United States and seems to be less achievable now than at any other time in U.S. history. Its most obvious contemporary manifestations are found today in parliamentary systems that follow the British model.

IN SEARCH OF PRESIDENTIAL PRIMACY

Because neither whiggism nor cooperation based upon shared party allegiances has been apparent for many years in the United States, presidential primacy, along with its imperial variant, and stalemate are the models with the clearest contemporary relevance. The presidential-primacy model has for many years stood as the implicit goal of each new president as he seeks to govern in the face of a constitution against government. The stalemate model, in contrast, symbolizes presidential failure and therefore has been a fate to be avoided. Presidents and political scientists have long pondered the factors that explain why some presidents seem to succeed (that is, achieve primacy), whereas others seem to fail in the sense that they are unable to break the policy stalemate to which the constitutional design seems so naturally to lead. The explanations have focused on two categories of variables: the individual characteristics of presidents and the nature of the times in which they govern.

The Person

The most common explanation for presidential primacy focuses on the qualities of the person who is president. James Sundquist asserted that shifts in the legislative-executive relationship are "attributable to the differing attitudes and objectives, and skills and determination, of the occupant of the presidential office."[12] Richard Neustadt's seminal work on the exercise of presidential power suggested that presidents needed to use the resources of their office to persuade others to follow their lead. Such persuasion takes the form of successful bargaining, and the president's capacity to do that depends upon the perception of others that "he has skill and will enough to use his advantages."[13]

James David Barber has focused attention on the personality of presidents as a key to what kind of leaders they turn out to be, while others have pointed to the presidents' rhetorical and management skills. Paul Light has provided for new presidents a list of strategic tips to enable them to control the national agenda and to achieve some degree of success in the Congress, and James Pfiffner argued for the importance of strategic planning during the transition period prior to the inauguration.[14] All of these diverse perspectives on presidential power share the idea that presidential primacy is always available to any president who has the right combination of personality, skills, and strategic know-how. In this sense, these scholarly perspectives merge with the views of political pundits as well as the general public, all of whom, once every four years, launch a search for the person with "the right stuff" to be a successful president.

The Times

In contrast to the emphasis on the traits of individual presidents, others suggest that there is a more or less natural rhythm, or cycle, to presidential power. From this perspective, presidential skills are less important because their impact is constrained by the nature of the times within which a president governs. Louis Koenig wrote that "an overview of the many decades of foreign and domestic policy-making reveals rises and falls, ebb and flow in the President's influence and impact." Activist presidents, in Koenig's view, who seek to dominate the national agenda with policy proposals, may succeed for a time but ultimately tire the people, provoke reaction from the Congress, and set the stage for a less aggressive presidency.[15]

Erwin Hargrove also emphasized the importance of cycles, especially those of the twentieth century, but pointed to an explicit policy dimension that underlies them. During a quiescent presidency or one characterized by policy stalemate, to use our terminology, demands for reform build up, Hargrove suggested. Ordinarily, the successor to such a president lacks the resources to respond effectively to these demands. About the best that he can do is to prepare the country for the next president who ultimately will be able to achieve major reform. After the latter presidency, a period of consolidation under a relatively weak president follows, before the next cycle of discontent, preparation, and achievement begins.[16] Stephen Skowronek brought a similar perspective to the issue, arguing that different stages of regime development and decay present different opportunities for presidential leadership.[17]

Regime changes or policy cycles of the sort described by Skowronek and Hargrove are sometimes accompanied by changes in the balance of partisan power in the electorate and in the Congress, changes that can have a significant impact on the president's chances of success. When the party that wins the White House also wins a large majority in the Congress, the odds that the new president will get what he wants from the Congress improve. Thus, the legislative achievements of Franklin Roosevelt's first hundred days were made possible by the huge majorities in both houses of the Congress that the Democrats gained as a result of the 1932 elections. In the Seventy-second Congress (1931–1932), the Democrats held a 6-seat majority in the House while the Republicans held a 1-seat majority in the Senate. In the next Congress, elected with Roosevelt, the Democrats held a 188-seat majority in the House and a 24-seat majority in the Senate. Similarly, as a result of the 1964 election, the Democrats increased their majority from 81 to 155 seats in the House while moving from a 34- to a 36-seat majority in the Senate. It was this Eighty-ninth Congress, elected with Lyndon Johnson, that approved so much of the Great Society legislation that he proposed.

In contrast, when successful presidential candidates do not arrive in Washington with a partisan majority in the Congress, things are more difficult for them. During Richard Nixon's almost six years in office, the Republicans were always a congressional minority, never getting closer to the Democrats than a 47-vote deficit in the House and a 10-vote deficit in the Senate. Ronald Reagan was helped immensely early in his presidency by the Senate majority that the Republicans gained in 1980, but one can only guess at how much more he might have achieved if his party could have also broken the majority that the Democrats have, since 1955, held in the House.

An even more deterministic theory of presidential success with the Congress has been advanced by Paul Light, who maintained that every presidency, no matter what the historical circumstances or congressional majorities that characterize it, will experience a "cycle of decreasing influence." Because the resources that a president needs to influence public policy—political capital, time, and energy—are at a maximum when he begins his term and diminish over his tenure in office, his capacity to lead must decline as he moves through his first term. Ironically, the president's decreasing influence coincides with an increase in his knowledge about policy and how to enact it, because the longer he and his staff are in office the more they learn about the national policy-making process. Light concluded that these concurrent and contradictory trends of increasing effectiveness and decreasing influence constitute "a pattern for all first term administrations." And during a president's second term, the situation gets worse. A successful reelection campaign provides a sharp, but very short-lived, boost to presidential resources; however, the subsequent fall-off is more rapid than that of the first term.[18] From Light's perspective, presidential primacy is quite likely for the first year or so of a president's first term, and for an even briefer period at the beginning of a second term, but after that, stalemate seems guaranteed. Quite apart from policy, partisan, and regime contexts, and even apart from the idiosyncracies of individual presidents, Light concluded that there is a life cycle for all presidencies, which ultimately limits what a president can accomplish and eventually places him in a no-win situation.

People and Cycles

These two categories of explanations, the one focusing on the man in office and the other on historical cycles, offer two levels of explanation for presidential success or failure. It may be hypothesized that the historical moment in which a president finds himself will establish the parameters, or the limits, within which he can act, whereas his own skills determine what he can accomplish within those limits. For example, Lyndon Johnson was cyclically well situated, after the Eisenhower administration, the Kennedy assassination, and the 1964 Democratic congressional landslide, to lead the nation toward major policy changes, and he also had the skill to do so. However, if through a feat of historical legerdemain, his and John Kennedy's positions had been reversed, Kennedy, as a president of lesser skills, presumably would have accomplished less than Johnson did, given the same historical moment.

Even Paul Light suggested that despite the cyclical forces that constrain every administration, there are things that presidents can do to win the no-win presidency. Thus it can be argued that Ronald Reagan's political and interpersonal skills allowed him to make the most of the early period of his first and second terms when Light's cyclical forces were aligned for success. His subsequent decline, although inevitable, was to some extent cushioned by his skills. Jimmy Carter, in contrast, as a less skillful president, could not take full advantage of the cyclical moments when he might have succeeded and could do nothing to cushion the decline in influence when that came.

Combining the individual and temporal perspectives in this manner suggests that whether or not a president achieves primacy depends on the historical era that he is in office, how much time he has left in his term, and factors such as his personality, his political skills, and his management style. Presidents, of course, are unlikely to recognize historical moments, so for them, that portion of our discussion is truly "academic." They will try, no matter what they are told, to achieve presidential primacy because such a quest is for them what the presidency is all about. In the sections that follow, I shall discuss how presidents organize their administrations and the strategies that they adopt as they seek the goal of presidential primacy.

THE MACHINERY OF PRESIDENTIAL POLICYMAKING

Developing the President's Program

Although the principle that the modern president would be actively involved in developing a legislative program and working for its passage through the Congress was firmly established during the presidencies of Woodrow Wilson and Franklin Roosevelt, it was President Harry Truman who, in 1948, submitted the first formal legislative program to Congress. Informally, the Congress now expects the White House to produce an annual legislative agenda, and it has more formally invited one by requiring the president to submit an annual budget message and an annual economic report in addition to the constitutionally mandated State of the Union address. These three regularly scheduled events, additional special messages submitted at the president's discretion, occasional news conference remarks, and daily presidential statements and addresses all provide opportunities for the president to tell the Congress what he expects of it and to focus the attention of legislators and the public on his most important policy priorities.

Ideas for the president's legislative program come from a variety of sources, but research has shown that relatively few originate with the president personally or with his staff. Rather, Congress and the bureaucracy are the primary sources for most of the ideas that find their way onto the president's agenda.[19] But all of those from whom legislative ideas might come will not necessarily share the president's overall goals for U.S. public policy. Individual members of Congress have their own policy agendas, parts of which may be consonant with the president's views and parts of which may not. Each executive agency has a policymaking agenda shaped largely by its permanent bureaucracy to serve their policy goals and aspirations for the agency, goals and aspirations that may be compatible or incompatible with those of the president. For example, the goals of the Reagan administration were less compatible with those of the Department of Education and more compatible with those of the Department of Defense. If each agency is allowed to speak out on its own, to advocate what those who staff it hold dearest, then there is no possibility of a coherent presidential program. The president must decide which ideas he wants to identify himself with, which he wishes to push, and which he wishes to ignore, postpone, or oppose. To this end, each administration must establish a process for assembling, evaluating, and developing the various possibilities in order to create a program that truly is the president's.

The Office of Management and Budget (OMB) is central to this process and has been since Congress passed the Budget and Accounting Act of 1921. The act delegated to the president the responsibility of preparing an annual budget and created the Bureau of the Budget (BOB), the agency that would eventually become OMB, to assist him. The act strengthened presidential control of the bureaucracy by prohibiting individual agencies from making their own appropriations requests to the Congress without first clearing them with the bureau. During Franklin Roosevelt's administration, this central clearance process was extended to nonbudgetary matters, and beginning in 1947, congressional committees instituted the practice of requesting from BOB the president's position on all pending legislation, including items that had not originated with the executive.[20] In addition to these clearance responsibilities, OMB solicits policy ideas and initiatives from executive agencies for possible inclusion in the State of the Union message or in the president's legislative program. After Congress acts, OMB develops recommendations for the president about whether he should sign or veto a bill. Finally, OMB serves as the executive's auditor of federal programs, regularly monitoring their efficiency, their effectiveness, and how they spend their funds.

For the first fifty years of its existence, the Bureau of the Budget performed its various functions in a professional manner, under the direction of career civil servants who served Republican and Democratic presidents alike. However, during the Nixon administration, the agency's role changed, as did its name. The new Office of Management and Budget was given additional management responsibilities and a decidedly more political orientation, as presidential appointees took control of the agency away from career bureaucrats. Concurrently, the White House staff became more active participants on legislative clearance decisions, particularly in regard to high priority items.[21] This new role continued through the Ford and Carter administrations and became even more pronounced during the Reagan administration when budget policy became the centerpiece of the president's domestic agenda.

The politicization of OMB was part of a larger movement toward centralization of executive-branch policymaking in the White House. In recent years, presidents have devoted more of their own and their staff's time to the process of policy development—to the assembling of ideas for policies, to the discussion of these ideas in the White House, and to the drafting and ultimate submission of legislative proposals embodying these ideas to Congress. The White House staff's original role of coordinating the executive-branch effort thus expanded to include the more proactive role of leading the policy development efforts of the various agencies. This White House–based policy development process became part of the institutional presidency with the creation of the Domestic Council during the Nixon administration. Nixon described the council as a "domestic counterpart of the National Security Council," which would be "primarily concerned with what we do," as compared with OMB, whose primary concern was "how we do it and how well we do it."[22] The council divided the work of the government into various broad policy areas, each supervised by an assistant director. Specific programs would be overseen by ad hoc working groups composed of White House personnel and, to a very limited extent, agency personnel.

The Domestic Council concept, though not the name, survived the Carter years but was replaced during the Reagan administration by a more complex structure involving a White House Office of Policy Development and a system of Cabinet Councils. Like the policy-making apparatus of previous administrations, the Reagan organizational scheme was designed to ensure that the policy process would stay under the control of the White House and that the influence of executive agencies would be minimized. But whereas in previous administrations the White House structures had helped to identify objectives, establish priorities, and construct policy agendas, in the Reagan administration objectives, priorities, and agendas were decided upon by the president and his transition people prior to taking office and by the president and his closest advisers after his inauguration.[23] The role of Reagan's White House policy structure was simply "to help the president implement his decisions by providing him an assessment of viable options" and "to mobilize support for these decisions within the Administration."[24] In short, presidential policy-making activities during the Reagan administration were even more centralized than in previous administrations.

The Congressional Arena

Although presidents, by issuing executive orders, by controlling the implementation of existing legislation, and by establishing and articulating U.S. foreign policy, can to some extent make public policy without involving the Congress, most of what the president wants to accomplish, particularly his most important initiatives, requires congressional consent. Congressional action is required to authorize new federal programs and to reauthorize existing programs. Constitutionally, no money may be spent by the federal government except as a result of congressional appropriation, and because Congress traditionally limits appropriations to a one-year period, the president must present and seek approval for his budget on an annual basis. Taxes, of course, can be neither raised nor lowered without congressional consent. In addition, Senate support is needed for administrative and judicial appointments and for treaties with foreign nations, and at least informal congressional support is desirable for the president's foreign policy initiatives.

After a presidential proposal is presented to the Congress by a member of the body—the president has no formal right to introduce legislation—it goes immediately to the committee or committees whose jurisdiction matches the content of the proposal. The committee has a number of options. It can choose to ignore the proposal altogether, or it can have its staff gather information on it. The committee can, if it wishes, schedule formal hearings at which administration representatives as well as representatives of affected interest groups testify. After the hearings, the committee can reject, modify, or approve the president's proposal, or it can write an entirely new bill on the same subject. In practice, presidential recommendations are seldom ignored by the committees to which they are referred. However, they are unlikely to be considered as completely or as expeditiously as the president would prefer, and there is certainly no guarantee that the committee will approve all or even most of what the president wants.

One variable affecting committee consideration is agenda space. The time that a congressional committee can direct toward the issues presented to it is finite, and therefore the president's proposals must compete for space on the committee's agenda with the proposals and preferences of committee members, party leaders, and other legislators, all of whom may have ideas different from the president's about what the committee should be doing with its time. The president's proposals also must compete for the attention of committee members, all of whom serve on other committees and have other policy priorities.

Whether and to what extent presidential proposals succeed in capturing the time and attention of the committee depends upon a number of factors. First, the president is likely to have more influence on committee agendas and decisions and on the congressional leadership if his party rather than the opposition controls the Congress. Because the Republicans controlled the Senate during his first six years in office, President Reagan usually could count on a friendly reception for his proposals in the

Senate committee to which it was referred, a factor that helped to offset Democratic control of the House, in whose committees his initiatives usually were treated less gently. With Senate support, the president could negotiate with the House from a position of strength and therefore get at least part of what he wanted in the compromises that eventually were reached. For example, the tax reform bill produced by the House Ways and Means Committee late in 1985 included several provisions that the president did not favor. Nonetheless, he urged House Republicans to support it on the assumption that once the House acted, the Senate committee would produce a bill more to his liking. The next year, that was indeed what happened, and the president happily signed the Tax Reform Act of 1986. Although it was inevitable that Reagan's legislative influence during his last two years in office was less than it had been earlier in his administration, his ability to move the Congress during the 1987–1988 period was severely hampered by the loss of a Republican majority in the Senate as a result of the 1986 elections.

A second factor affecting the president's quest for agenda space is the position taken on his proposals by the interest groups and the bureaucratic agencies to which they are relevant. Interest groups and agencies generally have strong and mutually supportive relationships with the legislators and staff members who serve on the committees and subcommittees that deal with measures of interest to them. These "subgovernments" have a great deal to say about the shape of public policy in their particular areas.[25] For example, President Reagan's proposal to abolish the Department of Education ran up against the solid opposition of interest groups such as the National Education Association that had worked for the establishment of the department as well as the opposition of those serving in the agency. These elements were supported by those members and staff of the House Education and Labor Committee who only a few years earlier had pushed the legislation that created the department. Not surprisingly, the president's proposal received only the most cursory attention from the Congress. Subgovernments can, of course, work for the president's proposals, as was the case when the Defense Department, military contractors, and the members of the House and Senate Armed Services committees generally accorded favorable consideration to the military buildup that President Reagan advocated early in his term.

Even if the president can win subcommittee and committee support, he still has no guarantee of ultimate success. In Chapter 3 we saw that power in Congress is highly decentralized, and the approval of a number of independent individuals and decisionmaking units is required before a bill becomes a law. For the president, the most frustrating aspect of this decentralized power structure is its bias toward inaction. That is, whereas a negative vote on a presidential proposal in committee or subcommittee may well doom it, a positive vote merely ensures that the proposal can move to the next stage of consideration, where, once again, a negative vote can defeat it. Positive recommendations from a House committee can be rejected or modified on the floor of the House. If the bill is accepted by the House, the entire process of subcommittee, committee, and floor approval must be repeated in the Senate, where, again, a negative vote at any stage can spell defeat; and where significant modifications of either the original proposal or the House-passed proposal are almost unavoidable. If the proposal passes in both chambers, its House and Senate versions may well be different. These differences need to be negotiated and reconciled in a conference committee, composed of members of both chambers, and there is no guarantee that these committees will reach an agreement. Every year, important legislation gets to the conference stage and then dies because neither the House nor the Senate is willing to budge. If the conference committee does reach an agreement, its report must be approved once again in both the House and the Senate before it can go on to the president for his approval or veto.

To summarize, the president's program, once conceived, must go through a complex, multistage legislative process where failure is much more likely than success because the process is designed to say no much more easily than yes. In recent years, the House has passed less than 10 percent of all the bills that have been introduced, and the Senate figure has been between 20 percent and 30 percent. And these figures have exhibited a declining trend during the postwar period. A bill introduced in 1983 had "about one-third the chance of success in the House that it would have had in the 80th Congress (1947–1948) and about one-half the chance of success in the Senate."[26] Although the chances that a bill backed by the president will pass are, of course, better than these averages would suggest, defeat is still a very real possibility and significant changes from what the president proposes are a virtual certainty. Approval requires successive affirmative decisions at each of several stages of the legislative process, but failure can come from one negative vote at any point along the way.

Congressional Liaison

Obviously, the task of seeing the president's program through this labyrinthine legislative process is both difficult and crucial. Any president foolish enough to think that his job is over once he delivers his proposals to the Congress will see little of what he wants approved. However, although all presidents, beginning with Washington, have made policy recommendations to the Congress, until the twentieth century aggressive presidential lobbying on behalf of these proposals was considered to be inappropriate, an infringement on the Congress's legislative power. In accounts of the Jefferson administration, for example, there are references to "secret agents" who worked in the Congress on behalf of the president. By the Wilson administration, overt presidential lobbying was still considered to be bad form and much had to be done behind the scenes. However, according to Stephen Wayne, these strictures did not deter Wilson from taking steps that would be considered routine today but that for his time, were rather bold. "He personally lobbied for his own proposals, utilizing the president's room off the Senate chamber to receive and confer with congressional party officials. The President had a special telephone line installed between the Senate and White House. Occasionally, the administration even supplied its supporters with draft bills and supporting material they could use in congressional committees and on the floor."[27]

The practice of sending personal representatives to the Congress to work for presidential proposals began with Franklin Roosevelt, who because of his limited physical mobility, could not go himself. This first liaison operation continued during the Truman administration, but because Truman, as a former senator, was more concerned than Roosevelt about seeming to infringe upon the Congress's constitutional responsibilities, his liaison people dealt for the most part with relatively low-level matters of patronage and favors. This pattern of low-intensity activity continued through the Eisenhower administration, although during this period presidential-congressional liaison became institutionalized with the creation of the first White House Office of Congressional Relations (OCR). OCR was supposed to maintain friendly relations between the administration and members of the Congress, but given Eisenhower's modest legislative agenda and his apparent reluctance to fight in Congress for what he wanted, the operation was neither large nor aggressive.

The Kennedy administration's more sweeping legislative agenda required a more active and prominent liaison operation, and OCR activities under the leadership of Larry O'Brien, a close friend of Kennedy's and an astute legislative tactician, became a model for future administrations.[28] This style continued and legislative liaison became an even higher priority during the administration of Lyndon Johnson, who had established a reputation as a master legislative strategist during his days as Senate majority leader. By the Nixon and Ford administrations the idea that a strong and effective White House Office of Congresssional Relations was essential to a president's chances of success had become so firmly established that these presidents and their successors thought of OCR as simply a part of the institutionalized presidency passed on to them by their predecessors that should be staffed with the best people available.

The standard method developed by O'Brien for organizing congressional liaison was to divide legislators into groups, usually based on geography, and then to assign one member of the liaison staff to each group. There would then be a single person in the liaison office to whom each legislator could go with any concern he or she might have, and, conversely, there would always be one liaison person who knew the needs of a specific member of Congress and who could approach that legislator to ask for support. The premise of this organizational style was that support for the president's policy initiatives would follow from established and friendly relationships between individual legislators and OCR, relationships based on services that the latter performed for the former. During the early days of the Carter administration, however, this approach was abandoned in favor of one in which each liaison staff member took responsibility for a particular policy area and dealt with legislators only with respect to that policy concern.

The problems with the Carter approach were manifold. If a legislator was not involved in an important policy area, he or she might never be contacted by a liaison person, or, even worse, the first time that the legislator would be contacted would be to ask for a vote. Also, the policy division meant that legislators had to deal with a number of different liaison people, and therefore no one got to know them very well. Finally, the emphasis on policy meant that the personal and political needs of legislators tended to be slighted. When these deficiencies eventually became apparent to the Carter administration, the more conventional "organization by people" was added to the "organization by policy area," but not before valuable time had been lost and a great deal of ill will created.[29] This revised approach, combining personal and policy interactions, was maintained by the Reagan administration. However, because it was used from the very beginning of the administration and because, unlike the Carter operation, it was run by people with a great deal of previous Washington experience and sensitivity to the needs of legislators, OCR rightly received much of the credit for Reagan's early success with the Congress.[30]

Presidential Approval

After Congress passes a bill and sends it to the White House, the president must decide whether or not to sign it. OMB polls the relevant executive-branch departments and White House staff people for their views on these "enrolled bills" and then prepares a memorandum for the president summarizing the various views and providing an OMB recommendation. Presidents usually go along with that recommendation; however, the views of the Domestic Council staff and its successor bodies have in recent years assumed increasing importance in shaping these recommendations and in determining what the president will do.

Summary

The key components of the president's legislative policy machinery are OMB, the White House staff, and OCR. Increasingly, the White House staff governs the process, OMB generates information and coordinates the process, and OCR sells the final product on Capitol Hill. All of these agencies and staff, working on the president's behalf to create his legislative program, are available to every president. The question then is what determines whether or not this machinery works successfully for a particular president.

DETERMINANTS OF PRESIDENTIAL SUCCESS WITH CONGRESS

Presidential policy success depends in part upon contextual factors that are beyond his control. There are, however, styles that presidents can adopt and strategic decisions they can make that will improve their chances with the Congress.

Personal Involvement

As a general rule, presidents who have been accessible to members of Congress and personally involved in the process of generating congressional support have been more successful than those presidents who have distanced themselves from legislators and left congressional relations to their subordinates. Richard Nixon and Jimmy Carter gave very little of themselves to the process of persuading legislators. For different reasons, both relied a great deal on their aides and were reluctant to call representatives, to stroke their egos, or to make the deals that win votes in the Congress. In Carter's case, his behavior was attributable in part to his staff's inexperience in Washington and in part to his desire to devote a great deal of his time to the details of public policy. Convinced that there were right and wrong answers to complex policy questions, he assumed that members of Congress would be able to differentiate between the two and act accordingly.[31] In Nixon's case, the explanation is based almost entirely on personality. He was, by all accounts, a very solitary person, unenthusiastic about speaking with members of Congress either in person or by telephone, someone who disliked confrontations of any sort, met regularly with only a few trusted aides, and was inclined to steal off to a hideaway office to work on his own. One Senator whom Nixon counted among his friends said of him, "I've never known a man to be so much of a loner."[32]

Lyndon Johnson and Gerry Ford were two presidents whose approach to Congress was antithetical to the Carter-Nixon model. It is perhaps not coincidental that both had long and successful congressional careers before becoming president: Johnson having served as Senate majority leader and Ford as House minority leader. Both men came to the White House with great respect for the Congress as an institution and with a keen sense of the personal and political needs of its members. Johnson devoted an extraordinary amount of his time to congressional relations. His frequent telephone calls to legislators and his willingness to spend time courting, pleading, and if need be, threatening those whose support he wanted was legendary. He always seemed to have a great deal of information about individual legislators and the political pressures that they faced, information gained through frequent, often informal meetings with them, and from his staff, which he constantly badgered for news about what was going on at the Capitol.[33] Gerry Ford also was "personally involved in his legislative battles and was willing to call, see, and keep in contact with many members of Congress."[34] Once every few weeks, Ford even made himself available to members of Congress on a walk-in basis.[35]

Lying somewhere between these two extremes were presidents such as Truman, Eisenhower, and Kennedy, none of whom were so personally involved with the Congress as Johnson and Ford nor so convinced that the president needed to lobby aggressively for his program. Truman had a number of friends in Congress from his years as a senator and breakfasted weekly with congressional leaders. However, because he thought it somewhat improper for the president to establish too close a relationship with the Congress, he tried to limit "both his personal interaction with Congress and that of his staff."[36] Eisenhower too met regularly with the Republican leadership but rarely made phone calls himself, and legislators seemed to find it difficult to get to him, either face-to-face or by telephone. However, it is possible that Eisenhower was in fact more active than he seemed to be. Fred Greenstein has argued that Eisenhower was pursuing a "hidden hand leadership strategy" that "camouflaged" his participation in a variety of political activities with a deliberately cultivated "reputation for not intervening in day-to-day policy-making."[37]

Although John Kennedy, like Truman, Johnson, and Ford, had served in the Congress, according to Arthur Schlesinger he "had always been something of an alien on the Hill."[38] Although as president he was more accessible to legislators than Eisenhower, he felt uncomfortable with many members of the Congress and "was less likely than Johnson to call legislators and ask for their votes."[39] However, Kennedy did score points with the Congress by including legislators in the exciting White House social whirl that he and his wife had created. Early in his administration, he had all of the members of Congress to the White House in groups of fifty for get-acquainted sessions and later regularly included selected senators and representatives on the White House dinner list. Schlesinger concluded that Kennedy "spent more of his time than people realized working with Congress. But it cannot be said that this was the part of the presidency which gave him the greatest pleasure or satisfaction."[40]

A president's personal involvement in congressional relations does not necessarily guarantee success. Two presidents who devoted the most attention to the Congress—Ford and Johnson—had very different experiences, with the former usually failing to sway the Congress and the latter generally quite successful, especially early in his term. The difference here is explained by context. Ford confronted a hostile Congress, embittered by Vietnam and Watergate, in which his party was a minority. Johnson, in contrast, dealt with a heavily Democratic Congress disposed, in the wake of the Kennedy assassination and the 1964 landslide, to support him. It is also worth noting that when the context changed in the last two years of the Johnson administration, with the escalation of the Vietnam War and an epidemic of urban riots, Johnson's vaunted skills in congressional relations could not prevent the erosion of his support in Congress.

Bargaining

In addition to personal involvement, a successful president also must understand that bargaining and compromises rather than rhetoric and demands are the way to move the Congress. A willingness to engage in political give and take and a certain flexibility about policy goals and how they should be achieved are therefore helpful. Franklin Roosevelt and Lyndon Johnson were the ultimate pragmatists, always willing to deal and always willing to take somewhat less than they wanted, in order to achieve incremental change. This too seems to have been the case with Ronald Reagan. Although Reagan had strong ideological beliefs, he was, in Fred Greenstein's words, "willing to adapt the positions he derives from doctrine if circumstances force him to recognize that they cannot be achieved or will not work."[41] Throughout his presidency, Reagan made a habit of stating his position, whether on taxes, contra aid, or government spending, in the strongest, most ideological terms, only to retreat in the face of legislative opposition to compromise positions that could command congressional majorities.

In contrast, Richard Nixon and Jimmy Carter were much more rigid. Nixon saw himself "more as an administrator and executive decision-maker and not as a power broker pushing to get his bills through Congress." Carter admitted in an interview that "horse trading and compromising and so forth have always been difficult for me to do."[42] One member of his staff recalled a meeting early in the administration when Carter reacted angrily to a suggestion that he consider the political feasibility of a policy proposal under discussion, saying, "I don't want to hear what the political implications are of this issue. I want to do what's right not what's political."[43]

Cordiality and Consultation

Bargaining is facilitated when presidents, through their personal involvement, have established cordial and cooperative relations with members of Congress. Cordiality can be diminished if legislators believe that they have not been consulted sufficiently. Legislators are embarrassed when they are the last to know about a new policy initiative, especially one that involves a policy area in which they have been working, or that falls under the jurisdiction of their committee, or that has a major impact on their constituency. To avoid these situations, most of the recent presidents have offered interested members of Congress previews of legislation that they intended to propose. Eisenhower would convene the Republican congressional leaders in December to let them know what was on his agenda for the next year. He would take their comments and occasionally make revisions, but this was generally as far as the consultative process went.[44]

Lyndon Johnson went much further, sometimes appointing members of Congress to task forces charged with designing policies, asking legislators, even Republicans, for their advice on questions of legislative content and strategy, and never sending anything to Congress until the appropriate members had been informed in advance. "We made many mistakes," said Johnson in his memoirs, "but failure to inform and brief the Congress was not one of them." This approach was important, Johnson said, because "when Congress helps to shape projects, they are more likely to be successful than those simply handed down from the executive branch."[45] Jimmy Carter, in contrast, was often criticized for failing to give members of Congress advance notice on matters ranging from major legislative initiatives to such minor but politically important items as patronage decisions and the allocations of funds for local projects. After his defeat, Carter complained in his memoirs of Congress's "insatiable desire for consultation which, despite all our efforts, we were never able to meet."[46]

Consultation has an obvious payoff: It helps the president to anticipate problems that might come up later, and if he is willing to revise his proposals based on these early reactions, what he submits may prove to be more acceptable. A more subtle, but more important, payoff is that a president's effort to consult with legislators makes them feel as if they are taken seriously by the White House, thus contributing to a cooperative atmosphere between the Congress and the president. Lyndon Johnson wrote, "If I were to name one factor above all others that helped me in dealing with Congress, I would say it was the genuine friendship and rapport I had with most congressmen and senators."[47] Although Johnson's estimate of how many legislators were among his "genuine" friends might be slightly exaggerated—he was harsh and unforgiving to those who crossed him—he nonetheless worked at these relationships. He went out of his way to recognize legislators for their contributions, he invited them to bill-signing ceremonies, he made it a point to thank them personally, and he demanded that his staff be constantly solicitous of legislators and their concerns.

Carter had a different attitude toward Congress, making it clear from the outset that he did not approve of the way Congress did its business. Early in his administration, he forced a confrontation with the Congress by moving to cancel several local water projects that he thought were environmentally unsound and fiscally unjustified. Not surprisingly, the legislators in whose states these projects were to be constructed had a somewhat different view of their worth. The fallout from this affair was lasting enmity between Carter and these legislators, of whom several occupied key committee positions.[48] Later in his administration, in 1979, Carter's veto of a public works appropriation bill containing numerous projects carefully designed for the electoral benefit of legislators occurred because, in the understated words of one of his aides, "This president just does not believe in project grants."[49]

. This obvious distaste for one of the Congress's primary operating principles—that federal expenditures should be widely distributed among members and their constituencies—won Carter few friends on the Hill. To make matters worse, Carter also lacked the personal touch. Although he began his presidency with a number of actions designed to symbolize his accessibility (he gave members of Congress his private telephone number, he and his wife, Rosalynn, took a postinauguration stroll down Pennsylvania Avenue, he was photographed wearing a sweater without a tie, and he was seen carrying his own suitcases), when the time for symbolism passed and the time for actual policymaking came, Carter usually refused to deal with legislators in a "personal or political sense" but instead stuck doggedly to the merits of the policy question at hand. Members of Congress were quite understandably upset when they received unsigned photos of the president for their offices and identical "personal" letters and when other little favors proved rare, such as invitations to the White House, rides on Air Force One, pens from bill-signing ceremonies, and evenings on the presidential yacht (the latter hardly possible because Carter had sold it).[50]

In this respect, Ronald Reagan was much more like Johnson than Carter. Fred Greenstein noted Reagan's "ability to be ingratiating" and called him "gifted at small group persuasion."[51] Although sometimes extraordinarily partisan and openly hostile to the Congress, Reagan nonetheless established strong personal relations with leaders on both sides of the aisle. His greatest opponent in the House, Speaker Thomas "Tip" O'Neill, though openly ridiculed by many of the president's people, and himself contemptuous of the president's conservative policies, nonetheless made no secret of the fact that he was more comfortable with Reagan personally than he was with his fellow Democrat, Jimmy Carter. Reagan, early in his administration, even invited O'Neill to two private dinners at the White House, much nicer treatment than he was accorded during the early days of the Carter administration.[52]

Hardball

Besides offering consultation and cordiality, a president must have the ability to be tough when necessary. If the president is to be a successful bargainer, according to Richard Neustadt, those in the Washington community with whom he negotiates must know that he has the "ability and will to make use of the bargaining advantages that he has."[53] Among the president's "advantages" are the services that he can perform for or withdraw from members of Congress, including support for their pet projects, invitations to the White House, help in raising campaign funds, and consideration of their nominees for federal appointments. The major formal advantage that the president has is his veto power. His single "no" can frustrate the will of majorities of senators and representatives and require them, if they wish to prevail, to round up another one-sixth of each chamber to override the veto. The infrequency of veto overrides suggests exactly how powerful this advantage is.

Hardball is an essential but at the same time a dangerous game for the president to play. Members of Congress do not like to be muscled, and too much of it will make congenial relations between the two branches unachievable. However, unless the president is prepared to lean on people at least occasionally, his threats to do so will have no credibility. Eisenhower, for example, did not like to engage in such tactics, and in the view of some of his staff members, his "reluctance to pressure Congress contributed to the floundering of his legislative program."[54]

John Kennedy made somewhat more frequent use of t
but generally preferred to avoid direct confrontations v
members of Congress. The Nixon administration, in contra‿
torious for arm-twisting and threats, and although the president u‿
distanced himself from such tactics, leaving them to his staff, thesᵣ
tactics nonetheless contributed to some estrangement between the White
House and the Congress well before the Watergate story broke.

Although hardball tactics do have a potentially negative impact, what
is probably worse for the president is to threaten such tactics but never
actually use them. Carter got off to a bad start with the Congress when,
confronted by a congressional uproar over his move to cancel the water
projects, he compounded his error by ultimately backing down and
accepting a congressional compromise on the issue. As Carter admitted
in his memoirs, the compromise "was accurately interpreted as a sign
of weakness on my part."[55] Ronald Reagan, in comparison, quickly
established a reputation for being tough when, a few months into his
presidency, he fired 11,500 striking air traffic controllers and absolutely
refused, in the face of much protest and pressure, to back down. The
added advantage of this episode for the president was that it allowed
him to demonstrate the strength of his resolve without directly confronting
the Congress itself.[56]

Using the veto presents another tricky problem for the president
because the veto is essentially a negative weapon that can stop the
Congress from acting but is of limited utility as an instrument to force
the Congress to act. However, by threatening to veto proposals he
dislikes, the president can encourage the Congress to make changes that
would render the bill more acceptable to him. But to make a veto threat
credible, the president does need to use the veto at least occasionally.
At one point in his administration, Franklin Roosevelt pleaded with his
staff to "give me a bill that I can veto" so that the Congress would
understand that he was willing to use that tool. And use it he did,
casting more than 25 percent of all presidential vetoes, and averaging
just under fifty vetoes a year while in office. Harry Truman also used
the veto aggressively, averaging thirty-five a year.

Despite the examples of Roosevelt and Truman, the most common
contemporary situation for the exercise of the veto occurs when a
conservative Republican president confronts a more progressive Congress
controlled by the Democrats. Thus, Dwight Eisenhower cast twenty-five
vetoes per year and Richard Nixon twelve. Gerry Ford, confronted with
a hostile post-Watergate Congress, in only two years in office cast
seventy-two vetoes, twelve of which were overridden by the Congress.
Ronald Reagan, however, cast relatively few vetoes (an average of about
ten a year), but his veto threats seemed quite credible and effective.

His oft-repeated promise to veto any legislation raising taxes ("Make my day!" he was fond of saying, quoting a celebrated line from a then current Clint Eastwood film) consistently discouraged the Congress from pursuing that line of attack on the budget deficit.

Agenda Control

An administration that comes to the Congress with a long agenda of major policy proposals often runs into difficulty, first, because it competes for agenda space with policy issues of interest to members of Congress and, second, because it may mean a series of tough high-pressure votes for legislators. However, the president's chances for success are greatest early in his term when he can take full advantage of high public support as well as initial congressional predispositions to support the new president. But these resources diminish markedly as time goes by, as do his chances of success. This phenomenon therefore argues for quick presidential action on a variety of fronts. Presidents face a dilemma: Keep the agenda short and manageable, but accept the fact that relatively little will be accomplished during the period when presidential resources are greatest, or try to get as much passed as you can as quickly as you can, thus making full use of your resources but also running the risk of overloading and thereby antagonizing the Congress.

Lyndon Johnson was keenly aware that his political capital had begun to diminish the day after his 1964 election victory and that he would have to move quickly if he wanted to accomplish much. However, his experience in the Senate had taught him the dangers of asking too much from the Congress. So he insisted that his initiatives go to the Hill gradually, rather than all at once. "It's like a bottle of bourbon," he said. "If you take it a glass at a time, it's fine. But if you drink the whole bottle in one evening, you have troubles."[57] Johnson also had learned from the Kennedy administration's mistakes. According to Arthur Schlesinger, during the early part of Kennedy's term, "there were too many new ideas coming too fast, couched in too cool and analytical tone and implying too critical a view of American society. Instead of being reassured, many Congressmen felt threatened."[58]

During the Carter administration, the decision was made to move as quickly as possible, and Congress reacted critically to what was perceived as an oversized administration agenda. Although Carter's agenda was in absolute terms not much different in size from those of his predecessors, it did include some very complex and controversial issues. Two members of his administration summed it up this way: "The President sent a flotilla of major proposals to the Congress in the first eighteen months of his Administration: cuts in water projects, social security finance, a comprehensive energy program, a tax rebate scheme, hospital cost containment legislation, comprehensive tax reform, welfare reform."[59] Carter also faced a great deal of competition for agenda space from Democratic members of Congress with their own policy proposals to push, proposals that had accumulated during eight years of Republican presidencies. As a result, Carter was sometimes perceived as making inordinate demands on the congressional process, and in hindsight he admitted that his relations with the Congress "would have been smoother" if his legislation had been proposed "in much more careful phases— not in such a rush."[60]

The Reagan administration, in contrast, brought a relatively brief agenda to the Congress and therefore succeeded by "limiting and staggering the issues." This allowed the administration to focus public, congressional, and presidential attention on a single major issue at a time, thereby maximizing its chances for success. Early in the administration, the White House spoke only about reducing federal expenditures and reducing taxes. Foreign policy issues were deliberately kept on the back burner, and initiatives in regard to the so-called social issues of abortion and school prayer as well as new proposals in other domestic policy areas were nowhere to be seen.[61]

Reagan's agenda-controlling strategy is generally viewed as having been much more successful than Carter's, but the method does have its limits. The one-big-issue-at-a-time approach was appropriate for a president who wanted the federal government to undertake no new initiatives, whose ideologically constrained agenda focused solely on reducing the policy scope of the federal government. Although Lyndon Johnson also kept an eye on the congressional agenda, his single-minded devotion to the art of legislative politics and his overwhelming support in Congress after the 1964 election enabled him to accomplish a great deal. As a general rule, the Reagan approach would be less compatible with the needs of a more activist president such as Carter, who had a broader vision of what the federal government could accomplish but also a much narrower legislative majority and much less zeal for legislative politics than Johnson had.

It is ironic that while Carter was criticized for overloading the Congress, he also was criticized by some members of Congress for not having specific policy proposals ready early enough in his administration and for taking too much time to work out the details, particularly in regard to energy policy. This view is supported by Paul Light's data showing that whereas John Kennedy made 76 percent of his first-year requests between January and March 1961 and Lyndon Johnson 94 percent in those three months of 1965, Carter sent up only 33 percent of his first-year proposals during his first three months. However, this compares with only 12 percent for Nixon in 1969 and 40 percent in 1973.[62] It is reasonable to conclude, therefore, that Carter was somewhat slower in making his proposals than other Democratic presidents have been, but that when they finally did come, they came all at once.

For an activist president, then, agenda control means walking a very fine line between too much too soon and being too late to take advantage of the honeymoon period. For such a president, the Reagan solution of accomplishing one or two big things early in his administration and accomplishing little if anything later on is unacceptable.

Going Public

Before he became president, Woodrow Wilson observed that the president's capacity to succeed with the Congress rested on the fact that he "has the nation behind him, and Congress has not. He has no means of compelling Congress except through public opinion."[63] One reason why presidents today are advised to move on their policy proposals as quickly as possible is that their public support tends to be higher earlier in their administrations. The evidence is that popular presidents can help shape the policy preferences of the American people and this public support for their policy priorities helps presidents gain the support of the Congress.[64] Samuel Kernell has documented, from the post–World War I period on, a steady increase in presidential activities designed to marshall public support for themselves and their programs. He detected increases in the number of presidential addresses, in the number of days that presidents spend away from Washington on political travel, and in the number of public appearances that they make. Kernell concluded, however, that although this "going public" strategy pays dividends early in the administration, the people eventually tire of the public presidency, and their public support diminishes.[65]

The capacity to generate congressional support by "going public" at least early in an administration constitutes another dimension of the Reagan-Carter comparison. Ronald Reagan's extraordinary ability to use televison to communicate directly with the American people has been recognized and admired by his friends and enemies alike. During the first months of his first term, as the administration focused all of its efforts on its economic agenda, Reagan carefully used nationally televised speeches, calibrated to important congressional votes, to generate public support for his position. These speeches explicitly encouraged citizens to communicate with their legislators and to urge them to support the president. In several cases, the television appeal and the follow-up constituency effort led to a major presidential victory in Congress, thereby further strengthening the Washington community's perception of Reagan as a public force to be reckoned with. However, as Kernell prophesied, Reagan's successful use of this strategy was confined largely to the first year of his presidency. After that, losses mounted in Congress, and as the state of the national economy began to deteriorate, his job approval ratings began to decline. Public appearances and televised addresses did little to stem the tide.[66]

When Jimmy Carter came to office, he too hoped to be able to appeal to the American people to support his legislative initiatives. Before the election, he told a reporter that if Congress proved reluctant to adopt his policy proposals, "I would use that influence of going directly to the people and identifying special interest groups that block good legislation."[67] Shortly after the election, Carter said that if Congress caused him any problems he would "handle them just as I handled the Georgia legislature. Whenever I had problems with the Georgia legislature, I took the problems to the people of Georgia."[68] Unfortunately for Carter, he did not have the same public skills as his successor would display. Although he made frequent use of television appearances, he never seemed able to strike a responsive chord with the public, and more important, he never seemed to link his public appearances with specific actions. Whereas Reagan's appeals were clearly linked to specific congressional votes, which more often than not he ended up winning, as Norman Ornstein noted, Carter did not recognize "how he would be perceived if he concentrated his resources, prestige, and determination, blew the trumpet, yelled 'charge!' and—nothing."[69] This is exactly what happened after Carter's various television appeals for his national energy policy, and as a result, Carter's capacity to intimidate Congress with the club of public opinion eroded.

In Carter's defense, one must say that few recent presidents have approached Ronald Reagan's public skills, with Franklin Roosevelt the most obvious exception. John Kennedy also had some of these same rhetorical talents, and his innovation of the live televised prime-time press conference added an important weapon to the presidency's public arsenal. However, Kennedy seemed seldom capable of translating his public activities into public and congressional support for his policy concerns. The other presidents who served during the television age— Johnson, Nixon, and Ford, as well as Carter—were all rather poor media performers. As Larry Berman concluded, "each had his credibility lessened by the mere fact that he looked and sounded as poorly as he did" on television.[70] Only on rare occasions were these presidents able truly to reach the American people or even to instill any fear in the hearts of members of the Congress that they might do so. Thus, on the one hand, television is available to all presidents, and all presidents can use the media to speak directly to the American people and to solicit support for their public policy priorities; on the other hand, not every president can pull it off, and even those who can, cannot do so for their entire term in office.

CONCLUSION

The lesson of this discussion for a new president who seeks to do well in the Congress is clear: Devote a great deal of your attention to congressional relations; treat members of Congress as important people, and as often as you can, talk to them personally; make certain that your congressional liaison operation is run by a staff that understands the Congress and is sensitive to the personal and political needs of its members; move quickly on your legislative agenda, but at the same time avoid overwhelming the Congress with too many proposals; be open to compromises and trades that may get you some but not all of what you want; make your bargaining position credible by playing selective hardball early in your term; and, try to cultivate and utilize your popular support.

If a president adopts the various elements of this recommended strategy, the literature on the American presidency has argued, he can make a difference, he can overcome the bias toward inaction created by the constitution against government, and he can overcome or at least mitigate the effects of adverse contextual variables such as the condition of the economy, the state of public opinion, the partisan balance in the Congress, or even the historical moment during which he is in power. Presidential primacy is, from this perspective, available to any incumbent as long as he plays his cards right. Stalemate or, worse, the loss of the policy initiative to the Congress can always be avoided. If they are not avoided, it is because the president has failed and not because of any endemic weaknesses in the structure of the political system.

In Chapter 5, we will see whether presidential success is really always available as long as the incumbent knows what he is doing. We will explore the record of presidential success and the consequences of following this recommended strategy on the quality of public policy.

5

The Failure of Presidential Domination: Stalemate and Bad Public Policy

The Congress today is one of the few legislatures that can regularly say no to a popularly elected president and make it stick. Even presidents such as Lyndon Johnson and Ronald Reagan, who seemed to follow the strategy for legislative success recommended in Chapter 4 and who for the most part avoided the personal and organizational failings that characterized legislative liaison during the Nixon and Carter administrations, often were unable to move the Congress on key issues. Nearly every president, no matter how adept he and his staff proved to be at legislative relations, and no matter how much success he had with the Congress early in his administration, has ended his term bitter toward the Congress and stalemated with it on the major policy issues of the day.

This has been particularly true for the most recent presidents. By 1968, Lyndon Johnson had reached a deadlock with the Congress on the conduct of the Vietnam War and on how the war, if it continued, was to be financed. Richard Nixon was forced to resign by a Congress infuriated by the Watergate scandal, but also resentful over the cavalier treatment that the administration had accorded it on issues ranging from budgetary policy to military policy in Southeast Asia. His successor, Gerald Ford, vetoed twice as many bills in his two years in office than Nixon had in his six. Jimmy Carter, after struggling with his legislative program for three years, blasted the Congress on national television as an institution controlled and twisted by special interests. And Ronald Reagan's second term ended with a rejected Supreme Court nomination, deadlock on the federal budget, and defeat for his Central American policy. In 1987, Reagan recorded "a string of defeats unmatched in the post-war era."[1]

In this chapter, the record of presidential success with the Congress will be presented, a record from which three facts seem to emerge. The first is that presidential success is far from certain. Presidential initiatives are about as likely to fail as they are to succeed, and the reason for this lies for the most part with the constitution against government. The second fact is that every president is more likely to get what he wants from the Congress early in his administration rather than later, a phenomenon explained by a seemingly inevitable dynamic of declining presidential resources and intensifying congressional resistance as an administration ages. The third fact is that over the past twenty years or so, it seems to have been getting tougher for presidents to succeed with the Congress. This trend is explained by the increasing degree to which power in Congress is fragmented, by the enervated state of U.S. political parties, by the robust health of interest groups, and by the growing dissensus among the American public about what government should be doing.

These three facts—the first attributable to the fundamental institutional arrangements, the second peculiar to the life cycle of each administration, and the third to the changing political context within which each administration functions—have proven to be mutually reinforcing and when combined, have significantly increased the likelihood of policy stalemates between the president and the Congress. However, on those occasions when policy stalemates are avoided and policy action does take place, the policies produced are likely to be poor by managerial standards. There are two reasons for this. First, if the president follows the recommended strategy for success outlined in Chapter 4, his actions will undermine what was hypothesized in Chapter 1 to be the superior capacity of the executive to produce managerially sound public policy. It is ironic that the president, it seems, must choose between being able to act and being able to act well, for under the current arrangements he cannot do both. The second reason for managerially poor public policy is that the generic characteristics of legislatures, which in Chapter 1 were hypothesized to lead to exactly such policy outcomes, continue to apply to—and are in fact accentuated in—the contemporary Congress. Finally, these managerially poor public policies also fail to meet democratic standards for good public policy.

THE RECORD OF PRESIDENTIAL SUCCESS

Measuring Presidential Success

What does it mean to say that a president has been successful with the Congress? *Congressional Quarterly* (*CQ*), the major source of information on the Congress for political scientists and journalists, has used two different measures of presidential success. One, reported annually from 1953 through 1975, identified the president's policy initiatives for the year and calculated the percentage that the Congress approved. A second measure, provided continuously by CQ since 1953, uses congressional roll-call votes on proposals on which the president took a clear public position, regardless of whether he initiated the proposal. Presidential success in the Congress is measured annually by the percentage of these votes on which the president's position prevailed. Both of these CQ measures are shown in Table 5.1.

Each of these indices has its limitations as a measure of presidential success.[2] The initiative-based measure depends upon answering the often tricky question of whether a particular bill is really a presidential proposal. For example, the 1981 tax reduction bill is viewed as one of the major accomplishments of the Reagan administration, but several years before Ronald Reagan became president the proposal had been drafted and pushed by Representative Jack Kemp and Senator William Roth. This legislative history suggests that the bill should be characterized as a congressional rather than a presidential initiative, even though it never came close to approval until it became part of the Reagan agenda. Similarly, if an initiative that is indisputably the president's undergoes significant modification before congressional passage, as was the case with the Carter administration's energy package, should its passage still be counted as a victory for the president?

The measure also misses the fact that what presidents propose (or fail to propose) can be affected by their assessment of what the Congress is likely to pass. The president may alter or delete elements of his program before they are announced because, on the basis of preliminary consultations, he anticipates strong congressional opposition. Even after the president announces a proposal, he may decide not to submit legislation, or if he does submit legislation he may decide not to push it because congressional opposition is expected. Thus, high presidential success scores may indicate that a president has introduced "fewer and less controversial bills" and has been "more willing to accept congressionally proposed changes."[3]

Finally, the measure fails to discriminate between those proposals that the president really wants and works for and those proposals that are lower on his list of priorities. Controversial policy proposals of major import are lumped together with minor, noncontroversial proposals. A narrow victory on the defense budget assumes the same significance as a unanimous vote to add land to a national park. Furthermore, the initiative-based score, by taking into account only what happened during the year in question, ignored the fact that complex proposals might take more than one year to pass. One study estimated that such a multiyear

TABLE 5.1
Presidential Success in Congress: Initiatives Approved and Roll-call Victories

	President's Party	House Majority	Senate Majority	Presidential Initiatives Approved (%)	Presidential Roll-call Victories (%)
Eisenhower					
1953	Rep.	Rep. + 8	Rep. + 2	73.0	89.2
1954	Rep.	Rep. + 8	Rep. + 2	65.0	82.8
1955	Rep.	Dem. + 29	Dem. + 1	46.0	75.3
1956	Rep.	Dem. + 29	Dem. + 1	46.0	69.7
1957	Rep.	Dem. + 33	Dem. + 2	37.0	68.4
1958	Rep.	Dem. + 33	Dem. + 2	47.0	75.7
1959	Rep.	Dem. +130	Dem. +30	41.0	52.0
1960	Rep.	Dem. +130	Dem. +30	31.0	65.1
Kennedy					
1961	Dem.	Dem. + 87	Dem. +28	48.0	81.5
1962	Dem.	Dem. + 87	Dem. +28	44.0	85.4
1963	Dem.	Dem. + 82	Dem. +34	27.0	87.1
Johnson					
1964	Dem.	Dem. + 82	Dem. +34	58.0	87.9
1965	Dem.	Dem. +155	Dem. +36	69.0	93.1
1966	Dem.	Dem. +155	Dem. +36	56.0	78.9
1967	Dem.	Dem. + 61	Dem. +28	48.0	78.8
1968	Dem.	Dem. + 61	Dem. +28	56.0	74.5
Nixon					
1969	Rep.	Dem. + 51	Dem. +16	32.0	74.8
1970	Rep.	Dem. + 51	Dem. +16	46.0	76.9
1971	Rep.	Dem. + 75	Dem. +10	20.0	74.8
1972	Rep.	Dem. + 75	Dem. +10	44.0	66.3
1973	Rep.	Dem. + 50	Dem. +14	31.0	50.6
1974	Rep.	Dem. + 50	Dem. +14	34.0	59.6
Ford					
1974	Rep.	Dem. + 50	Dem. +14	36.0	58.2
1975	Rep.	Dem. +147	Dem. +24	29.0	61.0
1976	Rep.	Dem. +147	Dem. +24		53.8
Carter					
1977	Dem.	Dem. +149	Dem. +23		75.4
1978	Dem.	Dem. +149	Dem. +23		78.3
1979	Dem.	Dem. +119	Dem. +17		76.8
1980	Dem.	Dem. +119	Dem. +17		75.1
Reagan					
1981	Rep.	Dem. + 51	Rep. + 7		82.3
1982	Rep.	Dem. + 51	Rep. + 7		72.4
1983	Rep.	Dem. +101	Rep. + 8		67.1

TABLE 5.1 (Continued)
Presidential Success in Congress: Initiatives Approved and Roll-call Victories

	President's Party	House Majority	Senate Majority	Presidential Initiatives Approved (%)	Presidential Roll-call Victories (%)
1984	Rep.	Dem. +101	Rep. + 8		65.8
1985	Rep.	Dem. + 71	Rep. + 6		59.9
1986	Rep.	Dem. + 71	Rep. + 6		56.5
1987	Rep.	Dem. + 81	Dem. +10		43.5
1988	Rep.	Dem. + 81	Dem. +10		47.4

Sources: George C. Edwards III (1980), *Presidential Influence in Congress* (San Francisco: W. H. Freeman and Company), p. 14; Norman J. Ornstein, Thomas E. Mann, and Michael J. Malbin (1987), *Vital Statistics on Congress, 1987–1988* (Washington, D.C.: Congressional Quarterly Press), pp. 203–204; *Congressional Quarterly Weekly Report*, November 19, 1988, p. 3327.

perspective would increase the overall presidential success rate from 43 percent to 60 percent.[4]

It was for these reasons that in 1976 *CQ* discontinued the initiative-based measure. However, the measure that *CQ* continued to report—presidential success on roll-call votes on which he took positions—also has problems. It too counts all votes equally and can be influenced by how frequently the president takes a position on legislation. It also ignores the possibility that the president may decide for strategic reasons not to publicize his support for a proposal.[5] Finally, the measure does not really assess the president's success in getting his program through the Congress. It does not consider whether the president is taking a position on a piece of legislation that is part of his legislative program or whether he is simply endorsing legislation generated elsewhere. However, in at least one important sense these scores are an indicator of the president's legislative success, for those presidents who seldom find themselves on the same side as a majority of the legislators hardly can be viewed as having established a successful record with the Congress.

How Frequently Do Presidents Succeed?

The *CQ* data on the fate of presidential initiatives indicate that presidents usually see less than half of what they propose enacted. The presidential success rate exceeded 50 percent in only five of the twenty-two years covered by the index, and the average success score for the entire period was 43 percent. The best performance was in 1965, when Lyndon Johnson saw 65 percent of what he proposed enacted by Congress, a particularly impressive showing because Johnson submitted a larger number of proposals to Congress that year than had been submitted in any other year during the 1954–1975 period. As for presidents' success on roll calls on which they took positions, this measure has fallen below 50 percent only twice, in 1987 and 1988, and nineteen times the rate was 75 percent or higher. Presidents do better on this measure because they can pick their spots. They can avoid public positions on issues on which they are likely to lose, and they can endorse proposals that are not particularly high-priority items for them but that are sure winners. Also, this measure is unaffected by congressional delay in passing the president's program.

Because of the ambiguities associated with the *CQ* measures, Mark Peterson's original analysis of a sample of 111 presidential proposals made between 1953 and 1981 provided perhaps the best indicator of presidential success. He found that in 49 percent of these cases either the Congress agreed with the president's proposal or he and the Congress compromised their differences. In 12 percent of the cases, the president overcame congressional opposition and saw his proposal pass. The Congress defeated the president 15 percent of the time and in 23 percent of the cases killed the proposal by failing to act on it. These data suggest an overall presidential success rate of about 60 percent, somewhat higher than the *CQ* score based on presidential initiatives to which Peterson's work is most comparable, but significantly lower than the success scores based upon presidential positions on congressional roll calls.[6]

All of these studies indicate that some presidents do better than others with the Congress, but the most rigorous study of the variables associated with presidential success concluded with the observation that the strategic decisions that presidents make are "not a predominant factor in determining presidential support in Congress on most roll-call votes."[7] One factor that is important is whether or not a president's party has a majority in the Congress and if it does, how large that majority is. One analysis of legislative support for the president concluded that "the average legislator of the president's party has backed the chief executive two-thirds to three-quarters of the time, whereas the average member of the opposition has done so one-third to one-half of the time."[8] A recomputation of the data in Table 5.1 shows that during the twelve years when Democratic presidents had Democratic majorities in the Congress (1961–1968 and 1977–1980) their success rate averaged 81.1 percent. In the two years (1953–1954) when Dwight Eisenhower had a Republican majority in Congress, his success rate averaged 86.0 percent. However, during the seventeen years that Eisenhower, Nixon, Ford, and Reagan dealt with Congresses with Democratic majorities in both chambers, their average success rate was 63.1 percent. With Republican control of the Senate, Reagan's average success rate during his first six years in office was only slightly better, 67.3 percent.

PRESIDENTIAL RESOURCES
AND CONGRESSIONAL RESISTANCE

Partisan considerations aside, the president's ability to move the Congress is usually greater at the beginning than at the end of his administration. This situation obtains because the resources that a president must draw upon if he is to succeed with the Congress are limited and they tend to diminish as he moves through his term in office. These resources include time, public support, personnel, and political capital, the last calculated in terms of the favors that he can do for, and the fear that he can engender among, those whose support he requires.

Time

When a president begins his term, he is immediately aware of the limited time that he has to accomplish his policy objectives. Eric Goldman said that Lyndon Johnson, even after chalking up a 16-million-vote victory margin in 1964, which brought him the largest congressional majority that any president had enjoyed in twenty-eight years, still "had a kind of mental clock ticking off the inevitable attrition of his control of the House and Senate."[9] Johnson knew that at the end of his first year in office, while he was still three years away from his next election day, all House members and one-third of the Senate would be perhaps three to six months away from a primary election. Increasing legislative resistance during his second year was virtually assured as the legislators' thoughts turned away from the president's political concerns and toward their own. Ronald Reagan discovered this in 1982 when, in the face of a sagging economy, his congressional support began to decline, even among his fellow Republicans. The president could ask the American people to "stay the course" and promise that if they did, the economy would improve, but this approach was unavailable to members of the Congress who were already on the campaign trail. Whereas 1981 was a year in which the president was able to convince Congress to approve significant reductions in federal expenditures, 1982 was a year of major defeats for him, with few legislators relishing the prospect of defending cuts in popular domestic programs while they were running for reelection.

The new president also knows that once past his second year, he must begin to think about his own reelection campaign, an enterprise that will consume increasing amounts of his own and his staff's time and attention, at the expense of resources that could be devoted to policy concerns. Should he be successful in that campaign, the euphoria of reelection will be quickly tempered by the knowledge that the Twenty-second Amendment has relegated him to lame duck status before he even frames his second inaugural address. Thus, the time that a president has to see his agenda through is bounded, both constitutionally and politically. He must move quickly or face the prospect of not being able to move at all.

The president's time is limited not only by the calendar but also by the clock. The recommended strategy for presidential success requires him to be constantly involved with congressional relations. Regularly seeing and speaking with representatives and senators, personally participating in the bargaining process, and doing the work necessary to understand, even in a rudimentary way, the specific policy areas being deliberated could take the greater portion of any president's day. All of this is in addition to those matters that claim the president's time that have little to do with congressional relations, such as the daily conduct of U.S. foreign policy, the supervision of the bureaucracy, and the countless ceremonial functions that he must attend. As Richard Neustadt put it, a president's time "is governed by the things he has to do from day to day: the speech he has agreed to make, the fixed appointment he cannot put off, the paper no one else can sign, the rest and exercise his doctors order."[10] So even a president willing to spend time on his legislative agenda will have difficulty finding all the time that the task ideally requires.

Not surprisingly, presidents carefully guard their time. One technique is to restrict to a few high-priority areas the number of issues that they must deal with personally, thereby assuring that the president's limited time is used where it counts the most. President Reagan's decision to make the economy his sole priority during his first year in office kept the attention of the Congress focused on a restricted set of issues and, just as important, helped a president notorious for his tenuous grasp on policy information to get the most out of his limited resources.

The president's time is also protected by a staff system designed to restrict the number of people who can see the president as well as the unprocessed information that reaches him. Every recent president has established elaborate arrangements for screening those who would like to see or speak with him, and members of Congress, except for the leaders, have not been very high up on these lists. Most presidents spend very little time with detailed policy information. Instead, they are "briefed" on policy issues only after the relevant data have been thoroughly analyzed and digested by the staff and a restricted list of options has been developed. In this way, the president's time is saved for final choices rather than for the more time-consuming exploratory discussions that go into framing these options.

Thus, even though presidents are advised to be accessible to members of the Congress and to be personally involved in shaping the policy proposals that they hope to advance on the Hill, presidents quite simply do not have the number of hours in the day that they would need if they wanted to follow this advice. Ultimately, presidents have been forced to decide between spending time on policy or spending time with politicians. The Carter and Reagan presidencies made quite different choices on this matter.

At the beginning of his administration, Carter promised members of Congress that he would be accessible to them and asked them to telephone him directly with their questions and concerns. However, Carter also was, in the words of one civil servant, "compulsively oriented in the detail direction," ignoring his advisers, many of whom urged him to "concentrate on the big policy issues and leave the details to them."[11] Although Carter worked harder and longer hours than most recent presidents, he soon discovered that he could not deliver on the congressional access that he had promised because his attention to policy left him little time to devote to personal interactions with legislators. This was probably a quite natural trade-off for a trained scientist such as Carter who liked policy details but, as one of his advisers noted, "simply did not like politicians."[12]

Ronald Reagan's administrative style was exactly the opposite of Carter's. On the one hand, he devoted a great deal of attention to personal interactions with members of Congress, but on the other, he conveyed a "nonchalance about the details of government," entrusting the latter entirely to his staff and "managing reasonably well on a diet of mini-memos supplemented by oral briefings."[13] Although this approach paid handsome legislative dividends early in his presidency, later on Reagan often found himself embarrassed by seeming to be the last person to know about the policy options that his administration was pursuing.

Public Support

Another important presidential resource—public support—also erodes over time (see Table 5.2). Every president's term begins with a so-called honeymoon period during which his public approval ratings are at their peak and his words and actions dominate the nation's political consciousness. During this period, Congress is reluctant to challenge the president and inclined to give his nominees for administrative positions as well as his major proposals the benefit of the doubt.

TABLE 5.2
Presidential Popularity, by Year

President	Year	Average Approval Rating (%)	President	Year	Average Approval Rating (%)
Eisenhower	1953	69.4	Nixon	1969	60.8
	1954	65.4		1970	56.9
	1955	70.9		1971	49.9
	1956	72.8		1972	56.4
	1957	64.2		1973	41.8
	1958	54.6		1974	25.9
	1959	63.1			
	1960	61.1	Ford	1974	53.9
				1975	42.9
Kennedy	1961	76.3		1976	47.6
	1962	71.6			
	1963	63.5	Carter	1977	62.3
				1978	45.5
Johnson	1964	74.5		1979	37.7
	1965	66.4		1980	40.6
	1966	51.0			
	1967	44.0	Reagan	1981	57.9
	1968	41.5		1982	43.8
				1983	43.9
				1984	55.5
				1985	60.6
				1986	61.5

Source: Charles W. Ostrom, Jr., and Dennis M. Simon (1987), "The Environmental Connection, Political Drama, and Popular Support in the Reagan Administration." Paper presented at the Annual Meeting of the Southern Political Science Association, Charlotte, N.C., November 1987.

However, as time passes the presidents' public support drops. Although the president continues to be featured prominently on the evening news and in the morning headlines, he attracts a good deal less attention than he did at the outset of his administration, and the weapon of public opinion that popular presidents try to wield against the Congress therefore diminishes in potency. Political scientists have developed a number of explanations for this decline. It may be that the novelty of a new president simply wears off and that "familiarity breeds discontent."[14] Or it may be that our expectations of presidents are so great and their capacities to deliver on these expectations so constrained that, once in office, presidents, no matter what they do, must inevitably disappoint the public.[15] It is also likely that once in office a president will antagonize some part of the coalition that elected him. During the campaign, elements of that electoral coalition perhaps allowed themselves to believe that the candidate could actually be all things to all people. As a president moves through his term, however, and as he makes policy decisions, some that were his supporters will become unhappy with what he does. Eventually, this "coalition of minorities" that thinks the president is doing poorly becomes as large or larger than the coalition that thinks he is doing well.[16]

This process of disenchantment may be accelerated by bad news or retarded by good news, and presidents like Ronald Reagan may continue to be personally popular throughout their terms in office, but support for the president's policy agenda inevitably erodes. Reagan was never so successful at mobilizing support for his legislative proposals after 1981 as he was during that first year in office, even though he continued to be viewed in affectionate terms by a public that gave him a landslide reelection victory in 1984.[17]

Presidents may respond to this decline in support by stepping up their public appearances, or by devoting more time to the ceremonial aspects of their public presidency, or by emphasizing their responsibilities for international relations by taking more trips overseas and by scheduling highly publicized summit meetings with foreign dignitaries. Ironically, responses of this sort may further diminish the presidents' chances of success with the Congress. The time to fight this doomed battle to maintain popular support must come at the expense of time that could be devoted to policy analysis or congressional relations. Also, as Sam Kernell has argued, repeated appeals by the president for public support may make it more difficult for him to reach agreements with the Congress; when the president "goes public," he is inclined to reduce issues "to black and white alternatives and to principles that are difficult to modify." The result is to "harden negotiating positions" on both sides.[18]

During his second term, Reagan escalated his public rhetoric in support of the Nicaraguan contras and in opposition to the Sandinistas. The former were freedom fighters, the latter, Marxist-Leninist terrorists, and Congress, he said, would have to decide whose side the United States would take. This fiery rhetoric seemed to have little effect on public attitudes, which continued to be at best skeptical about the administration's position. But the president's public offensive did serve to exacerbate his relations with the Congress to the point where inter-institutional negotiations on the issue became virtually impossible. Eventually, the president, operating from his dug-in position, came to have less and less influence on the policy decisions that Congress reached in regard to Central America.

The contra issue is in many ways typical of Reagan's second term. Accumulated resentment from years of unrelenting presidential attacks on congressional Democrats as the cause of all of the nation's ills, from the economy to the weakened state of the American family, contributed mightily to the confrontations and stalemates that characterized the twilight years of the Reagan presidency. On issues as diverse as budgetary matters, foreign policy, and Supreme Court appointments, legislative-executive agreements became difficult to reach. Congressional Democrats enjoyed "sticking it" to a president who had been sticking it to them for six years. The president, in response, virtually abandoned direct negotiation with the Congress, concentrating the bulk of his time on Soviet-American relations and strategic arms discussions, areas where he could proceed without much congressional involvement, bolster his sagging public image, and if all went well, secure his place in history.

Personnel

A third presidential resource that seems to come under increasing pressure as an administration ages is its people. Every administration begins with an enthusiastic cadre of presidential loyalists fresh from an exciting election victory and eager to take on the tasks of governing. There is ample testimony to the electric and heady atmosphere of a new president's White House and to the willingness of staffers to put in long days and nights in the service of the president and his programs. "The pace was frenetic," wrote one participant in the Kennedy administration. "Everyone came early and stayed late."[19] But this too comes to an end. The novelty and excitement wear off as the routine of government sets in. Eventually people leave, because they burn out, or because the pressure is too great, or because there are other things in either the public or the private sector that they wish to do, or because they have for one reason or another become political liabilities to the president.

In the case of the Reagan administration, personnel turnover among those responsible for foreign policy came early and often. Reagan's first National Security Adviser, Richard V. Allen, left early in 1982 under a cloud of scandal, and Secretary of State Alexander Haig resigned later that year after repeated conflicts with the president and his advisers over policy and turf issues. Whereas Haig's successor, George Shultz, stayed for the rest of Reagan's presidency, the national security post became a revolving door, with Allen followed by the president's old friend William Clark and then by Robert McFarlane, John Poindexter, Frank Carlucci, and Colin Powell.

In the domestic area, controversial Interior Secretary James Watt left in 1983 along with Environmental Protection Agency Director Anne Burford, the first because of his penchant for saying politically stupid things and the second because of alleged corruption and proven incompetence. As the first Reagan administration came to an end, the president's closest White House advisers, and those generally credited with his early policy successes, all left: James Baker for the Treasury Department, Edwin Meese III for the Justice Department, Michael Deaver for the public relations business, and David Stockman for Wall Street. As a result of the Iran-Contra controversy, Baker's replacement as chief of staff, Donald Regan, also was forced to leave his post, to be replaced by former Senator Howard Baker, who then also left, about six months before the end of Reagan's second term, to be replaced by Baker's aide Kenneth Duberstein. About the same time, Ed Meese resigned as attorney general after an independent prosecutor, while declining to recommend Meese's indictment, nonetheless raised serious questions about his ethical standards.

These high-level changes are only the tip of the proverbial iceberg. Before Meese himself decided to leave, several top Justice Department officials resigned, contending that the department was paralyzed because of the attorney general's continuing legal and ethical problems. Of course lower-level staffers also come and go with more frequency and less fanfare than is the case with the higher-ups. With each change, some degree of experience and expertise is lost and a significant amount of new on-the-job training has to take place. Although the president usually finds good people to replace the ones that leave, the necessary learning period that follows each transition can slow the policy process and waste a great deal of time. And time, unlike people, is a resource that the president cannot replenish.

Political Capital

Early in his term, there is much that a president can do for his friends and to his enemies. For the former, there are invitations to the White House, presidential support for pet projects, and jobs for political cronies. For the latter there are no invitations and little help on projects large or small. For those on the outside, it seems at the beginning of an administration as if their purgatory will last forever, and the pressures to get on board, to work with the president, are almost irresistible. Later in his term, although the president continues to be able to help his friends, the value of these favors diminishes relative to the cost of supporting the president for legislators in terms of their ideological or constituency concerns. And for those who have not been among the president's supporters, as the end of his term comes into sight, the pressure to go along is greatly reduced.

Especially during a president's second term, it begins to dawn on members of Congress that they are likely to be in Washington longer than the president, and their incentive for dealing with him thereby declines. More to the point, legislators realize that their electoral survival, upon which their continued residence in Washington depends, may in turn depend upon their assertion of a certain degree of independence from the president. The falloff is particularly marked among legislators who are members of the president's party. During his first year in office, Ronald Reagan could count on the near unanimous support of congressional Republicans. But as his administration continued, this partisan support became less dependable, and during his last two years in office, he regularly lost votes of Republican legislators on those issues that pitted the constituency interests of legislators against their loyalty to the president.

For example, in April 1987, 102 of the 177 House Republicans and 13 of the 46 Senate Republicans voted to override Reagan's veto of a bill providing $88 billion of highway and mass transit funds, despite direct appeals from the president and offers of various deals in return for votes against the override.[20] And in March 1988, Reagan suffered one of his most stunning defeats when 21 of the 45 Senate Republicans and 52 of 175 House Republicans deserted him on a vote to override his veto of a bill that expanded protection against discrimination by institutions receiving federal funds. Whereas the president was retiring, most legislators were running for reelection, and few wanted to do so with a vote against a bill entitled "The Civil Rights Restoration Act" on their record.[21]

As the president's popular support and political capital decrease, and as the rate of executive-branch-personnel turnover increases, the number of presidential policy initiatives decline. Each president makes more proposals during his first year in office than he does in any other year of his administration. As an administration ages, the number of old proposals that are simply dusted off and resubmitted increases.[22] The goal is "to conserve gains and not take chances" and the result is "programs that tend to be less innovative."[23] Quite simply, after the first year or so, presidents and their administrations already begin to run out of steam. Their resources for moving the Congress ebb, and because legislators have their own political and policy concerns distinct from those of the president, their resistance to his requests increases.

This discussion of waning presidential resources and waxing congressional resistance explains why presidents are less likely to succeed with the Congress as they move through their terms in office. The narrow window of opportunity for presidents to lead the Congress has meant that institutional stalemate on public policy has become an increasingly dominant characteristic of U.S. politics. What also needs to be explained, however, is why this bias toward stalemate is apparently becoming more pronounced.

FRAGMENTATION AND STALEMATE

As noted in Chapter 2, the authors of the Constitution were deeply suspicious of government power and wanted to minimize the likelihood of its unwise use. They did so by dividing political power among several independent institutions and endowing each with the capacity to check the other. Either these institutions would act cooperatively, or there would be stalemate and no governmental action. Institutional cooperation would occur and stalemate would be averted only if there was a broadly shared consensus on the policies that should be pursued. Such a consensus would occur if policy proposals clearly reflected the public interest, or if they were so moderate that they would not offend significant sectors of the society, or if the nation faced a crisis so grave that there was no alternative to strong albeit controversial governmental action. If policy proposals were not able to evoke this degree of institutional consensus, then for the Founders stalemate was the preferred alternative.

These days, consensus has been elusive and crises—at least what most people would recognize as such—have been scarce. Stalemate therefore has come to typify the U.S. political system, a stalemate engendered by the constitutional design and nurtured by an increasingly decentralized distribution of power within the Congress, persistently weak political parties, the increasing influence of interest groups on politicians and on the shape of public policy, and the fragmentation of public opinion concerning the proper goals of public policy and the appropriate means for achieving them.

Congressional Decentralization

Given their collegial characteristics, all legislatures are to some extent decentralized compared with more hierarchically organized executives. However, these decentralizing forces are in most legislatures balanced by the centralizing activities of legislative parties. But the evolved U.S. Congress is notable for the weakness of its party organizations; this weakness represents the result of a long-term decline in the strength of U.S. political parties, a decline that started around the beginning of the twentieth century. For most of the nineteenth century, party leadership in Congress was quite strong and party unity on roll-call votes was quite common. Larry Sabato summarized the era this way: "At the turn of the century, almost three quarters of all the recorded votes saw a majority of one party voting against a majority of the other party, and astoundingly a third or more of a session's roll calls would pit at least 90% of one party against 90% or more of the other party."[24] During this period, party leaders in the Congress wielded nearly absolute power, particularly the speaker of the House, who, among other things, could appoint all standing committees, name their chairs, select the members of the Rules Committee, and serve as that committee's chair.[25]

However, early in the twentieth century, the power of party leaders and the impact of party on the roll-call voting behavior of legislators declined. In 1910, progressives in the House led a revolt against the speaker, removing his power to determine committee assignments and institutionalizing the seniority system as a way to select committee leadership. These reforms increased the power of the committees because they enabled committee members and chairs to achieve a great deal of autonomy from the party leadership. On the floor, the frequency of party votes began to decline, with such votes often constituting less than half of the annual total of congressional roll-call votes.[26]

In recent years, there have been faint signs of the revival of party strength in the Congress. The percentage of party votes and the frequency of the average member's voting with his party on such votes increased, the power of the House speaker and the party caucus was enhanced somewhat, and the seniority system was modified so that the most senior member of the committee would not necessarily become its chair.[27] But although all of this suggests that the prominence of parties in the Congress may be increasing, the result, to this point at least, has not been significantly more centralized congressional decisionmaking. On the contrary, there has been a movement toward even greater dispersion of power, toward what Steven Smith called collegial patterns of decisionmaking.

The distinction between **decentralization** and **collegialism** is an important one. Smith put it this way: "Decentralization constitutes a fragmentation of legislative power with each subunit autonomous within its jurisdiction. Collegial processes do not fragment legislative power; all power is shared equally by all members." During the reform era of the 1970s, Smith concluded, both the House of Representatives and the Senate, but particularly the latter, "moved toward more collegial modes of decision-making."[28]

Whereas decentralization of power makes it difficult for the Congress to act *coherently* because there are so many autonomous decisionmaking units, collegialism makes it difficult for Congress to act *at all*. If all power is shared equally by all members, then it becomes virtually impossible to create and maintain stable or even temporary majorities. Such extreme fragmentation ("atomization" may be a better term) has been a major reason why presidents have been encountering greater difficulties in getting their programs through the Congress. Gone are the days when the president could speak to a few party leaders and committee chairs, gain their support, and then expect the rest of the Congress eventually to follow. Now, major policy initiatives involve the jurisdictions of numerous committees and subcommittees in each chamber, any of which is capable of obstructing passage of the legislation.

In addition, groups of legislators advocating a variety of specific policy concerns have increased in number and influence. The New England Congressional Caucus, the Great Lakes Conference, and the Sun Belt Caucus advocate interests associated with particular geographic regions and include members from both political parties. The Auto Task Force, the Congressional Arts Caucus, the Congressional Coal Caucus, the Metropolitan Area Caucus, and the Textile Caucus focus on specific economic and budgetary issues, while groups such as the Congressional Black Caucus, the Hispanic Caucus, and the Congresswomen's Caucus concentrate on issues of ethnic or gender discrimination. There are more than seventy such groups operating now, and they often have a crucial impact on the shape of legislation and certainly contribute to the further balkanization of the Congress.

With increasing collegiality, individual and unaffiliated legislators, even the most junior, expect to be addressed personally if they are to lend their support to some measure. In essence, no one's vote can be delivered by someone else. Norman Ornstein advised that if a president is to prevail in such a collegial Congress, he must accept the premise that "he will be required to know and deal regularly with a much wider array of players in the process, members and staff."[29]

Clearly, greater fragmentation in Congress does not mean that the president is always destined to fail, but just as clearly, the frequency with which he fails will increase and he will have to work harder than ever and expend more resources for his victories. If there is a bright side to all of this for the president, perhaps it is, as Charles Jones observed, that whereas the fragmented Congress cannot deliver for the president, it also cannot deliver against him.[30] Put differently, whiggism, meaning congressional domination of the public policy-making process, cannot occur because Congress more than ever lacks the capacity to develop its own policy-making options and to act upon them. But stalemate, meaning that neither the executive nor the Congress is capable of acting on its own and each is capable of stopping the other from acting, is the situation today as the transformed presidency collides with the fully evolved, fully decentralized, and now highly collegial Congress.

Weak Political Parties

The Jeffersonian model of institutional cooperation discussed in Chapter 4 held out the hope that strong national political parties would serve to bridge the constitutional gap between the president and the Congress. The assumption of the model was that if the president and a majority of the Congress were of the same party, that shared party allegiance would lead to a collective and cooperative responsibility for public policy. Unfortunately, this is not how U.S. political parties work today.

The American people continue to distinguish between their vote for president and their vote for members of Congress. In the nine presidential elections since 1952, the people have elected Republicans to the White House on six occasions but placed a Republican majority in the Congress only once. In 1984, Ronald Reagan won a huge electoral victory, but the Republicans were barely able to dent the Democratic majority in the House of Representatives and actually lost one seat from their Senate majority. And in 1988, George Bush soundly defeated Michael Dukakis, but the Democratic party still gained one seat in the Senate and three in the House. The reason for this ticket splitting, as one of the scholars most optimistic about the revival of U.S. political parties admitted, is that "there is little proof that most of the electorate cares about parties" and that in fact "most citizens do not understand or appreciate the role that political parties play in running government, organizing elections, or stabilizing society." He concluded that "as long as parties remain irrelevant to the public's view of the political world, ticket splitting will flourish."[31]

Although there is some evidence that the policy distinctions between Democrats and Republicans have become sharper, it is not yet clear whether this signals a reinvigoration of the party system or a temporary reaction to the pronounced ideological bent of the Reagan administration. What is clear, however, is that a shared party label and even a more homogeneous party ideology has not yet led to a cooperative, partisan approach to public policymaking, even when the Congress and the presidency are controlled by the same party. Legislative-executive policy stalemates cannot be prevented by the parties, reviving or not, if they lack an established means for articulating their policy priorities, if neither the president nor the legislative party leaders have effective means to compel or even encourage members to support the party's or president's policies, and if the constitutional differences between the constituencies and electoral cycles of legislators and presidents continue to take precedence over incipient claims to party loyalty.

Interest Groups

Whereas the policy influence of political parties continues to be problematic, the impact of interest groups seems to be increasing. Interest groups always have been important factors in U.S. politics, but during the second half of the twentieth century their number and influence have risen sharply. One study of 564 Washington lobbying organizations found that approximately 30 percent of these groups originated between 1960 and 1980.[32]

One of the primary tools that these interest groups use to influence public policy is contributions to political campaigns. In the post-Watergate era, Congress and the president agreed on major changes in the laws governing the financing of political campaigns. For presidential elections, a system of public financing was enacted. General election campaigns were to be financed entirely with public funds, while the nomination phase of the campaign was to be financed by a combination of private and public funds. These changes, although they did not eliminate the impact of interest group contributions on presidential elections, did restrict their influence somewhat.

For congressional campaigns, however, public funding was rejected in favor of a legislative strategy of legalizing, limiting, and publicizing campaign contributions by interest groups. The reform legislation of the 1970s recognized the existence of labor union political action committees (PACs) and extended the right to form such PACs to corporations and other interest groups. Ceilings were set on the amounts that PACs could contribute to each campaign, and candidates were required to file reports with the Federal Election Commission detailing who contributed to their campaigns and how much their contributions were.

These legal changes touched off a dramatic increase in the cost of congressional campaigns. In 1974, candidates for the House of Representatives spent an average of $53,384 on their campaigns. By 1986, this figure had increased to $260,032. In the Senate, the comparable figures went from $437,482 in 1974 to $2,578,016 in 1986. As elections became more expensive, the number of PACs and the proportion of campaign funds coming from them increased accordingly. In 1974, 1,146 PACs provided 17 percent of the funds raised by House candidates and 11 percent of the funds raised by Senate candidates. In 1986, the number of PACs had increased nearly fourfold to 4,157, and they provided 36 percent and 22 percent of the funds spent by House and Senate candidates respectively.[33]

To say that the votes of legislators are purchased through these campaign contributions would be, at the least, difficult to prove. To say, however, that groups buy access, or the capacity to present their case to legislators willing to listen and able to help, is undoubtedly true. The problem, of course, is that not all interests are equally represented by these groups, and those with wealth, therefore, have a disproportionate influence on the policy-making process. As Senate Majority Leader Robert Dole put it to columnist Elizabeth Drew, "there aren't any Poor PACs or Food Stamp PACs or Nutrition PACs or Medicare PACs."[34]

Interest groups, by definition, have a self-interested view of public policy, a view that will often stand in contradiction to broader public interests. This is particularly so of single-interest groups. Whereas groups such as organized labor, the National Association of Manufacturers, and Common Cause involve themselves in a broad range of issues, the number of groups that focus on a single issue or on a closely related set of issues has increased. Groups like the National Rifle Association, the National Abortion Rights Action League, the American Petroleum Institute, and the American Institute of Milk Producers exemplify this category of groups. They are distinguished by their tendency to take rather uncompromising positions on their specific issue and to view a politician's stand on that issue as a litmus test that determines whether they will support or oppose him or her at the next election. Faced with so many conflicting and specific demands and reluctant to antagonize anyone, members of Congress naturally search for compromises that can garner the support of a wide cross section of groups. But the huge number of groups and their increasing tendency toward nonnegotiable positions make such compromises difficult to achieve. This, in turn, may discourage legislators from taking any action at all, on the theory that not to act will be less offensive to interested groups than to act in ways that do not meet their demands.

From the point of view of the largest and most influential groups, such inaction may be quite acceptable. If one assumes that these groups and the interests that they represent enjoy the greatest benefits under current public policy, then governmental action that would change current policy is as likely to harm as it is to advance those interests. These organizations therefore can protect their interests not just by working for new public policies that they favor, but by acting as "veto groups" capable of defeating policy proposals that they view as a threat. Given the Congress's disposition toward inaction, the goal of stopping a policy proposal is more easily achieved than the goal of advancing a policy proposal. Established groups accomplish the former by concentrating their lobbying efforts on the congressional committees and subcommittees that deal with the policy areas with which the groups are most concerned. Members of these committees, particularly chairs and ranking members, receive special attention, including larger than usual campaign contributions, from their "client" groups. Established interests thus turn the decentralized power structure of the Congress to their advantage. Recognizing that a "no" at the committee stage will likely kill a proposal to which the group is opposed, they direct their efforts primarily toward those legislators who are in a position to deliver such a negative decision. In this way, the interest group system reinforces the political system's structural bias toward inaction.[35]

Public Opinion

The multiplicity of interest groups, the narrowing of their issue concerns, and the intensified level of conflict among them bespeaks a more deeply rooted cause of stalemate: the weakening of the national consensus about the goals of public policy. The New Deal consensus that accepted a larger government role in the distribution and redistribution of wealth, utilizing a generally progressive tax structure, underwent substantial erosion during the 1970s and 1980s. One recent analysis concluded that "the public has lost confidence in the answers and performance of the Democratic/Keynesian approach to the political economy." While people continue to support a role for the government in a wide array of policy areas, from health and education to defense and the environment, they also think that the government is "clumsy, inefficient, and wasteful."[36]

Public support for the idea of paying taxes has never been particularly high (its epigrammatic association with death is instructive); in recent years, however, public attitudes have become overtly hostile. By 1980, 68 percent of the population thought that the amount of federal income tax that they paid was too high, up from 58 percent in 1976.[37] At the state and local levels, referenda reducing property taxes have succeeded, whereas those asking for higher property tax rates to support local schools and services have often failed. State legislators as well as members of Congress seem absolutely terrified to vote for an increase in income tax rates, even more after Walter Mondale's 1984 presidential campaign was destroyed at the outset by his assertion that if elected, he would raise taxes. The conflicting expectations that the American people hold—that government will continue to provide them with essential services but that it also will reduce taxes—have raised a series of painful zero-sum issues, with new or expanded benefits for some coming either at the expense of benefits that others enjoy or from higher taxes. This reality has intensified the level of political conflict and made policymaking much more difficult.

One of the by-products of intense political conflict and seemingly intractable issues has been the erosion of the people's faith in government.

The percentage of the population that said that they trusted the national government to do the right thing "always" or "most of the time" dropped from 76 percent in 1964 to 25 percent in 1980.[38] The percentage that expressed high levels of confidence in the leaders of the executive branch dropped from 41 percent in 1966 to 17 percent in 1980, and for congressional leaders the drop was from 42 percent to 18 percent. Lipset and Schneider's analysis of these data concluded that confidence declined "because political leadership was proving ineffective in dealing with massive social and political problems like war, race relations, and the economy."[39]

Added to the cleavages in public opinion on economic issues are a range of noneconomic "social issues" such as affirmative action, women's rights, abortion, and school prayer, all of which now occupy space on the national political agenda. These issues, like the new economic issues, also seem to be zero-sum in the sense that it is extremely difficult to find compromise positions on them. This has led to further fragmentation of U.S. public opinion because cleavages on these issues do not necessarily coincide with the class-based cleavages that influence attitudes on economic issues. Particularly among the poor, tensions on racial and religious issues often stand in the way of unity on fundamental economic issues.[40]

Internationally, the post–World War II consensus on an activist and interventionist foreign policy, which sought military strength and the containment of communism all over the world, regardless of the cost, was shattered by the war in Vietnam. That this consensus is yet to be rebuilt is indicated by the inability to agree either at the mass or elite level on what military role if any the United States should be playing in regions as diverse as Central America, the Middle East, and Asia, or what the U.S. relationship should be with the Soviet Union. The struggle over the appropriate size of the defense budget has continued and intensified as zero-sum budget politics has highlighted the connection between the magnitude of these expenditures and the funds available for widely supported domestic programs. Even though Americans continue to support the principle of a strong national defense, it is not clear that they are prepared to pay for it with either higher taxes or reductions in domestic spending.

Stalemate

A cooperative policy-making arrangement between the president and the Congress has always been difficult to achieve because of the disposition toward stalemate that is sewn in the very fabric of the Constitution. Today, this bias toward inaction is reinforced by fragmented congressional power, by the continued failure of political parties to generate stable governing majorities, by increasing public dissensus on the role of government and the policy goals that it should be pursuing, and by a declining willingness to compromise competing positions among a populace fractured into countless interests and groups, each bent upon its own particular vision of what is good for itself and therefore good for the country.

The indicators of policy stalemate are abundant. By October 1, when the nation's fiscal year begins, the president and the Congress are supposed to have agreed on the spending levels for each federal agency. Between 1976 and 1986, only 31 percent of the appropriations bills setting these expenditure levels were approved by this deadline. During the Ford and Carter administrations, 41 percent of the appropriations bills were passed on time, but during the Reagan years this figure dropped to 12 percent.[41] Budget delays have been accompanied by mounting budget deficits. In 1976, the total national debt was $631.9 *billion*; by 1986, it had more than tripled to over $2.1 *trillion*, with individual-year deficits in 1985 and 1986 in excess of $200 billion.[42]

The stalemate on budgetary matters is replicated in other policy areas as well. For many years, nearly everyone has agreed that the welfare system is inefficient, unfair, and most important, that it does little to break the cycle of poverty. Yet year after year, nothing is done beyond some minor tinkering at the margins of the policy—a formula change here, an experimental program there. Similar statements could be made about agriculture policy, health care, and a legion of other domestic programs. It is difficult enough, it seems, for the Congress and the president to do those minimal things that need to be done to keep the system going—for example, to pass an annual budget or to reauthorize essential ongoing programs. Once these necessary tasks are accomplished, the institutional energy left is insufficient to overcome the strong bias toward stalemate that characterizes a policy area such as welfare reform.

This inability to tackle major issues is also apparent in international economic policy. Mounting trade deficits suggest a long-term loss of competitiveness for U.S. industry and a continued loss of jobs. When policy solutions are discussed, presidential biases in favor of free trade collide with congressional biases toward protectionism, producing, at best, half-hearted and short-term policies and, at worse, no action at all. More comprehensive long-term solutions involving the development of an industrial policy or more comprehensive national planning approaches are seldom considered. Similarly, Third World debt has enormous implications for the stability of the U.S. banking system and for the political stability of a large number of debtor nations. But it is also an enormously complex policy area and therefore one that is seldom mentioned either by the president or in the Congress.

The symptoms of deadlock are also apparent in foreign policy. In regard to Nicaragua, for example, the Reagan administration advocated continued military support for the contras, whereas the Congress was more disposed toward political solutions. However, because members of Congress feared being labeled soft on communism and being accused of having "lost" Nicaragua, they were reluctant to turn down completely presidential requests for support for the contras. As we will see in Chapter 6, the result, throughout the Reagan years, was a web of shifting and ambiguous presidential-congressional agreements that meant a mixture of military and nonmilitary aid to the contras, with various complex restrictions, however, on how the funds could be spent, restrictions that presumably would help the peace process.

The president and the Congress continue to be stalemated on the use of military power and the appropriate role for the Congress in such decisions. Faced with increased congressional reluctance to deploy military forces overseas, in light of the Vietnam experience, the president continues to maintain that he has unilateral authority in these matters by virtue of his role as commander in chief. Congress maintains that it too has a role by virtue of its constitutional power to declare war and the provisions of the War Powers Resolution. When the Reagan administration decided to use military force in Libya, Lebanon, Grenada, and the Persian Gulf, in each case the president faced substantial congressional opposition, but nonetheless did what he wanted to do. However, the impression created abroad was of a nation divided on its mission, and as a result, the actions that the president took had less impact than they might have had if the president and the Congress had been united.

This is not to say that the president and the Congress never reach agreement and that stalemate always characterizes every policy area. The routine of government has gone on and major policy initiatives are, on occasion, approved. President Carter was able to agree with the Congress on the Panama Canal treaties and, ultimately, on an energy program, although in the case of the latter, what Congress passed bore little resemblance to the comprehensive policy that the president had proposed. President Reagan and the Congress came into agreement on two major tax bills and on a rescue plan for Social Security. In other foreign and domestic policy areas, the fights between the president and the Congress for the most part have been on funding levels. Foreign aid, health research, student loans, other aid-to-education programs, environmental protection, federal highway construction, Medicare, and veterans assistance have continued from year to year, although funding has fluctuated considerably depending upon budgetary situations and the relative balance of power between the president and the Congress.

Because the system keeps running, it is easy to reach the conclusion that there is nothing wrong with it. Perhaps the big issues are avoided, one might argue, but when they reach crisis proportions, the leaders and the institutions seem equal to the task of finding solutions. Meanwhile, the basic body of federal policies and programs continue on a business-as-usual basis. The problem with this rather sanguine conclusion is that it ignores the system's implications for the quality of public policy. "If it ain't broke," goes the old saw, "don't fix it." But what happens if the questions that would allow one to determine if the system is "broke" are never asked? Are half-way and incremental policies that have the singular virtue of generating agreements at all effective in dealing with the problems to which they are directed? Does a strategy of accepting deadlock and waiting for a crisis before major issues can be addressed carry with it unacceptable policy consequences? When the system does operate, does it produce either democratic or managerially sound public policy?

WHEN STALEMATE IS AVOIDED: INSTITUTIONAL PERFORMANCE AND MANAGERIALLY GOOD PUBLIC POLICY

Recall that managerially sound public policy is informed, timely, coherent, effective, and responsible. Recall as well that in Chapter 1, I hypothesized that the executive would be more likely than the legislature to achieve such policy results. In the section that follows, we will put that hypothesis to the test.

Informed Public Policy

Because of the vast information resources resident in the bureaucracy and therefore available to the president, the Congress always is at some disadvantage compared to the president when it comes to making informed policy decisions. During the reform era of the 1970s, the Congress worked to correct this imbalance, primarily by improving its professional staff support. Between 1970 and 1986, the size of committee and subcommittee staff increased by 250 percent, the personal staff of legislators increased by 60 percent, and the staff of support agencies such as the Congressional Research Service, the Government Accounting Office, and the Office of Technology Assessment doubled.[43] The Congressional Budget Office was established so that the Congress could generate budget estimates and data, independent of what was provided to it by the Office of Management and Budget. By the end of the 1970s, one observer concluded, the Congress had "successfully established its independence of the executive branch for information, policy analysis, program evaluation, and legislative advice."[44]

However, although Congress succeeded in upgrading its information resources, it still lacks the ability to turn information into knowledge, to bring information to bear upon its public policy decisions. Whether the Congress can do this is open to serious question. Robert Reischauer, a Brookings Institution economist, writing about the way Congress deals with economic policy, concluded that even though the Congress generally gets good advice and has established an effective information-gathering system, it has proven itself "capable of ignoring the information when it contradicts powerful political forces. Whether Congress chooses to use information or not is a political question."[45] Mark Nadel reached a somewhat more harshly stated conclusion in his analysis of congressional activities in regard to regulatory policies. He wrote that "Congress is almost completely impervious to systematic policy analysis," and "the dominant factor in the use of analysis is not whether it is correct or technically competent, but which side it supports."[46]

An assessment of the president's information capacities needs to begin by distinguishing between him and his closest advisers on the one hand and the bureaucracy on the other. The latter has an extraordinary amount of information, but it is not clear that the president has access to all of it or that what he receives is always useful to him. Although the myth is that the bureaucracy is populated by loyal, nonpartisan civil servants who serve every president with the same professional efficiency, the reality is that presidential-bureaucratic relations are usually strained. According to one scholar, "willful permanent officials run the specialized policy shops that actually develop and implement specific government programs. These units repeatedly frustrate the best-laid plans of presidents, White House aides, career central agents, and appointed departmental 'masters' alike."[47] Presidents have frequently complained about their inability to control the bureaucracy and have voiced their suspicion that the information that they receive is designed to further the policy goals of the providing agency rather than their own. One of the keenest observers of the federal bureaucracy concluded that "for the President, his appointees, and high ranking bureaucrats, the struggle to control the bureaucracy is usually a leap into the dark."[48]

As we will see in Chapter 6, presidents have responded to this concern with a strategy of appointing political loyalists to administrative positions. The effect of this "administrative" strategy, however, is to sacrifice the policy expertise of the bureaucracy in order to enhance bureaucratic compliance with the president's political and ideological goals. During the Reagan years, "the role of OMB careerists and their program-specific knowledge diminished, thus increasing the chances that good programs get tossed out along with the bad."[49] What happened in OMB reflected a deemphasizing generally of "institutionalized expertise and professionalism" within the Executive Office of the President.[50]

Thus, the president confronts a dilemma. On the one hand, he can respect the expertise of the bureaucracy but run the risk that this expertise will work against his policy goals; on the other hand, he can politicize the bureaucracy, thereby ensuring its loyalty to his policy goals, but at the price of its professional expertise. No matter which approach he follows, the quality of the information in the hands of the president is to some degree suspect.

Even assuming that accurate policy information gets to the president, he may not necessarily be in a better position than members of Congress to understand or use it effectively. After all, like the legislators, the president usually lacks specialized knowledge in most policy areas and must depend heavily upon his staff to evaluate the information that he receives. In such a situation, he may well do exactly what representatives and senators have been accused of doing: He may use policy analysis only when it supports his view. And when the president has firmly held views, his advisers may be loath to tell him that his beliefs are not supported by the data. Examples abound. One thinks of the "best and the brightest" telling Lyndon Johnson that all was going as planned in Vietnam and Johnson's consistent refusal to acknowledge or even hear views to the contrary. One thinks of Ronald Reagan's decision, supported by his closest advisers, to ignore expert advice and to accept instead the supply-side economic fantasy that lower taxes would increase revenues and therefore achieve a balanced budget.

Finally, the recommended strategy for presidential success with the Congress articulated in Chapter 4 may militate against the president's careful use of information. If a president must move quickly, before his political capital erodes, he may have to postpone in-depth study and the appropriate utilization of policy expertise and instead take the first policy option that appears to meet his basic policy goals. As Ronald Reagan and David Stockman in the first days of the administration moved to slash the federal budget, they were working with very sketchy information. "None of us really understands what's going on with all these numbers," Stockman confessed to William Greider of the *Washington Post*. There was no time to stop to figure things out because they had to act quickly in order to take advantage of the president's honeymoon period: "We have to get a program out fast. And when you decide to put a program of this breadth and depth out fast, you can only do so much," Stockman said. "We didn't think it all the way through. We didn't add up all the numbers. We didn't make all the thorough comprehensive calculations about where we really needed to come out."[51] The accuracy of Stockman's self-perception is suggested by the comments of a lower-level budget official: "They didn't want analysis. They pretty much knew what they wanted to do. So, an analytic piece which either said, 'yes, you're right, go ahead,' or 'no, you're wrong, this is going to create havoc' wasn't the kind of thing they needed. They didn't want to hear if it was wrong."[52] So much for the quality of presidential information.

But if the president and his people take the time for careful, detailed analysis and if he personally involves himself in the process of acquiring policy expertise, he risks getting bogged down in details and wasting valuable time while his political capital inexorably erodes. This, presumably, was one of the great mistakes of the Carter administration, which was not repeated by the Reagan administration. For the latter, there were quick proposals, little attention to details, no presidential involvement with policy development, and stunning legislative victories. The only hitch was that no one in Washington, from the president to his budget director to the members of Congress, really understood what he or she was doing.

In sum, information is available to both the president and the Congress. Members of Congress seem unable and often unwilling to use it effectively because of the political pressures that they face as representatives of constituent and policy interests and because of their own lack of expertise. The president also seems condemned by political and strategic concerns to slight policy expertise. For him, the choice is between information and action: Taking the time to acquire and utilize information means that he may not be able to act when he has the best chance to succeed.

Timely Public Policy

As the preceding discussion makes clear, it is important to distinguish between quick action and timely action. The former is measured simply by speed; the latter refers to speed tempered by reason. In this context, the classic defense of the legislative process is that despite its being slow, the decisions that are reached reflect more careful deliberation because of the extra time taken. The classic defense of the presidency is that whereas it too can allow an appropriate period for deliberation, because of its hierarchical structure, it is capable of reaching closure on an issue and ultimately acting.

Congress is criticized not just because it is slow but also because its collegially oriented rules and procedures allow legislators who may be in a minority on an issue to delay and perhaps stop legislation by engaging in what has been called the "new obstructionism."[53] Countless amendments can be introduced, unlimited roll calls can be demanded, and at least in the Senate, debate can go on almost without end. Legislators as representatives of interests "are expected to struggle to the end and, if necessary, go down battling for their constituents." This leads to the "foot-dragging" and "sluggishness" that are so much a part of the popular perceptions of the Congress.[54]

Congressional reluctance to act in a timely manner also can be attributed to the open nature of the institution. Naomi Caiden suggested that it is easier to make tough budget decisions in countries where the issues are "fought out primarily behind the scenes in the closed world of cabinets and bureaucracies." In the United States, however, the difficulty of such decisions is compounded because "the budget drama is played out in the public arena of Congress."[55] In an open, collegial, and representative institution, with the eyes of constituents and lobbyists constantly on it, and with all members claiming a place at the bargaining table, congressional coalition building is extraordinarily difficult, and there is a greater likelihood that action will be delayed or avoided altogether.

Because he is one person, the president, simply by speaking, can state the executive branch's policy position and articulate a specific policy proposal. If he is willing to sacrifice detailed policy information, he can act quickly. However, if he is not prepared to make such a trade-off, then, as the experience of the Carter administration demonstrated, his capacity to act in a timely manner may be limited. If the president, to deal with a particular problem, needs policy information and options developed by his staff or the bureaucracy, he may have to wait a very long time, especially if the proposal involves a number of different agencies. Bureaucracies are notoriously slow-moving entities; to the extent that the president needs to employ them, he reduces his capacity to act in a timely manner. This is one of the reasons for the increasing tendency of presidents to centralize the policy-making process in the White House. What the president sacrifices in terms of detailed knowledge, he makes up for in terms of his capacity to act expeditiously.

In this sense, the strategic advice to the president to move quickly squares with the need for timely public policy. But once again, the distinction between timely and quick action needs to be drawn. If in order to achieve success with the Congress, presidents move too quickly, they may sacrifice the information that they need to make the best choices. In many cases, of course, they will never be able to have complete information because the pressure of events or statutory deadlines require them to truncate the information gathering process. But when they move quickly on the basis of insufficient information even when it is within their power to delay, presidential policy decisions will not meet the criteria of timeliness. As Ronald Reagan's budgetary decisions suggest, the desire to move quickly to maximize the chances for legislative success came at the expense of information about the exact dimensions and consequences of what was being done.

Coherent Public Policy

Even the most ardent defenders of the U.S. Congress admit to its disposition to move in opposite directions simultaneously. As Arthur Maass noted, members of Congress "feed their enthusiasm for certain programs by reporting authorizations from their legislative committees and guiding them through the House. They feed their belief in economy by supporting the Appropriations Committee when it cuts appropriations for various programs, including some of the very same ones that they have previously supported."[56]

Congressional policymaking has a tendency to proceed in disconnected chunks because of the open and collegial nature of the Congress. These generic characteristics were accentuated by the reforms of the 1970s, of which the overwhelming majority were designed to "provide more opportunity for members to express themselves in the legislative process." In comparison, "policy integration typically was not an intended consequence of reform."[57] With each subcommittee and its associated subgovernmental structure of interest groups and bureaucrats more firmly entrenched than ever, and with the whole process taking place in more open forums, it has become virtually impossible to "orchestrate the work of the disparate work groups into some semblance of an integrated whole."[58]

If the decentralized and collegial nature of congressional power contributes to incoherence, then the increasingly centralized nature of executive power should lead to coherence. Actually, to some extent it does. The Office of Management and Budget provides the president with the capacity to generate a coherent budget, a capacity that is still not apparent in the Congress despite the extensive budgetary reforms that it has undertaken.[59] Similarly, the growing strength of the White House national security apparatus relative to the Departments of State and Defense should provide the president with the capability of developing a coherent foreign policy.

Nonetheless, incoherence has characterized executive-branch policymaking. One of the problems is the size and diversity of the executive branch: The president is consequently unable, despite the trend toward centralization, to know what is going on throughout the entire bureaucratic structure and even if he were, to bring all of that together into some sort of coordinated whole. Colin Campbell concluded that executive-branch activity in regard to economic policy is "severely fragmented," that the Treasury Department cannot coordinate even its own affairs, let alone take the lead in integrating the activities of agencies such as OMB, the Council of Economic Advisers, the Office of the U.S. Trade Representative, and special economic units of the National Security Council, which all have a role in economic policymaking.[60]

Even in foreign policy, an area in which the White House role is more salient, incoherence can characterize executive policymaking. Harlan Cleveland's discussion of the Carter administration led him to the conclusion that although the president was well placed to be the "coherence factor" in U.S. foreign policy, examples of "ad hockery" abounded. Cleveland cited the administration's almost accidental decision to place a higher priority on the Panama Canal treaties than on the ratification of Strategic Arms Limitation agreements.[61] As for the Reagan administration, its simultaneous pursuit of a policy calling for an international arms embargo on Iran with a policy of selling U.S. arms to the Iranians in return for money to support the Nicaraguan contras and, perhaps, freedom for American hostages, stands as a prime example of foreign policy incoherence.

The Reagan budget proposals were also a study in incoherence. David Stockman, the architect of these proposals, explained how incompatible actions—cutting taxes, raising defense spending, cutting domestic spending, and balancing the budget—were all pursued simultaneously in the early days of the administration. "We should have designed those pieces to be more compatible," he admitted, but "the pieces were moving on independent tracks."[62] In large measure, this was because the president eschewed any broad comprehensive view of economic policy, concentrating all his resources on the goal of reducing the government's domestic spending. "The narrow compass of presidential priorities had little to say about industrial policies for particular economic sectors, about regional development, about industrial relations and wage bargaining, or about international economic relations. The presidential priority in economic affairs was to reduce the role of government."[63] Once again, then, the strategic advice to the president for success with the Congress ran counter to the needs of good public policymaking. Simplifying and restricting his policy agenda helped Reagan to win quick and stunning budget and tax victories during his first year, at the expense, however, of any comprehensive or coherent view of their consequences for other related policy areas.

Effective Public Policy

Compromise is generally viewed positively. To split the difference, to find policy formulations that can satisfy a number of diverse groups, to trade one policy for another—this is supposed to be the way of the world, the way to maintain peace in a society where there is a great deal of conflict about what to do and how to do it. In contrast, a refusal to compromise, to stand on principle and refuse to yield, is thought of as destructive. The only problem with such a mindset is that it tends to equate policy agreement with policy effectiveness and sometimes to view the former as more important than the latter. Put simply, a policy compromise that can garner majority support may not necessarily be the most effective policy to deal with the problem at hand.

Congress is frequently criticized for its disposition toward compromise, often at the expense of effective public policy. Catherine Rudder's study of the congressional negotiations surrounding the passage of the 1981 tax bill concluded that "the primary interest of the participants was in winning, that is, writing a bill that could attract a majority of votes in Congress. Absent were careful deliberation, a sense of limits, an ability to say no to claimants, and an overriding concern for the quality of the bill and for the integrity of the tax code."[64] The procedural reforms of the 1970s, creating a more open congressional decisionmaking environment, were partially to blame. Moving the final negotiations on tax bills out from behind the closed doors of the Ways and Means Committee, where these decisions used to be made, into open sessions attended by lobbyists and news media increased the responsiveness of members to particularized interests and decreased the chances for responsible and effective tax legislation.[65]

In the case of distributive programs that provide funds for highways, other public works projects, urban and rural development, agricultural research, and a host of other domestic needs, the classic question is, Who gets what? Ideally, these programs are supposed to be directed toward solving particular public problems, and the funds appropriated are supposed to be concentrated on those locales where the problem is the most acute. However, the representative nature of the Congress disposes it toward formula grants, which generalize such programs so that as many states and congressional districts as possible will reap the benefits, regardless of actual need. "This tendency to universalize the particular," Arthur Maass gently suggested, "does not necessarily result in good public policy."[66]

Once again, the executive branch, given its less-representative nature and more closed policy-making environment, has the potential to maximize effectiveness and to minimize those policy compromises that detract from program effectiveness. As Douglas Arnold noted, while bureaucrats too are concerned with political variables, they still "are much more likely than congressmen to target funds according to need" because "they are not faced with the task of writing blanket formulas suitable for every case."[67] The president, as a representative of a national rather than a local constituency, should feel less pressure to develop policies that trade effectiveness for a broader distribution of benefits.

Nevertheless, there are numerous examples of presidential decisions that make exactly these trades, and in fact, the recommended strategy for presidential success with the Congress leads directly to such decisions. Presidents who cling to their policy preferences and refuse to bargain with the Congress, as Jimmy Carter was accused of, usually fail to get their proposals approved. In contrast, one of the reasons why Reagan and Stockman were able to get their budget proposals through the Congress in 1981 was their willingness to trade in order to gain the majorities that they needed. There were several deals cut with moderate Republicans to go easier on certain domestic programs in return for support for the budget bill. And on the tax bill, far-reaching compromises and concessions were made to just about everyone. Included were "special tax concessions for oil-lease holders, and real-estate tax shelters, and generous loopholes that virtually eliminated the corporate income tax." According to Stockman, "the basic strategy was to match or exceed the Democrats and we did." These concessions, he concluded, "put us back in the game."[68]

Such strategy certainly helped the president to win this budget battle, but he did so at the price of an effective long-term budget policy. The huge budget deficits in the years following 1981 and the ensuing record of budgetary stalemate between the president and Congress, resulting in periodic budget crises, testify to that point. Once again, a strategy designed to attain quick short-term successes for the president proved incompatible with the requirements for managerially sound public policy.

Responsible Public Policy

As the budget debacle demonstrates, long-term national interests can be compromised for the sake of short-term political advantage. Such a bias is endemic to a Congress composed of members elected from state and local constituencies largely through their own efforts, with only the most marginal help from national political parties. Members view themselves first as representatives of their local constituencies and second as trustees of the national interest.

This orientation of legislators is reflected in the decentralized and collegial structure of the Congress. These organizational traits enable members to maximize their responsiveness to constituency pressures and thereby virtually assure their reelection.[69] Legislators seek and are granted committee assignments where they can best represent the interests that elect them, and then "whole committees become special pleaders for segmental interests. Agriculture committees are pro-farmer, interior committees pro-West, labor committees pro-labor, veterans committees pro-veteran, armed service committees pro-military, and so on." While this arrangement allows each legislator to protect his or her constituency interests, the more general national interest is often jeopardized because "a body made up of individuals looking out for themselves cannot, as a collectivity, act responsibly. It cannot govern."[70]

The president, in contrast, has "the structural capacity" to "rise above the pressures of local and narrow interests"[71] because he is "the only politician with a national constituency and thus with an electoral incentive to pursue some broader notion of the public interest."[72] The bureaucracy, with no electoral constituency at all, presumably should have only this public interest in mind. However, the orientation of the bureaucracy toward the public interest is to some extent questionable, given the dependence of agencies upon their friends in Congress for appropriations and their close relationship with the interest groups to whom the agency's policy mission is relevant. As for the president, during his first term, he, like the Congress, is concerned about reelection and needs to consider short-term policy results. During his second administration, he may be able to focus on long-term policy concerns, but by then he will no longer have the political capital necessary to secure these results. Strategically, the president throughout his tenure is urged to accept short-term solutions aimed at maximizing his chances in the Congress rather than to push for more responsible long-term solutions. Again the 1981 Reagan tax and budget exercise is a case in point. Also, Reagan's continued refusal, throughout most of his second term, to acknowledge that the deficit problem just might require revenue as well as expenditure solutions further suggests the presidential capacity for irresponsibility.

Summary

The Congress seems structurally incapable of producing public policy that is informed, timely, coherent, effective, and responsible. The president and the executive branch more generally seem in principle to have a greater capability in this respect but also seem unable to exercise this capability. The problem is that if the president follows the recommended strategy for success in Congress, he will move in a manner that reduces his information, that sacrifices timeliness for speed, that accepts relatively high levels of policy incoherence and ineffectiveness and that, in the end, will produce policy that is not as responsible as it could be. However, if he fails to follow the recommended strategy, policy stalemate is likely to be the result. In the end, then, it seems that the president can either succeed with the Congress or generate managerially sound public policy, but that he cannot do both, for what he needs to do to maximize his chances of gaining congressional approval for his policy proposals is exactly contrary to what he needs to do to maximize his chances for producing good public policy. Policy stalemate or bad public policy is the most likely result.

WHEN STALEMATE IS AVOIDED: INSTITUTIONAL PERFORMANCE AND DEMOCRATICALLY SOUND PUBLIC POLICY

But what of democratic criteria for good public policy? Public policies may be poor from a managerial standpoint, but the process by which they are reached may be democratic. And if stalemate is the result of the operation of democratic procedures, then those who value such procedures must accept stalemate as the will of the people, even if they are uncomfortable with the failure of the political system to respond. Unfortunately, there is little evidence that the system conforms any better to the democratic criteria of popular government, majority rule, responsiveness, and accountability than it does to the several managerial criteria that we have just discussed.

Popular Government

Whereas the policy decisions (or nondecisions) that we have been discussing are made for the most part by elected officials, we also have observed a growing role for the executive bureaucracy and, to a lesser extent, the legislative bureaucracy represented by Congress's greatly expanded professional staff. To the extent that the decisions of presidents and legislators are dominated by nonelected bureaucrats and experts, no matter how well-meaning or informed they might be, the system is less democratic. Moreover, the growing role of bureaucrats in the policy-making process seems beyond dispute.

The electorate, whose votes select presidents and members of Congress, is certainly in greater conformance with democratic criteria now than it was at the founding of the republic: Now virtually the entire adult citizenry is legally eligible to vote, regardless of race, gender, financial resources, educational attainment, or even language mastery. However, in most elections, more than half of those eligible to vote choose not to do so. And those who do seem for the most part not to be very well informed about either the candidates or the issues. Issues do play a part in presidential elections, but it is difficult to say how important a part, and it is particularly hazardous to interpret a vote for a presidential candidate as a vote in favor of his issue positions. For example, in 1980 and 1984, many public opinion surveys indicated that the federal government's various domestic programs continued to enjoy the strong support of the American people. However, Ronald Reagan, an enemy of most of these programs, was elected, receiving the votes of many people who said that they supported these programs.[73]

When citizens vote for members of Congress, a great deal goes into their decisions, but the most important variable continues to be the incumbency factor. Incumbents are almost always reelected because to voters they are much more visible than the person challenging them for the seats and because the people tend to evaluate incumbents and the services that they have performed for the district favorably. Whereas issues can occasionally intrude upon congressional elections—more frequently on Senate than on House elections—for the most part they play a limited role in election outcomes.[74]

The evidence is overwhelming that most people have little understanding of the issues with which the Congress and the president are dealing, of how their representatives or Senators vote on most issues most of the time, or of where the president stands on these issues. "No more than a third of the public recognizes legislative proposals that have been the center of public debate for months and sometimes years. Even among that third, few could describe the proposal accurately or in detail, and fewer could describe the intricacies and alternatives available to policy-makers."[75]

It is the rare congressional reelection campaign that turns on one particular legislative vote. In one study of voters in the 1982 House elections, only 15 percent of the respondents cited their agreement or disagreement with a particular vote cast by an incumbent in their evaluation of his or her performance. In comparison, 86 percent cited the incumbent's constituency service. Of the 15 percent citing a vote, less than half said they disagreed with the incumbent, and almost two-fifths of those respondents still voted for the incumbent. While 57 percent of the respondents cited the general voting record of the incumbent as a reason for their vote, only 8 percent of this number said that they disagreed with the legislator's voting record.[76] This study made no effort to determine if the voter had an accurate perception of the legislator's voting record, an important omission because there is some evidence that voters' perceptions of how their representatives vote may be wrong.[77] In conclusion, to say that a vote for or against a congressional candidate can be attributed to his or her stand on the major issues facing the country and therefore that legislative majorities on particular issues reflect public majorities on these issues is a leap of democratic faith that is simply unsupported by the data.

Majority Rule

Of perhaps greater concern from the perspective of majority rule is the growing dependence of elected officials on campaign funds provided by private interest groups. Whereas citizens may not elect candidates to Congress on the basis of their stands on issues and may have very little knowledge of how they vote, interest groups do contribute on those bases and are quite aware of who their friends and enemies in the Congress are. Even if it cannot be demonstrated that legislative votes are "purchased" by campaign contributions, it stands to reason that legislators, confronted by an inattentive general public on the one hand and very attentive interest groups on the other, will be highly responsive to the latter. As for the presidency, despite the public funding of the general election campaign, every presidential candidate has had to find wealthy people to support the expensive quest for the party's nomination. These debts come due after the election, and even during Democratic administrations access to the presidency will be heavily skewed in the direction of the rich and the powerful. The president's appointment calendar is less likely to show meetings with, say, representatives of welfare rights organizations than with representatives of the National Association of Manufacturers.

The interest group system thus tends to advantage those groups with financial resources while disadvantaging those without access to large sums of money. Intense, well-financed minorities such as the American Medical Association have a disproportionate influence on health care legislation compared with the consumers of health care, who are not organized and lack the resources that health care suppliers can generate. The democratic criterion of majority rule, of course, speaks only to numbers and not to financial resources.

Responsiveness

The structure of the U.S. political system generally and of the Congress specifically is designed to frustrate responsiveness to majorities. One of the goals of the Founders was to reduce the influence of majorities on public policy; the primary tool for accomplishing that goal was to divide political power. That division of power is further reflected in the organization of the Congress. Although the rules of the institution seem to say that majorities should prevail, in practice the legislative process is so strongly biased against policy action that it is relatively simple for minorities to prevent majorities from governing. Often, all groups need to do to prevent action is to convince a majority of the relevant committee, and in the Senate, minorities can prevent the majority from acting through extended debate. Thus, even though individual members of Congress may be highly responsive to the specific interests of their constituents, it is not at all clear that the Congress as a whole is responsive to the wishes of national political majorities.

Accountability

It is clear, however, that the mechanisms by which the people can hold the Congress as a whole accountable for what it does or fails to do are not particularly effective. Citizens tend to reelect their members of Congress, and they do so even when they are not very pleased with how the Congress has been performing. Quite simply, voters do not hold their own members of Congress to account for the performance of the institution as a whole. Voters, while they evaluate their representatives on the basis of their personal characteristics and the services that they perform for the constituency, evaluate the Congress on the basis of how well or how poorly they perceive the country to be doing.[78] The president, in contrast, is evaluated in terms of how well or how poorly the country is doing but is held accountable in a formal sense only once, when he runs for reelection, and then never again.

CONCLUSION

The analysis in this chapter indicates that the U.S. system of legislative-executive relations has failed to meet the challenge of producing public policy that can be judged as good according to both managerial and democratic criteria. Instead, the way in which the president and the Congress operate and the policy decisions that these institutions reach are difficult to defend on either democratic or managerial grounds. In addition, there is an increasingly strong likelihood that on many important issues the political system's bias toward stalemate will prevail and no decisions at all will be reached.

This tendency in turn has encouraged the Congress and the president to seek new mechanisms that will enable government to act, even in the absence of the legislative-executive agreements that the Constitution viewed as a prerequisite to such action. These mechanisms will be identified and their operation illustrated and evaluated in Chapter 6.

6

Living with Stalemate

Deadlock between the president and the Congress may be acceptable in many instances. If a failure to act means that bad policies are not improved or that nagging problems go unresolved, the political system is certainly the worse for it, but only slightly so if the policy stalemate leaves most people's lives unaffected in any immediate way. However, when policy stalemate is likely to have adverse effects on a significant segment of the population or when it prevents the government from making even the most routine decisions, then it becomes necessary to find ways to break the stalemate or, failing that, to find a way for the government to act even when there is no explicit agreement between the president and the Congress on what to do. As the political system has become increasingly disposed toward stalemate, such action-forcing devices have come into greater vogue.

One way to force action is to create a crisis. The theory here is that if the Congress and the president can be convinced that their failure to act will have grave consequences, they may be encouraged to suspend their hostilities and come to an agreement. One way to develop such an agreement is to establish a special commission charged with identifying presumably nonpartisan solutions to the policy problem that has provoked the crisis, solutions that the president and the Congress will have no choice but to accept if the threatened crisis is to be averted.

A second approach relies on automatic devices that require neither the president nor the Congress to act in order for policy to be made. For example, since 1972, Social Security payments have been indexed to the cost of living figures produced by the Department of Labor. As the cost of living rises, Social Security payments rise automatically, without the need for presidential or congressional approval. In recent years, other automatic provisions have been developed to reduce budget deficits and, in the War Powers Resolution, to control the commitment of U.S. troops to hostile action abroad.

A third approach emphasizes the unilateral use of presidential power to force government action either by removing Congress from the policy-making process or by minimizing its role. Congress often has been a willing participant in such a process, readily agreeing to legislation delegating broad policy-making power to the president and the bureaucracy. More recently, Congress has sought to condition such delegations with legislative-veto provisions designed to retain a congressional check on how the executive branch exercises these delegated powers. Another strategy focusing on the unilateral use of presidential power encourages the president to seek his policy goals through the exercise of his administrative powers of appointment and rule promulgation. Finally, an important step beyond this "administrative strategy" is an "imperial strategy" characterized by presidential actions, often taken in secret, that exceed his generally recognized constitutional and statutory powers or that are contrary to the expressed will of the Congress.

In this chapter, these various devices that allow government to act despite policy stalemate are illustrated with several case studies drawn from the Reagan administration. The capacity of such devices to generate public policies that are good by both managerial and democratic standards are assessed also.

CRISIS AND COMMISSION: SOCIAL SECURITY

The constitutional system of separate institutions sharing power makes it difficult for government to act on ordinary policy problems. However, government action is more likely to occur when the political system is confronted with an extraordinary policy problem. Proceeding on this assumption, political leaders often use the word "crisis" as they attempt to spur their colleagues to action. Of course, in many situations the existence of a crisis is not universally recognized. When President Carter declared an energy crisis at the beginning of his term and when he declared a crisis of confidence at the end of his term, nothing much happened after the presidential pronouncements. However, in situations in which political leaders can be convinced that a crisis actually exists, they can move quite expeditiously. In 1964, the Congress quickly passed a resolution authorizing a major escalation of U.S. military involvement in Vietnam when its members were led to believe that U.S. ships had been attacked in the Gulf of Tonkin. In fall 1987, the president and the Congress broke a seemingly intractable budgetary impasse only weeks after a stock market drop of more than 500 points in one day had touched off fears that an economic crisis had been precipitated by the government's inability to control the national budget.

Once a crisis is recognized, decisions need to be taken about what should be done. One traditional way of making such decisions has been to utilize bipartisan commissions to identify the policy course that should be pursued. These commissions, usually composed of politicians with differing points of view, representatives of the private sector, and experts in the particular policy area, all supported by a professional staff, are supposed to provide "nonpolitical" recommendations for dealing with the crisis. Presumably, when the president and the Congress are confronted with the fruits of this concerted expertise, they will display a new-found willingness to cooperate and adopt the recommendations of the commission. The 1983 agreement between President Reagan and the Congress about how to save the Social Security system from impending bankruptcy exemplifies the crisis-commission approach to breaking policy stalemates.[1]

Background

The Social Security system makes payments to program recipients out of trust funds financed by payroll taxes that wage earners pay and by matching contributions from their employers. This plan creates the illusion that worker and employer contributions are being held "in trust" for the worker until he or she reaches retirement age, but in fact the funds have operated on a revolving basis with revenues generated by current workers used to pay benefits to current retirees.

Signs of problems with the financial integrity of the Social Security system first became apparent during the Carter administration and reached crisis proportions early in the Reagan administration. The problem was that the trust fund from which most of the benefits were paid—the old age and survivors fund—was rapidly running out of money. One reason for this was that the Congress and the president had agreed in 1972 to index payments drawn from these funds to the cost of living. This meant that once each year payments would be automatically adjusted to the inflation rate. What those who designed the indexing device did not anticipate was the record inflation rates of the 1970s. The sharp increase in payments mandated by indexing, combined with lower than expected growth in wages and higher expected levels of unemployment, meant that money was going out of the fund much more quickly than new money was coming in. In February 1981, the Congressional Budget Office predicted that the trust fund would be exhausted by early 1983 and could have a $63.5 billion deficit by 1986.[2]

This was more than simply a short-term cash flow problem. Demographic data showed that birthrates were likely to continue to decline and that with improvements in health care, longevity was going to increase. Also, as retirement benefits improved, more people could be expected to consider early retirement. All of this made it quite clear that the number of retired people supported by Social Security would be growing at a faster rate than the number of working people who, through their payroll deductions and contributions from their employers, funded Social Security. If no changes were made, therefore, at some point in the not too distant future the deposits in the Social Security trust fund would be insufficient to support ever increasing payouts to an ever increasing population of retired people.

The policy options for dealing with the problem were, to say the least, unattractive. The strategy used in 1977, when the first cracks in the system began to appear, was to increase revenues by raising the payroll taxes of workers and the contributions of their employers. There were two problems with this option: First, it didn't work, and second, it was very unpopular. Double-digit inflation meant that the new revenues generated were insufficient to deal with even the short-term problem. Moreover, Social Security tax hikes antagonized workers and their employers. Because Social Security taxes are regressive—a flat rate applied to all wage income up to a certain cutoff figure—increases in payroll taxes, unlike increases in the graduated income tax, fall most heavily upon lower paid workers and small businesses and less heavily upon the most highly paid. Funding the Social Security system at least partially with general revenue produced by the graduated income tax would rectify this inequity but was never seriously considered. Fiscal conservatives viewed such a step as another potential drain on the federal budget, and most supporters of Social Security viewed the funding of the program through the trust mechanism as a way of insulating it from ordinary budget pressures.

To complicate matters further, by 1981 a president was in office who saw taxes of any sort as an unmitigated evil. Without higher Social Security taxes, the only way to increase revenue was to bring more people into the Social Security system. Government workers at the state and federal level constituted the largest group of employees outside the system. Bringing them in would increase the wage base of the program substantially, but the payroll taxes of these workers also would increase, and the financial viability of their existing pension plans might be threatened. Unions representing government employees, as well as state and local governments, had always opposed this step.

The alternative to increasing revenue—the mathematics of budgets are relentlessly simple—was to decrease expenditures. This could be accomplished in a number of ways, but all involved reducing benefits for current or future retirees. For current retirees, the automatic cost-of-living increase produced by indexing could be delayed or capped, or the minimum benefit paid to retirees who had contributed little to the system could be reduced, or the benefits of higher-income retirees could be taxed. For future retirees, the age at which one could retire with full benefits could be raised and payment levels to early retirees reduced.

The various groups representing retired or soon-to-be-retired citizens classified all of these options as benefit reductions and threatened political reprisals against any politician who did not see things their way.

Given Ronald Reagan's bias against taxes and the fact that he was some years away from a reelection campaign, his administration's first proposal, in May 1981, focused entirely on expenditure reductions: a reduction in benefits for those retiring early, delaying for three months the cost-of-living adjustment, thereby permanently saving the expenditures that would have been made during that period, and technical changes in the basic formula for computing benefits that would have had the effect of reducing payments by 10 percent for about 18 million recipients. The protests from the Congress and from interest groups were loud and immediate, and shortly after the proposals were announced, the president publicly abandoned them. Instead, he made a more modest proposal calling for the elimination of the minimum benefit as part of an overall round of budget reductions, but this as well as other attempts by the president and by Republicans in the Senate to reduce Social Security expenditures as part of a larger budget package either failed or were stillborn.

The Crisis and the Commission

By late 1981, the only step to which the Congress and the president were able to agree was to permit the endangered old age and survivors trust fund to borrow what it needed to meet its obligations from the other more solvent Social Security trust funds. This interfund borrowing authority was to last through the end of December 1982. At that time, the Social Security Administration would be allowed to borrow enough funds to cover payments for an additional six months. After that, the legislative authority for interfund borrowing would expire and the system would be unable to meet its obligations unless the president and the Congress could agree to significant changes. This time limit, engineered by Republican Congressman Barber Conable of New York as the price for his support for interfund borrowing, was crucial because it had the effect of creating a definite date beyond which a Social Security crisis would take place. It was hoped that the stark prospect of elderly people not getting their retirement checks would create a powerful incentive for action. But how to act, given the opposition of interest groups and most legislators to any significant benefits reductions, the president's opposition to increased taxes, and as his reelection campaign moved closer, his increasing reluctance to be associated with cuts in Social Security?

The crisis had placed the Social Security issue firmly on the agenda, and a method was needed to defuse the issue—to render whatever agreement that ultimately would be reached politically harmless to those who would have to vote to approve it. The answer was a bipartisan commission. In September 1981, the president proposed the creation of a National Commission on Social Security Reform, composed of five members appointed by him, five appointed by congressional Democrats, and five appointed by congressional Republicans. The members of the commission included representatives of the business sector, Democrats from across the political spectrum, and moderate and conservative Republicans. The commission chair was Allan Greenspan, a fiscally conservative Republican and a former chair of the Council of Economic Advisers. The commission's charge was to make recommendations to reform the Social Security system in time to meet the insolvency crisis scheduled by the Conable amendment. The lead time necessary to implement any reforms meant that a bill had to be on the president's desk no later than early spring 1983 if the crisis was to be averted.

The commission met for the first time in February 1982 and several times thereafter but made little progress beyond agreeing to general financing targets that would have to be met before the system could be declared "saved." Philosophical and partisan divisions within the commission proved to be as deep as they were within the Congress and between the Congress and the White House. After almost a year, no plan had been devised and the deadline for action was drawing closer. At that point, five commissioners representing the more moderate elements of the membership began to work secretly with four White House aides. In a two-week period in early January 1983, this "gang of nine" hammered out a compromise package calling for a six-month delay in the cost-of-living adjustment, taxation of Social Security benefits for upper-income recipients, the addition of new federal employees into the Social Security system, an increase in the tax rates for self-employed workers, and significant increases in the Social Security payroll taxes for workers and their employers. Once the "gang" had completed its work, and the agreement of the president and House Speaker O'Neill had been secured, the commission was hastily reassembled, a few reluctant members were leaned on by those who had appointed them, and with three dissenting votes, the commission publicly adopted the plan that had been privately worked out. With several additional, but for the most part minor, compromises, the package was approved by the Congress and signed by the president. The final product increased revenue and reduced expenditures for a net saving of $165 billion over seven years, thereby assuring the short-term solvency of the system. The long-term solvency of the system, although not quite so assured, was nonetheless on firmer ground than it had been before the legislation.[3]

Breaking Stalemates

Our concern here is less with the details of the social security bailout plan and more with the "crisis-commission" process for breaking the institutional stalemate between the president and the Congress. The Social Security problem and the paucity of politically acceptable solutions to it had brought the policy-making process to a halt, with neither the president nor the Congress willing to take the political risks that a comprehensive solution would entail. There the situation would have stayed but for an impending crisis. Perversely, the president and the Congress, unable to agree on what to do, were able to agree on the scheduling of a crisis that meant that something had to be done.

The national commission provided the president and the Congress with an arena to work out a solution. It also served to divert the political pressures generated by the issue away from the president and the legislators, all of whom could say, when asked, that they were waiting for the commission to complete its work. Actually, the commission and its members did relatively little to develop the final policy package. The savings targets that the commission had set did help to beat back last-minute attempts to find painless solutions based on wishful thinking, but the important compromises and decisions were reached by the "gang of nine," operating privately, without the participation of the other members of the commission. In this sense, the commission "succeeded mainly as a front for secret bargains." It provided "the political cover needed for compromise."[4]

As it operated, the commission can be viewed as a response to both the openness of the Congress and to the decentralized nature of power within it. It assembled a small group of legislators with whom the president could deal. Such groups have become increasingly difficult to find as power in Congress has become more fragmented. By providing these legislators and the president "with a place to hide,"[5] the commission countered the openness of legislative institutions generally and the evolved Congress particularly, an openness that often makes compromises difficult to reach. In the bad old days of closed meetings, committees provided this "place to hide," but in the new age of sunshine-filled and therefore often deadlocked committees, commissions of this sort may prove to be the new hiding place, especially when a crisis means that something has to be done.

In this way, the commission depoliticized the Social Security issue and broke the policy stalemate by providing a closed forum where the president and the speaker of the House could cut a deal that neither particularly liked, but that could be wrapped in the politically unassailable cloak of expertise, study, and bipartisanship and packaged as the only way to avert a crisis that all agreed was inevitable unless action was taken. Even though interest groups were heard from and caused some uncomfortable moments for a number of senators and representatives, the legislators as well as the president were able to say that they were simply implementing the commission's recommendations, and when challenged, they could blame the commission, which, quite conveniently, no longer existed, for anything in the final package that people did not like.

AUTOMATIC DEVICES: INDEXING
AND GRAMM-RUDMAN-HOLLINGS

The crisis-commission approach cannnot completely protect officials from complicity in difficult policy decisions; at some point legislators must vote and the president must sign the legislation. Also, for the approach to work, a generally recognized crisis must exist; the technique cannot break stalemates on noncrisis issues. In order to avoid even the modicum of public responsibility that the crisis-commission approach carries with it while at the same time providing a capacity for governmental action in noncrisis situations, an automatic mechanism for making policy decisions needs to be devised, one in which no individual political leader has a role. Such automatic devices are now playing an increasingly prominent role in the U.S. policy process.[6]

Background

In 1972, the Congress and the president agreed to index Social Security payments to the cost of living. That meant that each year payments under the program would be adjusted to keep pace with inflation; these adjustments would occur automatically, without the Congress or the president having to make that decision. On the contrary, the Congress and the president would have to legislate against these increases in order to prevent them from going into effect. Indexing was supported by Democrats as a way to ensure that benefits kept up with the cost of living and by Republicans as a way to avoid pressures for even higher payouts. Similar automatic cost-of-living adjustments, called COLAs, apply to other federal entitlement programs, and indexing also was a feature of the Tax Reform Act of 1981. Under the terms of the act, beginning in 1985, the exact income level at which one moved from a lower into a higher tax bracket would be automatically adjusted to the rate of inflation.

Indexing can be viewed in relatively narrow terms as simply a technical device for adjusting government payouts and revenues to the inflation rate so that citizens are not disadvantaged by unplanned economic trends. But indexing has had far broader policy consequences. As we saw, the decision to index Social Security payments played a crucial role in bringing the old age and survivors trust fund to the edge of backruptcy. And the decision to index tax brackets was one of the factors that contributed to the huge budget deficits of the later Reagan years. Previously, the government could count on the tax revenues generated by "bracket creep"—as salaries increased in response to inflation, earners were pushed into higher tax brackets with higher tax rates—to provide the extra funds that it needed to finance new programs, increases in existing programs, and the cost-of-living increases in entitlement programs that other indexing decisions had mandated. As long as inflation produced higher revenues, no one had to make the tough decisions to raise taxes to cover these expenses. By ending this annual source of new revenue but keeping COLAs and expanding other federal programs, the Congress and the president caused expenditures to increase relative to revenues and larger deficits to come about.

The Deficit

Even though these growing budget deficits were caused in part by automatic indexing devices, the solution to the deficit problem to which the Congress and the president agreed was, ironically, another, even more comprehensive, automatic policy-making mechanism. The legislation, known formally as the Balanced Budget and Emergency Deficit Control Act of 1985, and more informally by the names of two of its three cosponsors, Senators Phil Gramm and Warren Rudman, created an automatic device for reducing deficits to the point where ultimately the budget would be balanced between revenues and expenditures.

The Gramm-Rudman Act was most immediately a response to Reagan administration budget policies, which had reduced taxes by approximately $150 billion a year, increased military spending from $157.5 billion in fiscal year (FY) 1981 to $273.3 billion in FY 1986, and avoided significant reductions in most domestic programs. These policies caused the total accumulated national debt to double from under $1 trillion when Ronald Reagan took office to almost $2 trillion on the eve of the congressional vote on Gramm-Rudman. The situation was not likely to improve in the future; the best available estimates projected continuing annual deficits of approximately $200 billion for several years to come.[7] These numbers, quite apart from their dire implications for the economy, were particularly upsetting to many Republican legislators, torn between demands from the White House that they continue to support increases in the debt ceiling (Congress must set a maximum level for the total debt and periodically raise that level to accommodate mounting annual deficits) and their own commitments, as well as those of their fiscally conservative constituents, to the ideal of a balanced budget.

As with Social Security, dealing with the deficit problem meant choosing from among several politically difficult options. The painless supply-side fantasy that lower taxes would increase government revenues had by this time been abandoned. The starting point, therefore, was the mathematical certainty that reducing the deficit would require that expenditures be reduced and/or taxes increased. Neither approach was very appealing. For members of the Congress, particularly Democrats, the first option meant reducing programs that they had worked hard to legislate, that were important to their constituents, and that could be important to their own reelection. For the president, expenditure reductions might mean jeopardizing the major increase in military outlays to which he was committed and possibly going back on his promise to maintain the safety net of social welfare programs that protected the people he called the truly needy. Once the military and domestic programs to which the president was committed were excluded, the deficit monster could be tamed only by draconian and politically unacceptable cuts in most remaining federal programs.

The alternative, higher taxes, had always been anathema to President Reagan and also was politically dangerous for members of Congress, few of whom, in view of the antitax fervor afoot in the nation, were willing to run for reelection vulnerable to the charge of having raised taxes. Given the choice between savaging programs to which the president and members of Congress were committed or raising taxes, the response of both the legislature and the executive was "none of the above." In 1985, the Senate mustered a bare majority in support of a one-year freeze on Social Security COLAs and on the military budget along with cuts in several domestic programs. But the president pulled the rug out from under the Senate by striking a bargain with the House that resulted in increases for both Social Security and defense spending. This action resulted in a projected deficit for FY 1986 of $220.7 billion, the highest ever.

Gramm-Rudman

The Gramm-Rudman legislation was produced by conservative Republican senators frustrated by the budgetary disaster of 1985 and furious at the president for cutting a deal with the House after asking them to cast a potentially unpopular vote against Social Security and other widely supported domestic programs. Their chance for revenge came when the bill necessary to raise the debt ceiling to accommodate the new deficit arrived in the Senate. Without such legislation, the government could not legally borrow the funds that it needed to continue operations. Because the debt ceiling bill could not be killed and could not be vetoed, it was a perfect vehicle, both symbolically and politically, for legislation that promised to deal with the deficit once and for all.

The Gramm-Rudman approach to dealing with the deficit began by mandating a set of deficit targets for each fiscal year beginning with FY 1986. In that year, the budget would be permitted to show a deficit of no more than $171.9 billion. The target figure would drop to $144 billion for FY 1987 and then, in decrements of $36 billion a year, to zero by FY 1991. Because voting against these targets could be interpreted as a vote in favor of ever increasing deficits, getting legislators to support the targets would be relatively easy. Getting them to vote for budgets that would meet the targets would not be so easy.

The Gramm-Rudman legislation sought to reach the mandated targets by moving up the deadlines for the passage of congressional budget resolutions and by installing procedural checks that would prevent floor action on any legislation that would breach the figures in the budget resolution. However, its most novel and important feature provided that if the president and the Congress could not agree on a budget that came within $10 billion of meeting the annual deficit target, a mechanism would be triggered that would reduce expenditures automatically so that the deficit target would be met.

The mechanism would work as follows: Both the Office of Management and Budget and the Congressional Budget Office would make independent projections of the size of the deficit and the amount that it exceeded the limits set by the law. Differences between their projections would be arbitrated by the controller general, the head of the General Accounting Office (GAO), an agency of the Congress. The controller general's decisions would be announced in a GAO report, which would indicate how much would have to be cut from specific government accounts in order to reach the deficit target. The president would be required to issue a "sequestration order" implementing these cuts. Congress and the president would have a month between the issuing of the order and the date that it would go into effect to come up with an alternative package of expenditure reductions and/or tax increases that would produce a budget that met the deficit targets. If the president and the Congress failed to come to such an agreement, the cuts ordered in the GAO report, updated to reflect the latest budgetary data, would go into effect automatically. Some programs, such as Social Security, Medicaid, and Aid to Families with Dependent Children, were exempted entirely, while other programs such as Medicare and Guaranteed Student Loans were subject to special rules that limited the amount that they could be cut.

After all of the special rules and exceptions were taken into account, the total cuts necessary to meet the deficit target would be "across the board" and would have to come equally from defense and domestic spending.[8]

A diverse coalition supported Gramm-Rudman. Included were conservative Republicans who saw the device as a means to force cuts in the federal budget and as a way to protect themselves from the political repercussions of votes for raising the national debt or for trillion-dollar budgets. More moderate Republicans and Democrats hoped that the threat of indiscriminate and automatic cuts under the Gramm-Rudman process might create a crisis atmosphere that would force the Congress and the president to make hard budget choices. Many Democrats thought that the provision requiring equal cuts from domestic and defense spending would force the president to reverse his opposition to tax increases in order to protect the Pentagon's budget. Some members saw the legislation as a way to head off even more radical proposals that were in circulation, such as constitutional amendments requiring a balanced budget or giving the president a line-item veto. In the end, however, it was the inability of the Congress and the president to agree on fiscally responsible budgets through the normal policy-making process that made Gramm-Rudman an irresistible though not necessarily attractive alternative. As Senator Rudman said, it was "a bad idea whose time has come."[9]

It is not entirely clear whether Gramm-Rudman accomplished any of the several goals that its supporters had in mind. For example, as Gramm-Rudman neared final passage in December 1985, it was necessary to decide how it would affect government spending during FY 1986, which had begun two months earlier. The target deficit figure for that year, $171.9 billion, was unreachable without huge and, especially in an election year, politically unacceptable cuts. Therefore, the final agreement contained provisions limiting total FY 1986 cuts to $11.7 billion, enough to reduce the projected deficit to $208 billion, a "mere" $36 billion above the target figure. After various exemptions and special rules that applied to FY 1986 only were plugged in, cuts of 4.9 percent in defense accounts and 4.3 percent in nondefense accounts were ordered. Because these cuts had been tacitly accepted as part of the legislative package that produced Gramm-Rudman, and because they were so limited, there was no real attempt to head them off through alternative legislation. This was to be the first and the only time that the automatic process was actually used.

A further test of Gramm-Rudman was postponed by a July 1986 Supreme Court decision that held the automatic reduction mechanism unconstitutional. The Court ruled that because the controller general was subject to removal by the Congress, he was in fact subordinate to the Congress, and to permit an officer controlled by the Congress to execute the laws would violate the separation of powers between the president and the Congress. Other justices, concurring in the result, thought that it was inappropriate for the Congress to delegate its legislative powers to one of its officers rather than to go through the normal process described in Article I of the Constitution—House and Senate approval followed by presentation to the president.[10]

Constitutional problems with the act had been anticipated during congressional debate, and therefore a back-up budget-cutting procedure in case of an adverse judicial ruling had been included in the legislation. It provided for expedited congressional consideration of a joint resolution approving the OMB and the CBO reports and if both chambers approved, presentation to the president for his signature. The problem, of course, was that unlike the automatic process, the back-up procedure would require the Congress actually to vote on the budget reductions and the president actually to sign them into law. If it was that easy, then the law would not have been needed in the first place. Nonetheless, the back-up procedure was used to ratify the cuts that already had been made for FY 1986 but that had been invalidated by the Court's decision. This should not be interpreted as an atypical display of political courage on the part of the president or the Congress, but rather as a recognition that too much had happened and too much confusion would have ensued if these cuts had been junked eight months into the fiscal year.

Not surprisingly, the story was different for FY 1987. The prospect of having to stand up and be counted in favor of budget reductions proved too horrifying to all concerned, and the FY 1987 cuts required by the CBO and OMB reports were never enacted. Instead, "through legerdemain and blue smoke and mirrors" the Congress and the president declared that they had met the Gramm-Rudman target for FY 1987 or that at worst they were off by no more than $10 billion, the margin of error that the law allowed. They accomplished this feat "by selling some government assets, by postponing increases in pay or allowances due in fiscal year 1987 until the 1988 fiscal year, by underestimating agriculture payments, and by other forms of creative accounting."[11] This "solution" confirmed suspicions that the president and the Congress were unable to deal responsibly with the budget through the normal policy-making process and also raised substantially the amount of cuts that would have to be made if the FY 1988 Gramm-Rudman target of $108 billion was to be reached.

In September 1987, the president and the Congress responded to the Court's decision and to their own failure with the FY 1987 budget by agreeing to a revised version of Gramm-Rudman that eliminated the role of the controller general and gave the responsibility for designating and implementing the cuts to the Office of Management and Budget. OMB was required to explain any differences between its figures and those produced by the Congressional Budget Office and to operate within a set of constrained technical parameters spelled out in the law. Also, the balanced budget target date was moved back to fiscal year 1993, and higher and presumably more feasible targets were set for the years in between.[12]

Breaking Budget Stalemates

The beauty of Gramm-Rudman in both its original and revised forms is that it permits action on the budget deficit without requiring either the Congress or the president to make the tough decisions on what programs to cut and on whether to raise taxes. There was no provision for the latter in the Gramm-Rudman machinery, and the former would take place automatically, across a wide and mostly undifferentiated range of programs. As was the case with indexing, Congress and the president would have to agree to prevent the cuts from taking place, thus turning the system's disposition toward stalemate into a virtue by making the desired policy outcome, declining budget deficits, dependent on inaction rather than on action. And most important, no one—not the president nor any member of the Congress—would have to vote for the cuts or sign a bill mandating the cuts. Because no one's fingerprints would be on the budget axe, no one could be held responsible for the cuts when they took place.

Clearly, some who supported Gramm-Rudman hoped that the prospect of such wide-ranging expenditure cuts would be so frightening that the president and the Congress would have no alternative but to find a budget agreement that would be, for each, preferable to what the automatic mechanism would yield. The "blue smoke and mirrors" compromise of 1986 did constitute such an agreement, albeit one that depended on bogus accounting schemes. A somewhat fairer test of the hypothesis came in fall 1987, after the automatic process was revised and the cuts that it mandated for FY 1988 were announced. In this instance, the president and the Congress did agree on a last-minute budget compromise that averted these cuts, but not until a full month after the automatic cuts had been implemented. Even then, an agreement might not have been reached but for a sudden, steep drop in the stock market that created a crisis atmosphere around the deficit issue. Before the stock market crash, the president had indicated that he intended to accept the automatic cuts on the grounds that defense spending would fare no worse under those cuts than it would under an alternative package then under consideration in the House. He argued also that he would achieve more in domestic savings and avoid a tax increase by allowing the Gramm-Rudman process to run its course. The president's bluff (if he was bluffing) was called by the October 1987 stock market collapse, widely attributed to a lack of faith in the capacity of the president and the Congress to deal with the budget deficit. Senator Rudman said that the imposition of the automatic cuts told the markets that "the government isn't working, and that they don't want to hear." The crisis seemed to change the president's mind, for he agreed to summit negotiations between his aides and congressional leaders and announced that he was "putting everything on the table with the exception of social security" but including, presumably, tax increases.[13]

Two months later, these largely secret negotiations produced an expenditure and tax package to which the Congress and the president agreed, thereby overriding the Gramm-Rudman reductions that had been imposed a month previously. The package also contained a number of other provisions dealing with issues that had nothing to do with budgetary politics, such as funding for the Nicaraguan contras, an amendment ending tax breaks for companies doing business in South Africa, and an amendment banning smoking on domestic flights lasting less than two hours. These previously stalemated issues were added to the package because they would garner votes and also because their advocates took the view that with the president and congressional leaders so heavily invested in the budget compromise, no one would scuttle the whole bill over one additional unrelated provision.[14]

There are some similarities between the process for securing the December 1987 budget agreement and the one that produced the 1983 Social Security package. The stock market collapse created a generally recognized crisis, and the final arrangements were worked out by another "gang" of congressional leaders and White House aides, operating once again in secret. As was the case with Social Security, the legislators and the president, if forced to accept responsibility for the revenue and spending package or for the unrelated legislation that rode through with it, would argue that these steps had to be taken to deal with the crisis. On the unrelated issues, the "no fingerprints" approach could be used, with legislators claiming either that they were not aware that these provisions were tucked into the bill or that they knew that they were there but that the crisis left them no alternative but to vote for the bill. In any event, all complaints could be directed to the now dispersed negotiating gang.

Gramm-Rudman, like the crisis-commission approach to policymaking, represents an attempt to overcome the U.S. political system's bias toward stalemate. Unable to make the most basic governing decisions—what to spend money on, how much to spend, and how to raise the money—the Congress and the president decided on a hands-off approach. These decisions would be taken automatically by the OMB computers and the people who ran them. This specter might be sufficient to break the legislative-executive stalemate, or it might not, but at least decisions would be made. "It is a desperate act for a desperate situation," said House Minority Leader Robert Michel shortly after the passage of Gramm-Rudman.[15] Senator Lowell Weicker of Connecticut was more caustic: He called Gramm-Rudman a "legislative substitute for the guts we don't have to do what needs to be done."[16] We can call it just another way of getting government to act in a system designed to prevent action.

AUTOMATIC DEVICES
AND THE WAR POWER: LEBANON

Background

In 1973, Congress, in quest of a greater role in decisions committing U.S. troops to action overseas, passed the War Powers Resolution. The resolution was the product of growing congressional discontent over the developing concept of unilateral presidential authority to introduce U.S. troops into hostile or potentially hostile situations. The Vietnam conflict was the most striking case in point, but President Eisenhower had intervened with U.S. troops in Lebanon and President Johnson had introduced U.S. troops into the Dominican Republic. In taking these actions, each president had cited his explicit power as commander in chief of the armed forces and his implicit power to respond to emergency situations. However, many members of Congress, reflecting on the Vietnam experience, argued that these unilateral presidential actions circumvented and in essence made a dead letter out of the Congress's exclusive constitutional power to declare war.

If the Congress objected to these presidential wars, its only recourse was to instruments that were either too blunt or too subtle. Bluntly, the Congress could refuse to appropriate funds to support the foreign involvement, a risky course that could easily be depicted as failing to support U.S. troops in the field. Throughout the Vietnam conflict, even when domestic opposition to U.S. involvement was at its peak, Congress never seriously considered taking this step, even though it would certainly have brought the war to a halt. Rather, Congress used the more subtle instrument of holding hearings on the war, debating its merits, and otherwise focusing public attention on what was happening. These activities coincided with and reinforced growing domestic opposition to the war and eventually made it difficult for Presidents Johnson and

Nixon to pursue their policies. Although this approach was ultimately successful, it took a very long time, and a great deal of damage occurred, both domestically and internationally, before it worked.

The War Powers Resolution of 1973 sought a more timely and effective congressional role in decisions concerning the commitment of U.S. troops to foreign hostilities while at the same time retaining presidential discretion to respond to foreign policy situations. The resolution required that the president "in every possible instance shall consult with the Congress before introducing United States Armed Forces into hostilities or into situations where imminent involvement in hostilities is clearly indicated." Within forty-eight hours of the introduction of U.S. troops into such situations, the president was required to submit a report of his actions to the Congress. This report marked the beginning of a sixty-day period at the end of which the president would have to terminate the troop deployment unless the Congress had either declared war or extended the sixty-day period. Even before the sixty-day period was up, Congress could, by concurrent resolution, order the removal of the troops.[17]

The provision requiring the withdrawal of troops after sixty days in the absence of congressional action to prolong their stay is, like Gramm-Rudman, an example of an automatic decisionmaking mechanism. This provision of the War Powers Resolution means that a stalemate between the president and the Congress can force an end to a military conflict. Even though presidents have raised a series of constitutional objections to the War Powers Resolution, it is this provision that has made them most reluctant to comply with its terms. Their concern has been that once the sixty-day clock begins to run, adversaries, aware of the time limit, may calibrate their actions to that clock, avoiding certain steps that might encourage the Congress to support the president and prolong the involvement of troops, and taking other actions that might discourage the Congress from allowing U.S. involvement to continue. In the president's view, given the Congress's disposition not to act, the law most likely would lead to troop withdrawal. To prevent this from happening, presidents have simply avoided triggering the resolution's machinery by not formally reporting the introduction of troops, in most cases arguing that the troops were not really engaged in hostilities.

U.S. Intervention in Lebanon

The events leading up to the decision to commit U.S. troops to Lebanon began in summer 1982 when Israel invaded Lebanon.[18] In August of that year, after the Israelis had captured Beirut, the United States contributed a small contingent of marines to a multinational peacekeeping force whose sole mission was to evacuate Palestinian guerrillas from Lebanon in return for Israel's withdrawal. After this operation was completed, the troops were withdrawn. However, a string of violent events soon occurred, including the assassination of the Lebanese president, Bashir Gemayel, and the massacre of Palestinian civilians by Christian militia, all of which seemed to bring the country to the edge of anarchy. At the end of September, President Reagan sent 1,200 marines back to Beirut as part of a new multinational force designed to support the new government of Amin Gemayel, the brother of the assassinated president.

Upon ordering the marines back to Lebanon, President Reagan sent a letter to the Congress informing them of his decision but carefully skirting the terms of the War Powers Resolution. The letter, he said, represented his commitment to keeping Congress fully informed about the Lebanon situation; providing such information was, in his view, "consistent with the War Powers Resolution." The use of the term "consistent" rather than "pursuant to" was meant to suggest that the president, by informing Congress, was neither abandoning his constitutional objections to the resolution nor, more important, triggering the sixty-day clock, as a formal report, according to the resolution, would do. The president put even more distance between his actions and the War Powers Resolution by emphasizing his view that the troops were not being committed to hostilities or into a situation where hostilities were imminent. Their mission was to "facilitate the restoration of Lebanese Government sovereignty and authority"; he stated that "in carrying out this mission, the American forces will not engage in combat" and furthermore, that he had no expectation that they "will become involved in hostilities." Although the president refused to set a time limit on the involvement of the troops, he suggested that they were there "only for a limited period."[19]

In response to the Reagan letter, and on and off for the next year, Congress and the president argued about the meaning of the War Powers Resolution as it applied to the decision to send U.S. troops to Lebanon. Some legislators maintained that whether the president invoked the resolution or not, it was nonetheless in effect. Senator Charles Percy, chairman of the Senate Foreign Relations Committee, said that the sixty-day clock "began to run when the first Marine landed in Lebanon."[20] Congress, however, did nothing to back up these views. Meanwhile, it became evident that despite the president's assertions to the contrary, the marines were involved in a hostile and open-ended situation. In September, administration officials had implied that the marines would be out by the end of the year. They were still there on March 15, 1983, when five of them were injured in a sniper attack. The next month, the

U.S. Embassy in Beirut was attacked, and seventeen Americans, though no marines, were among the dead. The first two marine deaths from hostile activities occurred on August 29 and a week later two more marines were killed. It had taken about a year, but the administration's view that the Lebanese situation did not constitute one in which hostilities were imminent was finally untenable.

The changing situation brought the president and the Congress back into negotiations. On September 29, exactly one year after the introduction of U.S. troops, an agreement was reached in the form of a joint resolution passed by both houses of Congress and signed by the president. The resolution recognized that U.S. forces "are now in hostilities requiring authorization of their continued presence under the War Powers Resolution." This was the first time that a president had explicitly recognized the War Powers Resolution. In return for this concession, the president received authorization to keep the marines in Lebanon for eighteen months, provided that he report to the Congress at least every three months on the status of the forces.[21] Many in Congress opposed the joint resolution, viewing the broad terms in which the mission of the marines was stated—to help restore full control by the government of Lebanon over its own territory—as an open-ended invitation to a Vietnam-style escalation of American involvement. Others, however, believed that the resolution was the best that they could get out of Reagan and that if it were not passed, the president would simply continue as he had, without any congressional approval, thereby challenging the Congress to find a way to enforce the War Powers Resolution.

Even so, the Lebanon agreement did not constitute a wholehearted embrace of the War Powers Resolution by the president. Secretary of State George Shultz said that the president still reserved his right as commander in chief to keep the troops in Lebanon longer than the eighteen months that the resolution allowed. In a letter read during the congressional debate, the president used more circuitous phrasing to keep his options open, saying that if it was necessary to keep the marines there longer, "it would be my intention to work together with the Congress with a view toward taking action on mutually acceptable terms."[22] Later, it was revealed that the president had given private assurances to congressional leaders and to other wavering legislators that he would seek congressional approval if he wanted to extend the marines' stay in Lebanon.[23] However, the president, even while signing the resolution, continued to express his doubts about the constitutionality of the War Powers Resolution.

On October 23, four weeks after the president and the Congress had agreed on the Lebanon resolution, the true extent of the hostile environment in which the marines had been placed was brought home vividly and tragically when their compound at the Beirut airport was attacked and 241 marines were killed. One week later, an attempt by some House members to force U.S. withdrawal from Lebanon by cutting off funding was defeated. By early 1984, Democratic leaders in both houses were criticizing the administration's Lebanon policy, and on February 2, the Democratic caucuses in the House and Senate called for a "prompt and orderly" withdrawal of the marines. On February 7, Reagan threw in the towel, ordering a phased evacuation of the troops to ships stationed offshore.

Breaking Foreign Policy Stalemates

Those who designed the war powers machinery had some of the same motives as those who designed the Gramm-Rudman machinery. The president and the Congress had failed to reach agreement on the limits that Congress might impose on the war-making prerogatives that the president said he derived from his constitutional role of commander in chief. Congress, while upset at being cut out of the process, was at a loss to figure out exactly what to do. The solution, in the form of the War Powers Resolution, was a process that by its threat of automatic policy actions that the president and the Congress would find unattractive but that neither need be responsible for, would encourage the two to find an agreement. Presumably, the president would find withdrawing troops because of congressional inaction less desirable than a joint congressional-presidential commitment to keep the troops where they were, a joint commitment clearly consonant with the vision of those who framed the Constitution. Given the reluctance of the transformed presidency to share its greatly expanded version of the commander-in-chief function with the Congress, the War Powers Resolution was an attempt to force the President to involve the Congress: The resolution held over him the threat of forced withdrawal unless he did so.

What those who wrote the War Powers Resolution failed to reckon with was a presidential refusal to recognize or invoke its terms. Presidents repeatedly have found reasons to ignore even the relatively mild "consultation" requirement of the resolution as well as its stronger "reporting" requirement. In April 1975, President Ford said that he could not consult with Congress about the evacuation of Saigon because the Congress was on Easter recess at the time. In May 1978, President Carter failed to consult with or to report to Congress about the use of troops to stabilize the government of Zaire.[24] In 1983, President Reagan told the Congress about the invasion of Grenada after it was all over, and in 1986 the administration "violated both the spirit and the letter" of the resolution in its military actions against Libya.[25] And until the end of his term of office, Reagan refused to invoke the resolution in regard to his decision to provide U.S. naval escorts for foreign oil tankers in the Persian Gulf, despite the fact that these ships in several instances have had to engage in hostilities.

Presidents fear that by acknowledging the war powers machinery, they will in effect accept political and institutional limits to their capacity to use U.S. troops and, through the reporting mechanism, bind themselves to a time limit for the use of military force, thereby giving U.S. adversaries an advantage. On the grounds that it would constitute an erosion of executive powers, they resist the idea that Congress should be asked to sign on to such involvements. The argument that such institutional cooperation would be the most responsible way to exercise these powers falls on deaf ears at the White House. In the fifteen-year history of the War Powers Resolution, only in the Lebanon situation did the president and the Congress actually negotiate the specifics of a foreign military involvement. In this one instance, the resolution provided a vehicle to break the stalemate between the president and the Congress over war-making power. However, the machinery was abetted by external events— direct attacks on the marines and some deaths—that, while not constituting a crisis, did create a sense of urgency among the participants about the desirability of reaching an understanding. In that context, it is probably inappropriate to view the Lebanon case as precedent setting and more appropriate to view the War Powers Resolution as being of questionable effectiveness as a means either to break deadlocks or to forestall the unilateral presidential actions that are still the most effective deadlock-breaking devices.

THE LEGISLATIVE VETO

To this point, our discussion of methods to govern in a political system disposed toward stalemate has concentrated on combinations of crises and automatic devices that either force legislative-executive agreements or allow government to act in the absence of such agreements. Another approach focuses on a more expansive view of the power of the president to act unilaterally.

Origins and Purpose

As public policies became more complex, the Congress became more inclined to delegate the responsibility for determining policy details to the president. As such delegations of power became more extensive, the Congress began to seek devices for overseeing and controlling the exercise of these delegated powers by the executive. The legislative veto, narrowly conceived, is just such a device, but in a broader context, it also can facilitate government action in the absence of explicit legislative-executive agreements about what is to be done.

The legislative veto refers to a provision in a law that delegates to the executive the power to act but retains for the Congress the power to stop (that is, veto) that action if the Congress disagrees with it. Legislative veto power was sometimes vested in one house of Congress, in other instances in both houses, and, on occasion, in a committee or a committee chair.[26] Although forerunners of the legislative veto appeared in statutes passed during the nineteenth century, the origin of the current practice is usually traced to 1932 legislation that permitted the president to reorganize the executive branch by executive order as long as he allowed sixty days to elapse between the time that he announced the reorganization plan and the time that he implemented it. During that period, if a majority of either house of the Congress disapproved the reorganization, it could not go into effect.

At first glance, the legislative veto seems to be a method for expanding congressional rather than presidential prerogatives, an impression that is reinforced by an unbroken record of presidential opposition to such provisions. However, a closer look at the rationale underlying the legislative veto suggests its proexecutive intent. When presidents proposed executive reorganization legislation, interest groups that were clients of the affected agencies and therefore probable beneficiaries of the current organization were almost certain to oppose the restructuring plans. These groups would make their voices heard in Congress, particularly within the committees holding oversight responsibilities for the agency. There they would often find a sympathetic ear, for the committee members and their staff also were likely to have grown accustomed to the current organization, and if the proposed reorganization were to alter the jurisdiction or responsibilities of the committee in question, opposition from these quarters was virtually guaranteed. Given such potential legislative and group opposition, the chances of passing legislation authorizing any given reorganization were slim. Instead, it was easier for Congress to cede some of its authority to determine the structure of the federal bureaucracy to the president. But Congress would have been unwilling to do so unless it was able to retain a final check of some sort. By subjecting the president's executive reorganization proposal to a legislative veto, the opposition would be able to block the president's actions if it could generate a majority in either the House or the Senate. But if the Congress followed its usual disposition to avoid acting, the reorganization would go into effect.

In other policy areas where the legislative veto was used, the intent was similar: Delegate to the executive the power to decide, on the assumption that most of the time Congress would not act to block these decisions. Thus, whereas the legislative veto, seen in isolation, provides a congressional check upon presidential power, the act to which it is attached usually expands presidential authority. More to the point, Congress probably would not agree to expand presidential authority unless the veto provision is part of the deal. The legislative veto provides the Congress with a way to reconcile the need for executive discretion in administering the ever increasing responsibilities of the federal government with the need to maintain some semblance of congressional control over the decisions that are being taken. And, most important, it allows government to act without requiring explicit legislative-executive agreements.

Because the legislative veto proved so convenient, it became ubiquitous. James Sundquist counted 113 laws enacted between 1932 and 1979 that contained legislative-veto provisions; more than half of these laws were passed during the 1970s.[27] These provisions extended to issues as diverse as immigration matters, Federal Trade Commission regulations, and presidential decisions to defer the spending of appropriated funds and to deploy U.S. troops overseas. The last, a provision of the War Powers Resolution, allowed the Congress, through a concurrent resolution, to direct the president at any time to recall troops committed to hostile actions, even before the sixty-day time period that would trigger automatic withdrawal expired.

The Supreme Court Steps In

Despite its positive implications for presidential power, every president since Herbert Hoover has questioned the constitutionality of the legislative veto, and as veto provisions were applied to more detailed administrative decisions, presidential opposition to their use intensified. "Such intrusive devices," wrote President Carter to the Congress, "infringe on the Executive's constitutional duty to faithfully execute the law" and because they amount to lawmaking without presentation of the final product to the president, deprive him of his opportunity to exercise his veto power. More practically, Carter argued, although Congress can veto administrative decisions, it cannot rewrite them. "If the House and the Senate agree that a regulation is needed but disagree with the agency or each other on the specifics, the exercise of the veto can lead to indefinite deadlock."[28] Despite these constitutional and practical misgivings, most veto provisions have been signed into law by presidents who, presumably, valued the grant of discretionary power that accompanied the veto provision over the restrictions that the legislation seemed to impose upon the executive branch.

In 1983, in the case of *INS v. Chadha*,[29] the Supreme Court sided with the president on the constitutional question by declaring the one-house veto unconstitutional in immigration cases specifically and by extension in all other instances as well. The Court argued that the Constitution required the consent of both houses of Congress for binding action. But two-house vetoes also were unconstitutional because they violated the requirement that legislation be presented to the president for his signature or veto. While acknowledging the convenience of the device, the Court concluded that the Congress, through the legislative-veto provision, was usurping the executive power of the president.

Justice Byron White, dissenting from the Court's opinion, said that the decision sounded "the death knell for nearly 200 other statutory provisions in which Congress has reserved a legislative veto."[30] However, Louis Fisher of the Congressional Research Service reported two years after the decision that "the legislative veto is alive and well." He found that in the sixteen months between *Chadha* and the adjournment of the Ninety-eighth Congress, 53 laws were added to the books that sought to accomplish the same goals as the legislative veto while avoiding the objections raised by the Court.[31]

In many instances, these new provisions actually made life more difficult for the president. Some of the redrawn measures required the consent of the appropriations committees before an expenditure was made. Others invoked internal congressional rules, and still others required joint resolutions of approval before the president could proceed. The latter was particularly difficult for the president because both houses had to agree before his proposal could go into effect. The requirement that he go through the equivalent of the usual legislative process largely negated any discretionary power that had been assigned to him. Because of this, numerous informal arrangements have been entered into between committees and agencies that provide de facto, if not de jure, legislative vetoes. Though many of these measures are legally questionable in light of *Chadha*, agencies and even presidents readily accept them in return for the discretionary authority that they carry. This suggests that *Chadha* may prove to be as effective in limiting legislative vetoes as the Eighteenth Amendment was in limiting the consumption of alcohol.[32]

Breaking Stalemates

From the perspective of legislative-executive stalemate, the legislative veto is instructive because it uses the systemic bias against action to make governmental action more rather than less likely. If Congress needed to muster majorities to approve each administrative action covered by a veto provision, the chances for approval of any particular proposal would be reduced, and given the heavy legislative workload that such an individual approval process would entail, the entire system would likely come to a halt. However, because it is just as difficult to marshall a majority against an administrative proposal, the likelihood that Congress will exercise its veto in any particular case is also reduced and therefore the likelihood that a proposed administrative action will go into effect is increased. In sum, the legislative veto admits that, given the broad scope of government, Congress is simply incapable of making detailed policy decisions; the legislative veto permits the president and the bureaucracy to run the government, even in the context of underlying presidential-congressional dissensus, while reserving to the Congress the capacity to intervene when it chooses.

Presidents usually have welcomed the broad authorizations of power that Congress has conferred upon them, despite resenting the legislative veto as an unwanted string attached to such legislation. But presidents would not be very pleased by the alternative to the veto: a requirement for affirmative legislative action on all measures now subject to the veto. That is no doubt the reason why presidents have quietly acquiesced to the quasi-legal devices that have, after *Chadha*, provided functional equivalents to the legislative veto. In the end, the legislative veto contributes more to the power of the executive and to the government's capacity to act than it takes away; strategically, if not constitutionally, presidents probably have been ill advised to resist these steps.

ADMINISTRATIVE STRATEGIES

Although the legislative veto ultimately strengthens the president's capacity to act, such provisions cannot be used in every policy area, and when they are used, they can, as President Carter pointed out, lead to deadlock on those occasions when Congress does decide to intervene. An even more effective means to deal with legislative-executive stalemates is an administrative strategy that emphasizes what the president can accomplish by controlling the bureaucracy rather than by seeking the approval of Congress.

The Strategy and Its Uses

The basic premise of the administrative strategy is that the president can change the shape of public policy if he places people in charge of the bureaucracy who are completely loyal to him and his policy priorities and if he avoids staffing agencies with people whose first loyalty is to the agency's missions. The strategy provides the president with a way to implement his policy priorities without going through the normal legislative process, thereby avoiding even the possibility of deadlock with the Congress.[33]

The administrative strategy is part of a more general trend toward the centralization of power in the White House that began during the Kennedy administration and continued through the Johnson and Nixon years. Because established bureaucracies often pose as many difficulties as the Congress does for activist presidents seeking to achieve ambitious policy goals, presidents have to an increasing extent attempted to direct policymaking from the White House. The Ford and Carter presidencies represented a pause in this process, but during the Reagan administration, the Kennedy-Nixon strategy of centralization to avoid bureaucratic obstruction was joined with administrative policymaking to avoid legislative obstruction.

The heart of the Reagan administrative strategy was the appointments process. To receive an appointment in the Reagan administration, the primary qualification "overshadowing managerial competence and experience or familiarity with the issues appeared to be the extent to which an appointee shared the president's values and would be reliable and persistent both in transfusing these values into agency practices and in executing central directives bound to be unpopular in his or her agency."[34] In several cases, the appointees manifested an "open hostility to the mission of the agencies" they were asked to lead.[35] During the Reagan years, such appointments reached farther down into the operating staffs of agencies than was the case in previous administrations. By September 1983, noncareer appointees constituted, for the first time ever, over 10 percent of executive-branch personnel.[36]

During the Reagan administration, examples of the administrative strategy in action have abounded. In the area of environmental protection, the administration decided not to seek changes in the laws, most of which had strong support in the Congress. Rather, people were appointed to run the Interior Department and the Environmental Protection Agency (EPA) who were hostile to the goals of these laws and who could alter their impact through enforcement decisions. The director of the EPA, Anne Gorsuch (later Burford) "had little management experience or familiarity with the major environmental programs" and relied only minimally on the advice of the professional staff. "Contacts with regulated industries were frequent; meetings with environmentalists and other interested parties were almost non-existent."[37] With no significant changes in the underlying legislation, "the end result was that the environmental policies of the prior fifteen years were substantially diluted."[38]

In the Department of Labor, Assistant Secretary Albert Agrisani suspended all grants and contracts that were in the pipeline when he took office. He went after the Employment and Training Administration with singular zeal, drastically cutting staff and using transfers and position downgrades against those who remained. In Housing and Urban Development, Secretary Samuel Pierce reduced the agency's oversight activities and staff and reversed Carter administration policies that had targeted community development block grants to distressed neighborhoods and the poor.[39] In the Department of Interior, Secretary James Watt went after the Office of Surface Mining, cutting its staff in half and purging the more zealous regulators. He then instituted policies that returned the primary responsibility for implementing strip-mining legislation to state governments, where, historically, business influence always had been stronger than at the federal level. Federal strip-mining laws were disregarded when they "contradicted the drive to cut business regulatory costs," and state laws were permitted to stand "even when they were contradictory to the federal statute."[40]

The Reagan administration's emphasis on administrative policymaking was most apparent in those agencies with regulatory responsibilities. The administration was ideologically committed to the notion of deregulation and expected its appointees to see that this commitment was reflected in the activities of their agencies. Thus, the Mine Safety and Health Administration and the Occupational Safety and Health Administration (OSHA) "began to stress cooperation with business rather than confrontation in achieving regulatory compliance." The Federal Trade Commission, the National Highway Safety Administration, and the Antitrust Division of the Justice Department all exhibited "a general easing of regulatory vigor."[41] Even when agencies retained their aggressiveness, their proposed regulations had to pass muster with a newly invigorated Office of Information and Regulatory Affairs (OIRA), a part of the Office of Management and Budget. Staffed by presidential partisans, the OIRA became "the President's agent in screening and shaping decisions that would otherwise be lost to the permanent government."[42] OIRA was particularly aggressive in delaying and obstructing regulations proposed by OSHA, by the National Highway Traffic Safety Administration, and by EPA, but that were opposed by the affected industries.[43]

Whether one approves or disapproves of the administrative strategy, one must admit that it is an effective way for presidents to continue to pursue their policy options beyond the early part of their administrations, beyond that brief period when their resources are at a maximum and congressional opposition is at a minimum. The strategy allows a president to circumvent the legislative labyrinth and use the hierarchical administrative powers that all agree he possesses. It is a way to break the legislative-executive stalemate by taking unilateral action, especially in those areas where agreement from the Congress is very unlikely to be forthcoming. A Congress so committed to a cleaner environment that over the past decade it has passed a series of increasingly stringent laws dealing with that issue is not about to repeal or soften this legislation. To attempt to get the Congress to do so would be a waste of effort. Achieving the desired change in policy through administrative actions is easier and because it is less visible, less likely to provoke opposition. Similarly, it would be politically difficult for any member of Congress to cast a vote that could be interpreted as weakening occupational safety and health regulations. Why ask them to do so when OMB can accomplish the same goal by blocking specific OSHA regulations?

PRESIDENTIAL IMPERIALISM: NICARAGUA

There are limits to the effectiveness of the various devices and strategies discussed to this point as ways to break or avoid presidential-congressional stalemate. A crisis cannot be generated nor a commission appointed for every issue. Quite the contrary: A point of diminishing returns may be reached; if a new crisis is declared every few weeks, people will come to accept crises as normal occurrences rather than as action-forcing events. Automatic devices cannot be devised to solve complex problems that require that choices be made. There are also limits to the discretionary power that the Congress will delegate to the president, even with the check of the legislative veto. Administrative strategies seem most effective, but at the extreme, they may raise legal questions—when unilateral presidential actions move beyond generally recognized statutory and constitutional limits. At that point, an administrative strategy turns into an imperial strategy. Reagan administration policy in Nicaragua provides a case study of how a president, confronted by deadlock with the Congress, tested and then stepped beyond these limits.

Background

When the Reagan administration came to power, its highest foreign policy priority was to stop the spread of communism in Central America. These efforts focused on El Salvador, where a right-wing, pro-U.S. government was under pressure from left-wing rebels, and on Nicaragua, where in 1979 a leftist revolution had overthrown the right-wing, pro-U.S. Somoza dictatorship. The administration's goal in El Salvador was to prop up the government and to help it put down the guerrilla uprising. Its goal in Nicaragua was more ambiguous. Initially, the administration asserted that all it wanted to do was to stop the flow of arms from Nicaragua to the El Salvadoran rebels. Later, after it became clear that Nicaragua had halted its support for the rebels, the administration's stated goal shifted to preventing the creation of a Marxist state in Central

America and, according to President Reagan, encouraging the government to restore "democratic rule and to have elections."[44]

As first steps toward accomplishing its goals, the Reagan administration ended a modest program of economic aid to Nicaragua, which had been instituted during the Carter administration. Then in December 1981, the president signed an executive order authorizing covert actions by the Central Intelligence Agency (CIA) in support of rebels operating against the Nicaraguan government. The rebels, who later came to be called "contras," were a loose coalition of a number of factions, including soldiers and police who had worked for former President Anastasio Somoza and certain centrist elements that had split with the new revolutionary government. The ostensible purpose of the Honduras-based CIA operation was to stop the flow of arms from Nicaragua into El Salvador, but for the contras, and probably for the administration as well, the real objective was to weaken the Nicaraguan government by confronting it with a civil war that would sap the country's economic resources and possibly provoke the regime into dealing with dissent in a more authoritarian manner. The administration hoped that the combination of economic hardship and political repression would, in turn, produce even higher levels of internal dissent.[45]

By early 1982, the CIA operation was no longer covert. The news media carried frequent stories of a secret U.S. war that, with approximately 10,000 rebels in the field, clearly had moved well beyond simple harrassment of the Nicaraguan government. As information about the operation became public, members of Congress became more critical. And as the financial needs of the contras escalated, the Congress was presented with a series of opportunities to act on its doubts because the necessary funds needed to be legislatively authorized.

These "contra-aid" votes were difficult for the Congress. On the one hand, many members, particularly Democrats, were skeptical about the president's stated intentions, suspecting that his real goal went beyond simply interdicting the flow of supplies from Nicaragua to El Salvador and was the overthrow of the Nicaraguan government. Whereas most legislators held a dim view of communism, many did not share Ronald Reagan's world view of a monolithic international communist conspiracy, with Nicaragua as the current battlefield. They saw, instead, a pitifully poor country with myriad social and economic problems, a country that posed no military threat to the United States or its allies. Although neither the Nicaraguans' approach to dealing with these problems nor their friendship with the Cubans was to be applauded, what the Nicaraguans were doing, argued the congressional critics, was none of our business. They saw the administration starting down the same road that had led to disaster in Vietnam.

However, there also was concern among some of the president's opponents in Congress about what seemed to be an increasingly authoritarian cast to the Nicaraguan government, and despite their reluctance to support the administration's efforts to overthrow that government, they also did not want to be seen as supporters of a dictatorial communist regime. They also considered the possibility that the president might be right in some respects about Nicaragua. If so, when the dust settled, they did not want to be held responsible for "losing" Nicaragua. As Kenneth Sharpe has observed, many Democrats found themselves "trapped between their opposition to communism and their opposition to U.S. troop commitments, between 'no more Cubas' and 'no more Vietnams.'"[46] Thus, all-out opposition to the administration's policy in Central America entailed serious political risks that many congressional skeptics were not prepared to take.

As his administration progressed, President Reagan became committed to an increasingly aggressive policy toward the government of Nicaragua, and as his priority economic issues began to move off his agenda, he invested ever larger amounts of his political capital in support of that policy. As he sought the cooperation of the Congress, he confronted an institution with attitudes ranging from strong support for his course of action among conservatives to ambivalence and opposition among moderates and liberals. Once again, therefore, a government constitutionally designed not to act was confronted with the need to make policy decisions on a highly visible issue where there were significant political costs attached to any option that might be taken. The usual choice in such a situation was to do nothing, but in this case that option also was risky, for not to act when the president was demanding action meant that the Congress would have to accept responsibility for any adverse consequences of inaction. In this context, the Congress and the president arrived, over the years, at a long series of twisting, turning, and often contradictory policy decisions concerning support for the contras.

Congress and Contra Aid

Congress dealt with the issue for the first time in April 1982, when the House Intelligence Committee, under the chairmanship of Representative Edward Boland of Massachusetts, rejected efforts by some Democrats to kill the Nicaraguan operation entirely. Instead, the committee inserted into the bill authorizing CIA funding for FY 1983 language requiring that the agency use funds in Nicaragua solely to interdict arms shipments to the rebels in El Salvador, and that it use no funds for the purpose of overthrowing the government of Nicaragua. Later in the year, when the defense appropriation bill came up, another attempt to cut off aid was quashed when Boland offered a different version of his amendment, barring the CIA and the Department of Defense from spending any funds "to furnish military equipment, military training or advice, or other support for military activities, to any group or individual not part of a country's armed forces, for the purpose of overthrowing the government of Nicaragua or provoking a military exchange between Nicaragua and Honduras." The Boland amendment, approved by Congress as a part of the FY 1983 appropriation bill, would expire on September 30, 1983 when the fiscal year ended.[47]

Throughout 1983, the fighting in Nicaragua continued. Clearly, funds and supplies were still reaching the contras, despite the Boland amendment. The House at this point would have been willing to bar all aid to the contras, but the Republican-controlled Senate was not yet prepared to go along. The best that Boland could get for FY 1984 was a cap of $24 million on the amount that could be spent in support of the contras. Early in 1984, Reagan asked the Congress for an additional $21 million, but this was not forthcoming. Despite Reagan's assurances that his goal was not "to destabilize or overthrow the government of Nicaragua nor impose or compel any particular form of government there,"[48] the House rejected the additional funds, and ultimately the Senate backed down. Congress, for the first time, seemed on the verge of halting all support for the contras.

Reagan, however, was not prepared to take no for an answer. As he would do throughout his presidency on the issue of contra aid, he persisted, returning to Congress in 1984 to ask for $28 million in the FY 1985 budget. This time, the now-traditional delay in dealing with budget issues had put the Congress under strong end-of-the-session pressure to pass an omnibus continuing-appropriation bill that in essence tied all the regular appropriations together into one large funding package. The president's request for funds for the contras became part of that legislation; thus deadlock on that issue would jeopardize passage of the continuing resolution. With the House opposed and the Senate in favor of contra aid, a House-Senate conference arrived at a truly bizarre compromise, agreeing to ban all aid, but also agreeing that a few months later, the president could submit a report to Congress asking for a resumption of the aid. If at that time both houses of Congress, acting under expedited procedures, agreed by joint resolution to resume contra aid, up to $14 million would become available. To get the aid authorized, the president's report would have to state that Nicaragua was supporting guerrilla activities against other Central American countries, show that such support was militarily significant, and justify the money requested for the Nicaragua operation as well as the goals that were being pursued.

This compromise guaranteed that the 1984 "no" would not be final and that the issue would come back to the Congress. In an attempt to blunt the opposition, Reagan coupled his new request for the $14 million with a Central American "peace plan" calling for a cease-fire in Nicaragua. If the Sandinistas accepted the cease-fire, the president promised to use the $14 million for humanitarian aid to the contras, but if the Sandinistas did not agree, he would use the money for additional arms shipments. The Congress, sensing quite correctly that the president was making an offer to the Sandinistas that they were likely to refuse, was reluctant to support the president's request, and Reagan agreed to another compromise, this time saying that the $14 million would be used solely for humanitarian aid. This was a compromise that a majority of the Senate was willing to buy. The House, however, refused, with members arguing that the distinction between humanitarian and military aid meant little if the contras could use the funds that they received from other sources to buy weapons while using U.S. funds to buy everything else that they needed.

So, once again, the House said no, but once again, the issue refused to die. Two months after the House rejected the president's $14 million request, the Senate approved $38 million in nonmilitary aid to be spent over the remainder of FY 1985 and through FY 1986. In an extraordinary reversal, the House agreed to $27 million in aid. The change of heart was provoked in part by an ill-timed trip to the Soviet Union by Nicaraguan President Daniel Ortega—immediately after the April House vote against the president's request. Some moderate Democrats, worried that their April vote against contra aid left the impression that they wished to do nothing at all about Nicaragua, took the opportunity to demonstrate that they were not being soft on communism. A vote for humanitarian aid provided them with a politically appealing option to support.

The 1986 installment of the by now annual contra-aid battle began in March when the president raised the ante considerably, requesting $70 million in military aid and $30 million in humanitarian aid. In a rerun of the 1985 scenario the House once again said no, whereas the Senate supported the president. In April, the president's request reappeared in the House as part of a supplementary appropriations bill but was again rejected. However, in June, the president finally prevailed, with the House performing its annual backflip, approving virtually the same $100 million request that it had rejected in March.

The president began 1987 with a victory when the Senate, then under Democratic control, still refused to go along with a move in the House to block an installment of the aid package that had been agreed to in 1986. The president, sensing a weakening of congressional opposition, again raised the stakes, requesting $270 million for the contras for FY 1988. But this time he was forced to back down after the Central American presidents signed an agreement that set in motion a process aimed at achieving a negotiated peace. However, the president did not give up entirely; in the last-minute December 1987 budget compromise, he got the Congress to approve $14 million for the contras as part of his price for going along with provisions of the bill that he had opposed. The compromise also mandated a vote in early February 1988 on additional aid, which would carry the contras through the balance of the Reagan administration. The familiar scenario seemed once again to be playing itself out. The House rejected the president's request for $36 million, the Senate supported it, and the House seemed poised to reverse itself once again. But this time, the Nicaraguan leaders and the contras agreed to peace negotiations and the Congress, despite the president's pleas to keep the pressure on the Sandinistas, postponed further action indefinitely.

Failing to Break the Stalemate

As the president and the Congress fought to a standstill on contra aid, with the president usually emerging with some though not all of what he wanted, various devices for breaking the deadlock were brought into play. In July 1983, the president tried the commission approach, appointing a National Bipartisan Commission on Central America, chaired by former Secretary of State Henry Kissinger and including prominent citizens from the public and the private sectors. The commission recommended increased military aid to El Salvador, continued aid to the contras, and an economic aid package for the Central American countries.

However, the commission's recommendations were generally ignored because, unlike the Social Security commission, it did not adequately represent some of the major "players" in the game. Those in Congress who were opposed to the president's policies claimed that the commission was stacked with supporters of the president and that it was designed simply to place a bipartisan stamp of approval on what the president wanted. Just as important, despite often inflammatory statements by the president about the dangers of communism on the doorstep, the crisis element never really entered into the conflict. Whereas all of those involved in the Social Security issue came to believe that the fund was going to run out of money if no action were taken and that the consequences of such a default would be unacceptable to the American people, few believed that either the defeat and disappearance of the contras or their victory over the Sandinistas would make much difference one way or another to anyone. It seems clear that without a crisis, commissions do not work.

With the commission approach a failure, the president turned to unilateral actions. In 1983, he used the traditional U.S. tactic of gunboat diplomacy, ordering naval maneuvers off the coast of Nicaragua and mock landings on beaches in Honduras, a few miles from the Nicaraguan borders. He increased the number of military personnel stationed in Honduras and spent large amounts of money to upgrade the military facilities there. In 1984, the CIA escalated its involvement by mining Nicaraguan harbors, causing damage to ships from the Netherlands, the Soviet Union, and Panama. The administration defended the mining as "a legitimate means of exercising the right of individual and collective self-defense in appropriate circumstances," an argument Congress rejected in a nonbinding "sense of the Congress" resolution.[49] In 1985, a week after he lost a contra-aid vote in the House, the president imposed a trade embargo on Nicaragua, saying that the "policies and actions of the government of Nicaragua constitute an unusual and extraordinary threat to the national security and foreign policy of the United States."[50]

These tactics were not particularly effective. The mining of the harbors had a negative effect, intensifying congressional opposition to Reagan's policies and creating international embarrassment for the nation, especially after the World Court condemned the action. The trade embargo was largely symbolic. By this time, there was very little trade between the United States and Nicaragua anyway, and no one doubted that what little there was would be absorbed by other nations. Moreover, the increasing U.S. military presence in Honduras was making other Central American countries edgy; they were traditionally worried about Yankee imperialism, and U.S. policy probably spurred on their own peacemaking efforts.

The Iran-Contra Scheme

When an administration cannot accomplish its goal through the normal legislative process and when legitimate and visible unilateral actions by the executive prove to be of limited effectiveness, the president may be tempted to try an imperial strategy to accomplish his goals. Thus in 1983, despite the first Boland amendment prohibition against the expenditure of funds to overthrow the government of Nicaragua, the administration expanded support for the contras, a group whose goal from the beginning was to overthrow the Sandinista regime. The spending limits imposed by the Congress were regularly circumvented by charging expenditures to other accounts. The military buildup in Honduras, for example, precipitated entirely by the desire to put pressure on Nicaragua and to support the contras, was charged for the most part to the Defense Department.[51]

When in 1984 the Congress adopted another version of the Boland amendment prohibiting the Defense Department, the CIA, or other intelligence agencies from spending funds to support the contras, the National Security Council staff, under Colonel Oliver North's leadership, organized a private aid network. North not only helped to generate the funds but also worked to reorganize and coordinate the operations of the different contra groups, gave tactical advice, and arranged for resupply operations. As the Iran-Contra hearings made clear, these efforts were supported with funds solicited by the president and other administration officials from private citizens and foreign countries and also with funds derived from the illegal sale of arms to Iran. These efforts turned out to be part of a larger Project Democracy authorized by the president and designed to finance and carry out worldwide intelligence operations outside the normal congressional funding and control procedures. Involved in these decisions in one way or another were the president, his national security advisers, various State Department officials, and the director of the Central Intelligence Agency.[52]

Whether President Reagan knew the full details of all that was going on, particularly the diversion of funds from the Iran arms sales to the contras, is subject to some dispute. According to his national security adviser, Admiral John Poindexter, the president approved efforts to circumvent the congressional ban on funds for the contras by seeking contributions from other countries and from private individuals. Colonel North's testimony before the Congress and memoranda that he wrote while in the White House indicate that he assumed that the president knew about his various activities.[53] In Poindexter's view, the money from the Iran arms sales fell into the same category as the other techniques that were being used to get money to the contras during the period of congressional restrictions. He concluded that diverting the Iranian funds "was a matter of implementation of the president's policy with regard to support of the contras." Nonetheless, Poindexter said that he decided not to tell the president about the diversion because he wanted to insulate him from the political repercussions that would surely follow if the enterprise was ever exposed. But in perhaps the most revealing part of his testimony, the admiral said that he was "sorely tempted" to tell the president about the diversion when the president, frustrated by a negative vote in the Congress, inquired whether he could aid the contras "unilaterally." In this context, it was not unreasonable for Poindexter to conclude that the president would have supported the scheme had he known about it. The president, after the facts had become public knowledge, said that this conclusion was erroneous.[54]

Whether Reagan knew about or explicitly authorized all that was being done to allow him to act "unilaterally" in support of the contras or whether he would have allowed these operations to continue if he knew about them is beside the point. The fact is that members of his administration took steps to implement his frequently and fervently expressed Central American policy goals, steps that they kept secret because they knew that the Congress and the nation would react harshly if they became public. Colonel North admitted to preparing documents for the Congress that were "erroneous, misleading, evasive and wrong."[55] Admiral Poindexter justified the record of deception, describing his and the president's frustration at the "underhanded tactics" employed by the Congress on the contra issue and attacking Speaker O'Neill for using his power to delay contra-aid votes.[56]

Although one can argue that the Congress had been behaving in an unreasonable, irresponsible, erratic, and even "underhanded" manner, it is interesting to note that neither the president nor his aides argued that Congress's actions on Nicaragua exceeded its legal or constitutional authority. In contrast, the Reagan administration dealt with the policy stalemate engendered by congressional opposition and ambivalence toward its Central American policy by stepping outside recognized constitutional boundaries to pursue the president's goals. The administration's actions, of course, have their historic precursors. Richard Nixon, for example, convinced that he had few friends in Congress and that after the 1970 election, he was unlikely to get very much of what he wanted from them, launched a set of actions abroad and at home that ended ultimately in his forced departure from office. The illegal bombing of Cambodia, the war on domestic dissent against his Southeast Asia policy, the use of the Internal Revenue Service to "get" his administration's enemies, the break-ins and wiretaps aimed at getting information about these people, and the complex cover-up that ensued when these events became public taken together constitute one of the more sordid chapters in the history of the American presidency.

Nixon's Watergate experience and Reagan's Iran-Contra affair are easily viewed as deviant cases. And to some extent, they are. To conclude that presidents regularly break the law would be overly cynical. However, to view these episodes as unrelated to the general state of presidential-congressional relations would be overly naive. Clearly, a president's rocky relationship with Congress, particularly in the years beyond the early honeymoon period, may encourage him to give up on Congress, to view the world from the perspective of "us against them," with "them" including the Congress and all other opponents of the administration, and to go his own way, convinced that he is on the side of the nation's interest, if not its laws.

BREAKING STALEMATES
AND GOOD PUBLIC POLICY

We have seen that the various mechanisms discussed in this chapter can break policy stalemates. The question remains, are the policies that are thereby produced good by either managerial or democratic standards?

Crisis Commission

The crisis-commission approach seems to achieve managerially sound public policy but does so at a considerable cost to democratic criteria for good public policy. The National Commission on Social Security Reform provided a setting within which there could be developed a rescue plan that was informed, coherent, effective in the sense that future payments were secured, and responsible in the sense that a relatively long-term solution involving some difficult choices was developed instead of the short-term painless solutions that are usually favored in these circumstances. The timeliness of the action was assured because all the concerned parties accepted the crisis deadline established by the Conable amendment, and a policy option was selected prior to that deadline.

However, whereas the final package was ultimately modified and approved by elected officials, the details of the measure were worked out by a small, anonymous group of commissioners and White House aides working, for the most part, in secret. Although the policy that the commission produced was responsive to majority wishes that the Social Security system be saved, the commission provided a means to insulate the elected leaders from accountability to that majority for the choices that they made to achieve this goal. By insulating them from public visibility and pressures, the commission allowed the president and members of Congress to suspend their roles as elected policymakers and to avoid responsibility for their decisions. In this way, managerially sound public policy was achieved, but primarily through the suspension of democratic policy-making procedures.

Automatic Government

Automatic devices such as the Gramm-Rudman machinery also suspend democratic procedures but, unlike the crisis-commission approach, do not have the saving grace of achieving managerially sound decisions. By definition, decisions that take place automatically, such as across-the-board budget cuts, are uninformed by data on the comparative success or failure of individual programs or of their relative need, efficiency, or effectiveness. Rather, all programs are treated alike, the good and the bad, the necessary and the unnecessary. Funds for military bands and for cancer research receive equal treatment, as do funds for environmental protection enforcement and for corporate subsidies, aid to a foreign country's hungry and aid to its police force. These decisions are timely only in the sense that they happen automatically and therefore on schedule. Although the policy that results may be effective in terms of achieving the short-term goal of reduced budget deficits, it fails to meet the criterion of responsibility because it is untouched by any long-term calculations of the merits of individual programs.

Automatic devices fail utterly on democratic criteria because they constitute a refusal on the part of elected officials to make governmental decisions. Gramm-Rudman in effect cedes budgetary authority to un-elected bureaucrats and to the calculations that their computers make. Accountability is also abandoned, for when the budget axe falls, no elected official need take responsibility; in fact, even the unelected officials who implement the cuts are not really responsible. Rather, the law, working as a machine unto itself, is responsible. The reductions arrived at are responsive only in the very narrow sense that citizens expect that government will act to reduce spiraling deficits; they are nonresponsive in the more significant sense that citizens expect that this problem will be dealt with intelligently. Similarly, tax and spending decisions that are made automatically, in response to changes in an economic indicator, or a decision to withdraw troops from a foreign involvement because Congress has failed to act also must be viewed as retreats from both democratic and managerial principles of good government, no matter how pleasing the result may be in a particular instance.

In fact, the policy that results from the workings of automatic devices is usually not very pleasing. It is instructive that the Gramm-Rudman machinery was allowed to work only once and that on two other occasions Congress and the president went to extraordinary lengths to prevent it from working. It is equally instructive that in dangerous military situations, neither the president nor the Congress has come anywhere near risking the withdrawal of U.S. troops through congressional inaction. In the Lebanese case, the single time that the War Powers Resolution was invoked, the time frame agreed upon for the commitment of troops was so long and the escape hatches built into the agreement by the president so numerous that it is doubtful that had events in Lebanon gone differently, withdrawal ever would have been forced, using the resolution's machinery. As it happened, the troops were withdrawn, but it took place the old-fashioned way, through domestic opposition, articulated in the Congress, and provoked by the death of U.S. soldiers.

The Legislative Veto

In contrast to automatic devices for dealing with stalemate, the legislative veto can meet both managerial and democratic standards. Managerially, it allows sufficient executive discretion to encourage policy decisions that are informed, coherent, effective, and responsible. Letting these decisions go into effect unless the Congress vetoes them makes a timely policy decision more likely, because the constitutional and congressional bias toward inaction will in these cases allow the policy process to proceed. Although democratic standards are to some extent undermined by the greater discretionary power that the presence of the legislative veto encourages the Congress to delegate to bureaucrats, the fact that Congress retains the final say and that the president can, if he wishes, still intervene in these bureaucratic decisions, contributes to the adherence of the device to democratic standards. Unfortunately, the Supreme Court has placed the legislative veto under a constitutional cloud, although this has not stopped the president and the Congress from entering into equivalent arrangements when it has proven convenient for them to do so.

Administrative Strategies

The adherence of administrative strategies to managerial and democratic criteria is more problematic. On the one hand, such strategies negate the policy expertise of civil servants by placing them under the control of people known more for their loyalty to the president than for what they know about a particular policy area. During the Reagan administration, this phenomenon often resulted in administrative decisions innocent of policy expertise. On the other hand, as with the legislative veto, administrative strategies enhance executive power, and to the extent that executive discretion is associated with more timely, more coherent, more effective, and more responsible policymaking, it can be argued that such strategies can produce managerially sound public policy.

The verdict is also somewhat ambiguous on the question of whether administrative strategies meet democratic criteria. To the extent that the approach encourages presidential control of the bureaucracy rather than bureaucratic independence from the president, these strategies enhance democratic values. When bureaucrats operate on their own, independent of the elected chief executive, what they do, no matter how laudable by managerial criteria, cannot be called democratic. However, when the president, through the use of administrative strategies, attempts to reverse the intent of the Congress when it passed the legislation in question, such actions are difficult to justify according to democratic criteria. During the Reagan years,the federal courts overturned several administrative decisions that they concluded had violated congressional intent, most notably in the area of Social Security disability pensions and National Highway Transportation Administration regulations.[57] Constitutional issues aside, a question of accountability surfaces when the meaning of a law is substantially changed by the bureaucrats who implement it, even if they are operating under the authority of an elected chief executive. And the accountability of presidential power itself is questionable, particularly during a president's second term, when he is barred from facing the public again and therefore need never be held to account.

The Imperial Strategy

From a managerial perspective, imperial strategies are suspect because the president, acting in secret, must necessarily restrict the number of people who know what is going on to a small circle of his closest advisers, a step that necessarily restricts the information and advice that he receives. In the Iran-Contra affair, Reagan consciously cut himself off from the governmental expertise that might have shown him the folly of his course of action. The episode also had adverse consequences for the coherence of larger U.S. foreign policy objectives as well as for the effectiveness of the policy—few of the hostages were released, Iran did not moderate its anti-American attitudes, and the contras ultimately failed. The responsibility of the policy in terms of long-term national interests is also questionable given the damage that it did to U.S. credibility overseas, the ambiguous message it sent on how the United States deals with terrorist groups, and the additional strain that it placed on presidential-congressional relations.

When the president orders violations of laws that Congress has passed and that he or his predecessors have signed, it is difficult to square such behavior with democratic criteria. Although the argument can be made that occasionally laws need to be violated for certain higher goals or principles, such an argument amounts to nothing more than saying that even democratic nations must sometimes act undemocratically. Even if this is so, such actions certainly cannot be justified according to democratic criteria, unless one is willing to redefine democracy as being embodied in the discretionary power of a single elected chief executive. This, noted Theodore Lowi, comes uncomfortably close to viewing "the presidency and the state as one and the same," a modernized version of Louis XIV's assertion, "L'état, c'est moi."[58] Only from that imperial perspective could President Reagan say that his decision that the contras should receive aid should take precedence over legislation to the contrary.

Instances of presidential imperialism are attributable in part to the constitution against government. Presidents, conscious of the limited time that they have in office and acutely aware of the substantial obstacles that the Constitution and the Congress present to the accomplishment of their goals, are tempted to act unilaterally when confronted by stalemate. And because stalemate is the probable state of presidential-congressional relations after the president's early months in office, the temptation to act unilaterally becomes difficult to resist. Presidents know that their predecessors who have chosen this course and gotten away with it—one thinks of Jackson and Lincoln—are the heroes of the American presidency and that those who, for a variety of reasons, did not get away with it—one thinks of Richard Nixon—have ended up as villains. But what is most perverse, they also know that those who did not even try, such as Jimmy Carter, who succumbed to the stalemate system, were viewed simply as failures.

CONCLUSION

A president apparently can provide creative and strong leadership for the Congress early in his administration if he follows the right strategies, but these approaches seem likely to produce less than optimal public policy results. Later in his term, stalemates with the Congress can be expected, stalemates that mean either that major public policy problems go unresolved or that they are resolved with poor policy decisions, whose only virtue is that they can command the agreement of the major players. The methods for breaking policy stalemates, such as the crisis-commission approach and the various automatic mechanisms, often seem to be aimed less at providing good policy solutions and more at allowing political leaders to avoid responsibility for their actions. More disturbing is the fact that the automatic mechanisms turn the process of government on its head, with the inaction of political leaders rather than their actions producing policy results. In contrast, the strategy of avoiding stalemates through strengthened presidential prerogatives does make public policy decisions contingent on the actions of a political leader and does fix responsibility for these decisions with that leader. However, approaches that rely on unilateral presidential action deprive the policy process of the deliberative capacities of the Congress and invite extraconstitutional or imperial behavior on the part of the president and his people.

The U.S. political system can and should be structured in such a way that the choices are not between stalemate and imperialism, between automatic actions for which no one is responsible and presidential dominance that vests a great deal of responsibility but also a great deal of power in one man. These alternative structures will be discussed in Chapter 7, the concluding chapter.

7

Beyond Stalemate

My aim has been to examine the policy-making performance of the president and the Congress from a critical perspective. The discussion moved from the premise that political institutions should be expected to make good public policy to the conclusion that the president and the Congress have failed to meet this expectation. Before we proceed to the question of what can be done, let us take a few moments to review the argument that has taken us from premise to conclusion.

THE ARGUMENT IN REVIEW

After exploring the origins and functions of legislative and executive institutions, we tackled the knotty question of what constitutes good public policy. From one perspective, policy could be defined as good if it was arrived at by procedures that were in accord with democratic principles. Alternatively, public policy could be defined as good according to managerial criteria, with good public policy being informed, timely, coherent, effective, and responsible. An examination of the generic characteristics of legislatures and executives led us to theorize that the more that legislative institutions were involved in the formulation of public policy, the more likely it was to meet democratic criteria; the more that executive institutions were involved in its formulation, the more likely it was to meet managerial criteria. This posed a particularly acute dilemma for those political systems committed to democratic principles. It suggested that if political institutions were organized to produce managerially sound public policy, such institutional arrangements might not be very democratic and that, conversely, the price of a democratic political system might be managerially poor public policy. Thus, a fundamental challenge facing democracies is to find institutional arrangements that will produce public policy that is good from both a managerial and a democratic standpoint.

This was a challenge much on the minds of those who wrote the U.S. Constitution. Although at one time their republican beliefs had convinced them that legislative institutions were the place to make good public policy, by the time that they arrived in Philadelphia in 1787 they had reached essentially the same conclusion that we reached in Chapter 1: Legislative domination of the policy process led to managerially poor public policy. They sought instead a more balanced relationship between the president and the Congress, one that ideally would temper the democratic biases of the latter with the managerial capacities of the former. To achieve that balance, they designed an elaborate system of separate political institutions sharing power, with each institution possessing the capacity to check the other, and with no one institution being able to predominate. But their system, rather than encouraging managerially sound public policies, actually turned out to have a pronounced bias against policy action of any sort. In truth, what the Founders had created was a constitution against government. Perhaps they did not fully anticipate the tendency toward governmental inaction that would characterize their new constitutional arrangements, but such a result would not necessarily have displeased them. For the Founders were people who had come to fear the abuse of governmental power, especially power exercised in the name of popular majorities; thus, implicit in their design was a preference for the risks associated with inaction over those associated with unwise action.

It was with this constitution against government that the United States set out to deal with problems of ever increasing scale brought on by the physical expansion of the nation, its larger and more diverse population, an increasing role for the federal government, and the internationalizing of the political environment in which it functioned. Politically, three major changes took place. First, the political system became much more democratic than the Framers had intended. Second, the responsibilities of the American presidency were transformed. As presidents moved to meet new governmental challenges, they interpreted the vague generalities of the Constitution so as to move their office to a central position in the political system and in the minds of the people. In so doing, presidents relied heavily upon the increasingly democratic character of their office to legitimize their actions. They also were assisted by the Congress, which as policy became more complex, tended to delegate even greater policy-making power to the executive branch. Third, the Congress itself changed, evolving into a larger, more complex, more locally oriented, and more professionalized institution.

Whereas the balance of power between the president and the Congress would shift from one decade to the next, over the long term the presidency emerged as the more dominant policy-making institution. The transformed presidency seemed the answer to the question of how policy could be produced that was both managerially sound and democratic. The president, chosen by a national electorate consisting, as barriers to the franchise fell, of a larger and larger proportion of the population, would be the quintessential democratic leader and, from his vantage point as chief executive, would preside over that branch of government with the greatest capacity to produce managerially good public policy.

Proceeding on this theory that presidential government would produce good public policy, presidents sought to dominate the policy-making process by controlling the Congress. Models of presidential-congressional power that reflected a more balanced or more cooperative relationship between the two institutions, and arrangements that emphasized congressional prerogatives, were discarded or ignored because they were thought to be emblematic of a failed presidency. If a president aimed to be great, he had to dominate the Congress; during the twentieth century particularly, the American presidency expanded as it sought to carry out this newly defined role not only of chief executive but also of chief legislator. The literature on the presidency began to emphasize a strategy, ostensibly available to all presidents, that if used correctly would produce presidential mastery of the Congress and its policy decisions. The president was advised to involve himself personally with the Congress, to consult with, be courteous to, and bargain with its members, while at the same time letting them know that if necessary, he could be tough as he pursued his goals. Furthermore, he should avoid overloading the Congress with a large policy agenda, but at the same time he should be aware that the faster he moved on his priorities, the better his chances for getting the Congress to approve what he wanted. Finally, he should cultivate his relationship with the American people so that he could be in a position to mobilize their support in his battles with the Congress.

There were several problems with this strategy for presidential success, however, not the least of which was that it worked only occasionally. What turned out to be crucial, quite apart from the rest, was how quickly he moved, for his window of opportunity for leading the Congress was very much restricted to at most his first year in office. At other points in his presidency, it seemed that no matter what he did or how he did it, he was likely to fall short of his goals. The second problem with the recommended strategy was that even if it worked—that is, even if the Congress went along with the president—the result was unlikely to be public policy that was good by managerial standards. Ironically, the very things that the president needed to do to maximize his chances for success with the Congress were contrary to what he needed to do to produce good public policy. And the inability of the Congress to produce good public policy, an inability rooted in its generic characteristics as a legislative institution, had not gone away; therefore, on those occasions when the president and the Congress succeeded in breaking the disposition of the system toward stalemate, the result was likely to be managerially poor public policy. To make matters worse, the processes used adhered no more closely to democratic than to managerial standards, so it could not even be said that democratic criteria had been maximized, even if managerial criteria had not been met.

With the option of presidential government a failure, stalemate became the usual condition of a U.S. political system confronted anew with the question of how to govern given a constitution against government. The new answers centered on techniques and strategies that would enable the government to operate in the absence of explicit presidential-congressional agreements. Automatic devices were designed that would allow governmental decisions to be made without the need of either presidential or congressional action. Commissions were utilized to arrive at policy choices that the president and the Congress could adopt without taking explicit responsibility for them, especially during times of crisis. Other devices emphasized unilateral presidential powers, either through the traditional process of delegation of congressional authority to the executive or through administrative strategies emphasizing what the president could accomplish through enhanced control of the bureaucracy. On some occasions, presidents resorted to imperial strategies by which they sought to accomplish their goals by stepping outside recognized constitutional and statutory limits to their power. An evaluation of these various devices for living with stalemate suggested that although a few seemed to produce managerially sound public policy, most failed utterly in regard to democratic criteria.

The U.S. political system, I concluded, needs to do better. It needs to have a policy-making arrangement that offers more than continuing stalemate on the major issues of the day, punctuated by sporadic episodes of presidential leadership and occasional examples of presidential imperialism. It needs a government with a dependable capacity to act and to act well from both a managerial and a democratic perspective. It should not have to rely upon jury-rigged automatic devices to make governmental decisions, and it should not have to wait until crises arise that force it to act.

WHAT CAN BE DONE?

If the political system is to do better, significant changes need to be made in the way U.S. political institutions operate. Simply put, the constitutional scheme of shared powers between an independent president and an equally independent legislature needs to be altered, first, so that the executive has the dominant role in the policy-making process and, second, so that the two institutions are more intimately involved with each other than is currently the case. The effect of these changes will be to move legislative-executive relations in the United States from what I described in Chapter 1 as a balanced system characterized by an activist president and an equally activist Congress to a representational system characterized by a dominant executive role in the policy-making process. Although the legislature in such a system will possess the ultimate authority to say no, ordinarily the executive will have its way. The legislature, by pursuing its representational activities, will establish the parameters within which the executive can act, will seek modifications in public policy proposals designed by the executive, and will hold the executive publicly accountable for what it does.

Given such an altered relationship with the legislature, the recommended strategy for presidential success that the current arrangements mandate can be modified. The president, freed from the need to commit all of his resources to the constant battle to gain congressional approval for every policy proposal that he makes, will be able to devote his attention and that of the various executive agencies to the quality of their proposals. No longer will ill-considered proposals need to be rushed to the Congress so that the president can take advantage of a brief period when he has the best chance to succeed. No longer will the president have to spend so much of his time bargaining with the Congress in order to gain congressional support for his initiatives. And no longer will presidents have to bargain away the managerial quality of the proposals that they make in order to generate a legislative majority. Although a president certainly will have to attend to the Congress and discuss seriously with the legislators what he proposes to do, such discussions will take place under a presumption that the legislature will approve most of what the president asks.

The argument for a representational system is built upon the reasoning that the executive has a capacity, which the legislature lacks, to make managerially sound public policy, whereas the legislature's special strength is its capacity to ensure that the policy-making process meets democratic criteria. Under current arrangements, neither the presidency nor the Congress has fully realized its individual institutional capacities; as a result, public policy that is managerially poor and democratically suspect too often characterizes the U.S. political system. A representational system holds out the possibility that the system can work better. To move to such a system, however, it is necessary to strengthen the ability of the presidency to make managerially sound public policy and the ability of the Congress to ensure that public policy meets democratic criteria. With these tasks accomplished, the presidency and the Congress, so carefully separated from each other by those who designed the Constitution, need to be reconnected in a manner that encourages a cooperative, action-oriented exercise of governmental power rather than the current stalemate-oriented system of mutual checks.

The first and in some respects the most difficult step toward securing these changes is to change the way Americans think about their political institutions. Political systems survive over the long term because their structure and performance match the expectations of their citizens. As these expectations change, a political system must adapt or else risk losing the allegiance of those who live under it. For one who decides to advocate and work for significant political change, it is important to understand the attitudes upon which the current institutional arrangements depend and to think about how these attitudes need to be altered so that the desired institutional change can occur. Little can be done to improve the operation of the U.S. political system until the public understands and changes its expectations about the respective roles of the president and the Congress, about how these two institutions should interact with each other, and also about the role of government in U.S. society.

REFORMING THE PRESIDENCY

Expectations

The American people have come to expect that their presidents can do anything, solve all problems, deal with all crises. These inflated expectations are largely the product of early socialization experiences: The president is the first political leader about whom children learn, often in a classroom with his picture and pictures of his most famous predecessors hanging on the wall, in close proximity to the American flag. Contemporary presidents are depicted as successors to certified heroes and martyrs: George Washington, Thomas Jefferson, Abraham Lincoln, Franklin Roosevelt, John Kennedy. And as these past presidencies retreat in time, they seem to take on added luster, with their virtues and accomplishments magnified and their failings and failures diminished. Monuments are erected to presidents, highways, schools, and children are named after them, and they are accorded the same respect that in other countries is reserved for hereditary monarchs.

As the nation lavishes this attention on the president, other components of the federal government—the Congress, the courts, the bureaucracy, the White House staff—recede in the political consciousness. By the third grade, most children can name the president, whereas they have only the vaguest notion of the other branches of government and those who populate it. For children, the federal government, the presidency, and the nation itself are virtually coterminous concepts. Actually, most people become somewhat more sophisticated and knowledgeable as they mature, but few completely shake off the effects of that initial overdose of presidentialism, and for many adults the presidency still remains their primary institutional link with the political system.[1]

The result of all of this is a presidency based on such an inflated set of expectations that no president could possibly fulfill them.[2] Therefore, reforming the presidency requires, first of all, lowering the public's expectations about presidents. Quite simply, more is expected from presidents than they can deliver under the current, or for that matter under alternative, constitutional arrangements. That last point is important: Even if they had more power, presidents could not meet the expectations. As it is now, the job is simply too large; making it larger will not help. Making the job more manageable can help, but only if people begin to think of the presidency in a collective rather than a singular sense, as part of a larger governmental apparatus. The president should be viewed as a single political actor connected with the rest of the executive branch and the Congress and sharing with these institutions and their incumbents the collective responsibility for governing.

Once people begin to think of the president in this collective manner, the representational model and its plan to enhance the president's capacity to control the policy-making process start to make sense. Shifting the policy-making burden from the **singular** president to the **collective** executive, along with reducing the expectations focused on the president himself, will make it more likely for the presidency, as the representational model promises, to be a source of managerially sound public policy. In short, a prerequisite to strengthening the capacity of the presidency to make good public policy is to lower the expectations about what the president acting alone can do.

Tinkering with the Presidency

The proposals most commonly advanced for reforming the presidency fall into three categories: those that would increase the power of the presidency, those that would restrict the power of the presidency, and those that would change the selection process to increase the likelihood that better presidents will be chosen.[3] Among the proposals aimed at strengthening the presidency are repeal of the Twenty-second Amendment limiting the president to two terms in office, giving the president the power to item-veto parts of legislation, especially appropriation bills, enhancing the president's capacity to control the bureaucracy, and various proposals that by changing the election calendar and strengthening political parties, would increase the likelihood that the president's party would also have a majority in the Congress. Also included in this category would be repeal of the War Powers Resolution and other measures that seem to place congressional restrictions on what presidents argue are their prerogatives.

Naturally, these proposals are opposed by those who view an overly strong presidency as a danger to the nation. They advocate steps that would strengthen the policy-making powers and prerogatives of the Congress and restrain the presidency. Such proposals seem to arise cyclically, typically after periods when presidents appear to have exercised extraordinary power. Thus, the Twenty-second Amendment was passed after Franklin Roosevelt had been elected president four times. The apparent abuses of presidential power during the administrations of Lyndon Johnson and Richard Nixon led directly to a series of reforms aimed at restricting the power of the presidency by increasing the power of the Congress. These measures include the War Powers Resolution, the more frequent and varied use of the legislative veto, the strengthened congressional budget process, the greatly enhanced legislative staff support, the increased attention to legislative oversight of the bureaucracy, and the quest for greater congressional access to intelligence data.[4]

As for the quality of the people who become president, it has been argued that the reformed nomination process—the long primary season, its lack of logical order, the expenses associated with it, its intricate and varied rules, and the disproportionate impact of the media—has scared away the best and the brightest, many of whom do not wish to subject themselves or their families to its physical, psychological, and political strains. It has been argued as well that what it takes to win the nomination struggle is not necessarily what it takes to be an effective president. Although certainly the rhetorical and organizational skills that lead to a successful presidential candidacy will contribute to a successful presidency, campaigns also tend to deemphasize policy knowledge and expertise as virtues either for the candidate or for his managers, elevating in their stead glitzy media skills. Thus, to the extent that presidents rely upon the people and skills that got them elected to help them govern, they are likely to govern poorly.[5]

Reform proposals aimed at the selection process usually focus on reversing or revising the democratizing reforms of the 1970s—instituting national or at least regional primaries to bring more order to the nomination season, restoring the role of the party organization to the nomination process, expanding government funding of campaigns, and facilitating access to the media.[6] And the perennial proposal to change the president's tenure to one six-year term in office, although it would do little to improve the current selection process, presumably would allow presidents, once elected, to accomplish more and better things by giving them more time and by eliminating the distorting impact that the prospective reelection campaign has on what they do during their first term in office.[7]

The problem with these various reform proposals is not that they are wrong or undesirable (although some may be) but rather that they lack a systemic perspective. In other words, they assume that the problem is solely with the presidency rather than with the U.S. political system. Thus, proposals for increasing the power of the presidency perpetuate the myth that the office would be able to work, in the sense that the president would be able to control the Congress and produce good public policy, if only he had more power. The argument of this book is that the presidency as currently conceived is impossible no matter who is there and that given the current constitution against government, no matter how much one tinkers with the relative balance of congressional and presidential power, good public policy is unachievable. Unless reform proposals speak to these systemic concerns, they amount to little more than adjusting a carburetor or changing the oil for a motor that is about to conk out.

Rethinking the Presidency

To do more than tinker, one must focus on the real problem—that the presidency is unable to deliver on the promise that executives will produce managerially sound public policy. One reason for this is that the presidency has separated itself from the rest of the executive, from the permanent bureaucracy over which it ostensibly presides. Within that bureaucracy reside the qualities that led us to the hypothesis that executives are the most likely source of managerially sound public policy. When too much emphasis is placed on the president as policymaker and too little on the executive as policymaker, the benefits of those executive qualities are lost. A second systemic reason for presidential failure is that the president comes to office with little in the way of a policy constituency. His proposals are very much his own; indeed, few members of Congress, even those in his own party, have any stake in them or any sense of responsibility for them.

As we have seen, presidents have come to view the bureaucracy as almost a hostile power, and they have responded to this perception by increasing the degree of centralization of executive-branch decisionmaking in the White House. Furthermore, they have combined this centralization strategy with an administrative strategy of putting presidential loyalists in charge of the bureaucracy, loyalists whose policy knowledge is often suspect. All of this serves to cut off the president from the expertise and personnel of the federal bureaucracy, resources that he absolutely must have if he is to be a source of managerially sound public policy.

Rather than separating themselves from the bureaucracy, presidents need to devise organizational strategies that allow them to utilize its resources. Presidents must seek mechanisms that allow them to exact a degree of responsiveness from the bureaucracy while at the same time making full use of the policy expertise that it offers. Such arrangements require a willingness upon the part of the president to defer to the expertise of the bureaucracy and a willingness upon the part of career civil servants to accept the political leadership of the president and his people. There is no surefire way to achieve this cooperative relationship between the presidency and the bureaucracy, but certainly the "bureaucracy as enemy approach" favored by recent presidents is not the way to do it.[8]

A second reason for presidential failure is the "partyless" process by which presidents are selected. Presidents today are nominated and elected very much on their own. Candidates raise their own funds, hire their own campaign staff, and take great pains to emphasize their own personal qualities and competencies. During their campaigns they convey no sense of the collective nature of government and of their need for people to govern with them. They give no hint—perhaps because they do not know—that they will need the support of the relatively permanent Congress and bureaucracy if they are to achieve any of the policy goals that they have outlined during their campaigns. As Lowi argued, U.S. presidential elections are very much a plebiscite focusing exclusively on the qualities of the competing candidates. For the winning candidate, his is very much a personal victory that leads inevitably to a personal presidency composed of himself and the small coterie of people who helped him to get elected.

The problem is that whereas a personal campaign, in this media age, can be highly successful, a personal presidency cannot succeed. In contrast, the collective responsibility that would come from a selection process that emphasized the president's connection with his party organization could well lead to a collective commitment to work for the success of the party's and the president's policy proposals. The current system of every person for him or herself, characterized by only episodic collaboration and cooperation between the president and his copartisans in the Congress and the state houses, could yield to a more consistently cooperative pattern of behavior. Such a presumption of support would make the president's job more manageable because he would not be going it alone. He would not have to work to develop a new constituency for everything he wanted to propose. Rather, his policy constituency would largely coincide with his electoral constituency. Such an arrangement would require the president to shelve his ego and to recognize that successful government must be collective government in which partisan support is earned by appropriate deference to the collective wisdom of one's partisans. And with the party and the president connected in such a manner, it is possible that more experienced and perhaps more capable presidential candidates will emerge, candidates whose association with national policy and politics extends back further than the primary season.

To recapitulate, a reformed presidency must be more firmly integrated with the administrative apparatus of the state and with the political apparatus of his party than is currently the case. In any event, presidents will have a difficult time succeeding, perhaps because no matter how hard the people work at it, they will probably continue to expect too much of presidents. However, presidents who are brought to Washington by a personal campaign and who arrive with little understanding and often a great deal of hostility toward the more permanent government must fail, no matter how the selection process or the length of the presidential term is changed or how the relative balance of presidential and congressional powers is altered.

REFORMING THE CONGRESS

Expectations

Most Americans assume that the main job of the Congress is to make laws. This activity is the focus of press discussions of congressional doings, and it is the activity that is most likely to be emphasized when, much later than they learn about the presidency, children first learn about the Congress. At that point in their education, they will encounter the "How a bill becomes a law" diagram, complete with cartoon-character legislators and arrows showing the course that a bill follows through the Congress from the time that it is introduced until the time that it is presented to the president for his signature.

The problem with this lawmaking expectation is not that it is incorrect—the Congress does indeed make laws—but that lawmaking is neither the only function of the Congress nor the one that it performs best. We have noted that members of Congress devote a great deal of their time and resources to their representational as compared with their policy-making responsibilities—in other words, to responding to the demands of their constituents. Moreover, legislators tend to view national policy proposals from a local perspective, asking, before anything else, how the proposal will affect the various interests that they represent.

Our earlier discussion suggested that this primary concern that legislators have for their constituencies detracts significantly from their capacity to make managerially sound public policy decisions. However, this consequence does not mean that legislators are wrong when they are being responsive to their constituencies. On the contrary, legislators should be concerned with representing their constituencies and should devote their resources to that task—one that they are able to perform well—rather than to the tasks associated with public policymaking, tasks that they are typically unable to perform well. What Americans need to do is to shift their expectations concerning the role of the Congress from those that emphasize its role as an initiator and designer of public policy to those that emphasize its role as a representative body.

Actually, public expectations concerning the Congress may be somewhat more congruent with the representational model than the expectations of political leaders. Although the mass public undoubtedly believes that Congress should make laws, the evidence is clear that the primary expectation that citizens have of their individual legislators is that they attend to the interests of the constituency. Citizens evaluate their individual legislators on the basis of how they perform these representational activities and these evaluations are in turn major factors in determining how people vote in congressional elections. It is also true that Americans expect the Congress as a whole (as compared with their individual legislators) to make good public policy, and they do not think that the Congress does a particularly good job in this respect. But most important, they do not evaluate their individual legislators in terms of their perception of how well or how poorly the Congress as a whole is performing.[9]

At the elite level, however, the story is very different. Simply put, although members of Congress recognize the importance of their representational responsibilities, they are still convinced that making public policy is their primary job.[10] Legislators regularly initiate, consider, and sometimes pass reform proposals that their designers claim will help the Congress regain policy-making powers that it has lost to the executive and that will enhance the institution's capacity to exercise these powers. This tendency was in evidence most recently during the 1970s, when Congress placed various new restrictions on the president while at the same time it sought to improve its own collective level of policy expertise by increasing its own staff support and proliferating specialized subcommittees. Thus, although the general public may have given up on the Congress as a source of good public policy, the legislators themselves do not seem to have given up. Unfortunately, the steps that they have taken, while partially successful in helping the Congress to achieve a more prominent role in the policy-making process relative to the president, have not been at all successful in helping the Congress to make better public policy.[11]

The recent history of congressional reform efforts and the theoretical analysis of the policy-making capacities of legislatures argue that this quest for a structure that will enable Congress to make better public policies is in the end futile. Instead, the role of the legislature needs to be reconsidered. That is, members of Congress must come to accept what the American people seem to have already at least tacitly accepted— that the Congress should be a representational rather than an activist legislature.

The Congress as a representational legislature would not design public policy, but it would continue to affect it. First, a representational Congress would engage in open debate on the issues of the day. Assuming that such debates are publicized and that the Congress can claim to be broadly representative of public opinion, the executive will ignore at its peril what is said in the legislature. Congress will become, metaphorically, a lens, the function of which is to reflect and intensify public opinion on policy issues. The prospect of an adverse congressional reaction to its policy proposals may dissuade the executive from going ahead or at least persuade the executive to pause and reconsider, even if the authority or the votes to win are available. Or legislative debate may prod the executive into action in areas where left to its own devices, it might choose not to act. Moreover, legislative discussion, if taken seriously by the executive, can improve the managerial quality of public policy. As the views and opinions abroad in the land are articulated in the legislature, the information base upon which the executive acts can be improved and a clearer conception of the public interest developed. By way of summary, it would be easy but incorrect to conclude that a legislature that seldom says no to the executive has little influence on public policy. Debate in a representational legislature, far from being "just talk," can inform executive action and can establish the boundaries within which the executive is free to act.

A representational Congress also would take responsibility for over-seeing the executive. Aggressive oversight activities can enhance public policy from a managerial standpoint by generating information about how policy is working and about how it might be revised to make it more effective. From a democratic perspective, the dangers of unbridled executive power are clear, and reforms that advocate an even stronger policy-making role for the executive are, in this respect, very risky. Protections against abuse of power by the executive are therefore a high priority for the representational model and are provided by vesting in the legislature the unquestioned authority to require the executive to account publicly for what it does.

Finally, in the sense that legislators convey the problems of individual constituents to the bureaucracy and seek to resolve them, all legislatures link citizens with political elites. The provision of this "service repre-sentation," as well as lobbying on behalf of the constituency as a whole for its fair share of distributional programs, is a nearly universal legislative function, the performance of which injects an important element of democratic responsiveness into the policy-making process.[12] The executive responds to these requests not only because it wishes to remain on good terms with the legislature but also because of its own interest in generating mass support for its policies. In activist legislatures, members devote a great deal of their own and their staff's time to these service chores, but such activities are viewed as less legitimate than, and coming at the expense of, the legislature's policy-making activities. In representational legislatures, this linkage role is recognized as a principal legislative function.

Thus, a Congress organized in accord with the representational model would not be viewed as the incubator and designer of public policy— something that it does poorly—but instead as a body that would publicly discuss policy problems and potential solutions, aggressively oversee the executive as it develops and implements public policy, continuously hold the executive to account for its actions, and through its members, represent to the executive the needs of individual constituents, the interests of the constituency as a whole, and collectively, the opinions of the nation at large. A Congress so conceived would be doing what legislatures do well—ensuring the democratic nature of the public policy process.

Congressional Reform and Interest Groups

Proposals for reforming the Congress should be directed toward enhancing the institution's capacity to ensure that public policy meets democratic criteria. The single factor that most diminishes Congress's capacity to accomplish this goal is the intimate relationship between its members and moneyed interests. Members of Congress are heavily dependent upon interest groups for funds to finance their election campaigns, and even legislators who are unopposed for reelection receive sizable campaign donations. For incumbent legislators, campaign fundraising is no longer restricted to the months before an election but rather is an activity that continues throughout their term. In addition, under the rules of the Congress, members are permitted to receive honoraria (up to 30 percent of their annual salary for members of the House, 40 percent for Senators), along with travel expenses for attending and speaking at interest group–sponsored "seminars" or meetings. Whereas legislators argue, often persuasively, that their votes cannot be purchased either by these "perks" or by campaign contributions, there is no argument that the effect of these arrangements at a minimum is to facilitate access to legislators and to the legislative process for organizations that have funds. Groups without funds, including disorganized interests such as consumers or the poor, are in contrast at a marked disadvantage.

Among the factors fostering the dependence of legislators on interest groups is the weakened state of U.S. political parties and the highly decentralized nature of congressional elections. Like presidents, members of Congress are elected largely on their own: They raise their own funds, hire their own staff, develop their own campaign organizations, and establish independent relationships with the constituencies and interest groups that get them to the Congress and keep them there.

The tie between legislators and moneyed interests can be broken by two simple reforms. First, legislative campaigns should be financed with public funds, with candidates barred from receiving any contributions from private sources. Second, legislative salaries should be raised substantially, and legislators should not be permitted to receive additional stipends, or honoraria, or salaries from outside groups or business activities. As an alternative to public funding, the role of party organizations in legislative campaigns could be strengthened, with the party's receiving campaign contributions and then disbursing them to candidates.[13] Moneyed interests would enjoy preferred access to party organizations, but such a reform would diminish group influence over individual legislators. As for raising congressional salaries, this has proven to be a politically difficult step to take because members of Congress would have to vote to raise their own salaries. Congress tried the commission approach to this issue but even that failed. In February 1989, a fierce public outcry forced the Congress to reject a proposal by the Quadrennial Commission—a blue ribbon panel that is supposed to meet every four years to make recommendations on salary increases for top federal officials—to raise congressional salaries by 51 percent. Even a provision in the proposal that would have required members to forgo honoraria from outside groups in return for the salary increase did not provide sufficient political cover for members confronted by enraged constituents focusing on what appeared to be an overly large pay raise. Although this proposal failed, it is still important to recognize that if the connection between moneyed interest groups and members of Congress can be severed or at least made more tenuous, the likelihood of members of Congress acting in a manner that enhances the democratic nature of public policy will be increased.

The Distribution of Power in the Congress

Power in the Congress is extremely fragmented. Reforms that would achieve greater centralization of power are often advocated as a way to enhance the Congress's policy-making capabilities, but they are also important steps to take if the legislature is to perform the activities associated with a representational model. The power of representational legislatures to say yes or no to the executive must be exercised in a timely and responsible manner. Currently, the Congress can ignore presidential requests entirely or subject them to prolonged delay. If the Congress is organized in such a way that minorities may prevail over majorities through the capacity of the former to influence small groups of legislators sitting on key committees or through devices (in the Senate) such as the filibuster and various other dilatory methods for prolonging debate, the Congress will not be able to fulfill its democratic function. Power in Congress needs to be more centralized and less dispersed, not because such changes will enable the legislature to make better public policies, but so that the Congress will not be able, by its inaction or by undue deference to minority wishes, to prevent a reformed presidency from doing so.

The solution to the organizational problems of Congress lies with strengthened legislative parties. Just as presidents need to be more closely connected with their political parties, members of Congress must be more closely connected with theirs. Although there is evidence that political parties are becoming somewhat more prominent in the politics of the Congress, there is also evidence of their continuing weaknesses. In the House, the Democrats have increased the power of the speaker so that he is now able to control the Rules Committee, strongly influence the Steering and Policy Committee's decisions about committee assignments, and on occasion, set up ad hoc committees to handle specific bills. In addition, the Democratic party caucus assumed the right to vote on committee chairmanships and instituted various rules that increased the power of the party members on the committees at the expense of committee chairs. Nevertheless, the caucus is often at odds with the party leadership and exercises very little influence over substantive policy decisions, usually deferring to the committees and subcommittees. And whatever tentative movement there has been toward greater party influence in the House has not been reflected at all in the Senate. There, "rampant individualism" is as strong as it has ever been, with each senator willing and able to use the rules of the body to advance his or her own personal policy agenda, even when that is at odds with the wishes of party leaders.[14]

There is no mystery to what needs to be done to strengthen party leadership in the Congress. The caucuses must achieve a strong voice in substantive policy matters, and in the Senate, procedural rules that can be manipulated by small minorities to frustrate majorities and prevent action need to be changed. Campaign finance reforms that will strengthen the role of political parties and reduce the role of interest groups will also reduce the independence of representatives and senators from their legislative party leaders. The problem, of course, is how to get legislators to approve steps such as these that in essence ask them to surrender a great deal of their individual power and prerogatives in order to increase the effectiveness of the Congress as a whole.

Oversight of the Executive

One of the primary responsibilities of a representational legislature is oversight of the executive branch, a task to which the Congress currently devotes much time, but with uneven success. The size of the executive in terms of money, people, information, and programs helps to make congressional oversight activities a hit-or-miss operation. Furthermore, oversight continues to be one of the grubby chores of Congress, usually far removed from public view and often unrelated in any direct way to either the reelection or policy concerns of legislators. Either they are loath to undertake such responsibilities, or when they do, they pick occasions when their constituency interests or their pet programs are directly involved or when a scandal in the executive branch promises favorable publicity to those legislators doing the investigating. Seldom are legislators motivated in their oversight activities simply by a desire to review systematically the effectiveness and efficiency of a federal progam. But it is also argued that when a congressional committee or subcommittee does involve itself in overseeing a specific program, its efforts can amount to micromanagement. As legislators attempt to specify the details of administrative decisions that should necessarily be matters of executive discretion, they may cross the admittedly ambiguous line between "constructive oversight and irresponsible intervention."[15]

Whether congressional oversight activities are generally constructive or irresponsible, there is no doubt that the process is, for administrators, extraordinarily repetitive and time consuming. As policy has become more complex, what any one agency is doing may be relevant to the jurisdictions of a number of congressional subcommittees each of which feels it has the right to summon and hear from a representative of the agency involved. Therefore, at any one time, duplicative oversight hearings may be going on in several committees and subcommittees, in both chambers of the Congress, and top-level administrators will find themselves spending a great deal of their time at the Capitol telling essentially the same story to different groups of legislators.

There are no easy ways to improve the oversight process. Legislators are generalists concerned with their representational activities, whereas administrators are specialists concerned with the policy areas for which they are responsible, and to some extent, never the twain shall meet. But under current arrangements, it is not at all clear to legislators where oversight "fits": as an extension of their policy-making prerogatives, as a part of their representational activities, or as simply a dreary and unimportant governmental housekeeping task that all but the truly masochistic probably avoid. Under the representational model, however, oversight is a core legislative responsibility because the legislature is charged with holding the executive to a public accounting of its actions. As the responsibilities of the legislature and the executive are redefined to conform with the representational model, it may be possible to draw with greater precision the boundary between appropriate legislative concerns and the micromanagement of the bureaucracy.

Oversight also would be improved if steps were taken toward greater centralization of congressional power, especially if these steps resulted in some consolidation of oversight responsibilities. One study found that in 1983, Pentagon officials spent 1,453 hours testifying before ninety-one congressional committees and subcommittees.[16] If all of this meant more effective oversight, it might well be worth the time and effort spent. But as matters now stand, what is everyone's job is in fact no one's job. As administrators rush from one committee meeting to another, they find themselves on the receiving end of conflicting advice and instructions from different members of Congress. Paradoxically, all of that advice may provide administrators with more rather than less latitude for action because they can always justify what they have done by pointing to some suggestion voiced by at least one of the various congressional groups with which they have met. All the time that those Pentagon officials spent on Capitol Hill in 1983, and in the years before and since, did not prevent, and may well have contributed to, the major weapons procurement scandal that broke during summer 1988. With greater centralization of oversight responsibilities, administrators would be spared the necessity of doing repeat performances for different audiences as well as responding to the conflicting comments and suggestions that arise in each forum. Congress in turn would be able to speak to the executive more coherently and would be in a better position to monitor the executive's responses to the issues raised during the oversight process.

JOINING THE CONGRESS WITH THE PRESIDENCY

Separation of Powers

Part of the folklore taught in civics classes deals with the importance of separation of powers to the U.S. political system. Like other examples of folklore, however, there is much that is misleading about that term. The Constitution, as we have discovered, separated institutions and required that they share governmental powers, an arrangement that remains today the cornerstone of the constitution against government.

If the constitution against government is to become a constitution that facilitates government, this system of institutional separation and mutual checks needs to be modified. The problem is that this notion of separation—whether correctly conceived as separate institutions or incorrectly as separation of powers—has become part of the public's expectations about government. Mass publics probably have only the vaguest sense of what separation of powers actually means, but they have been socialized to the slogan and are likely to support the principle if they are told that it is threatened. Certainly, the public has seemed willing to accept presidential arguments that the executive needs to maintain its independence from congressional interference, while presidents seem to have taken it as an unwritten part of their oath of office that they must at all costs protect the independence and power of their office against every threat, real or imagined, from the Congress. Similarly, the incessant preoccupation of the Congress with its own institutional prerogatives and powers suggests its collective commitment to resist presidential encroachments. And in recent years, the Supreme Court has become quite finicky about the issue of institutional separation, rejecting as threats to this principle both the legislative veto and the Gramm-Rudman automatic budget-balancing mechanism.

If the president and the Congress are to work together to make good public policy, these expectations need to be altered and the two institutions must be brought together. Today, contact between the president and the Congress is largely voluntary. The president need not meet with members of the Congress and the Congress need not meet with the president. Constitutionally, each institution is free to go its own way until the policy plans of one require the approval of the other. Even then, communication need be no more personal than the president's sending a written message to the Congress or the Congress conveying an enrolled bill to the president. If under a representational model, the executive were to have a more dominant policy-making role and the Congress were to have the job of ensuring the responsiveness and accountability of the executive, then the president would have to interact regularly and publicly with the Congress as a whole rather than sporadically and privately with individual members on those occasions when it pleases him to do so. Means need to be found to require a continuous dialogue between the Congress and the president. Means need to be found to require the president to account to the Congress for his actions. And means need to be found to require the Congress to account for its actions, particularly when it refuses to follow the lead of the president.

Joining the President with the Congress

The set of reforms typically advocated to bridge the gap between the president and the Congress would move the U.S. political system toward a parliamentary version of the representational model. In such systems, the political leaders of the executive branch are simultaneously members of the legislature and serve in their executive capacities as long as they can command the support of a legislative majority. Such legislative majorities are usually generated by unified and disciplined political parties.[17]

It is not at all clear, however, that the U.S. political system needs to be converted to a parliamentary system in order to rectify the problems that have been identified. It is possible that more modest and therefore more feasible changes could be made that would accomplish the same goals. For example, many have advocated a more responsible political party system for the United States.[18] Such a system seeks a cooperative legislative-executive relationship premised upon the shared membership of the president and a majority of the Congress in a national political party much more prominent and stronger than the current U.S. political parties. Policy goals would be determined within the party, and candidates for Congress as well as presidential candidates would run for office committed to support those policies if elected. The president and the Congress would cooperate on public policy because of their joint commitment to their party's success. This plan also would strengthen the presidency because the policy options that the president would be pursuing would be collective party policies and not just his own preferences.

The structural changes that most need to be implemented would require the president and the Congress to interact with each other. Specifically, the president should be required to come to the Congress regularly and in person to discuss with its members the issues of the day and what he and his colleagues in the executive propose to do about them. He also should be ready on such occasions to respond to questions and criticisms about the governmental programs for which he is responsible. Such a procedure comparable to the question period used in many parliamentary systems, should be adopted in the United States, not to create a parliamentary system here, but rather to provide a mechanism for executive accountability.[19]

The weakness of mechanisms for public accounting is one of the great failings of the U.S. constitutional system and one of the factors that make any thinking person reluctant to place additional power in the hands of the presidency. Presidents, as long as they can choose when and under what terms they meet and answer questions from people who are not in their employ, have numerous opportunities to abuse power. However, if a president is required to meet regularly with the Congress and to defend his policies in the face of hostile questions from his political opponents, his tendency to abuse power will be reduced. The inadequacy of the current mechanisms for holding presidents accountable no doubt contributed to the imperial episodes of the Nixon and Reagan administrations. If Nixon had not been able to hunker down in the White House, waiting for the Watergate scandal to blow over, but instead had been required to appear regularly in the Congress to respond publicly to the various allegations against him, that long national nightmare (as President Ford characterized it) would have been a good deal briefer. Similarly, had Reagan not been able to pick the occasions and forums in which to respond to the Iran-Contra scandal, it would not have been possible for him to escape that episode as relatively unscathed as he did.

Public accounting is not simply a mechanism for guarding against the possible imperial tendencies of presidents. In the normal course of events, a president should be required to explain and justify his policies before those who have an incentive to subject him to tough questions. Otherwise, all the country has is the president's own rendition of the facts, a version that inevitably will be self-serving and will remain so unless it is directly questioned. After the marine barracks in Lebanon were attacked and 241 marines were killed, President Reagan simply announced to reporters that he took full responsibility for the deaths. After that announcement, however, he never discussed the incident again. It is one thing to accept responsibility at a brief meeting with the press and quite another to assume responsibility before the Congress and then deal with questions about what happened, why it happened, and its implications for the administration's Middle East policy. That, rather than a staged confession, is what public accountability is all about.

The concept of public accountability should be mutual, applying to the Congress as well as to the president. Just as presidents should respond to congressional critics, these critics also should be required to account publicly for their opposition to the president. Just as the president should have to explain why he acted as he did, it should be incumbent on his congressional critics to make clear the reasons for their opposition. Just saying no to the president should not be sufficient.

A prerequisite to a system of mutual accountability is mutual access to information. In discussions with the Congress, the president is often at an advantage, or at least claims to be so, by virtue of the superior information at his disposal, particularly in regard to foreign and military affairs. Means need to be found to make the same information that is available to the president available to the Congress. In most matters, this should present no practical problems, although the constitutional issue of executive privilege may have to be reviewed. However, in foreign and defense matters, there is a legitimate question of secrecy that needs to be considered.[20]

The premise upon which any discussion of governmental secrecy must be based is that the very idea is antithetical to democratic principles. Any system that is committed to popular control of political decisions and to the public accountability of its leaders must opt for the most widespread dissemination of information. But one can think of information that for good and proper reasons of national security should be kept confidential, information concerning, for example, troop movements during wartime or negotiating positions during arms control discussions. The problem is that under current procedures the power to decide what information should be kept confidential is exercised solely by executive branch personnel who are ultimately responsible to the president. Given such arrangements, there is a strong temptation to declare information secret because of its implications for the *political* security of the president and his people rather than its implications for the *national* security of the United States and its people. Surely, nearly everyone knew that the Reagan administration, despite a congressional ban, was funding the contras—everyone, that is, except the Congress and the American people. Certainly, the supposed enemies—the Sandinistas, the Cubans, and the Russians—knew. As Colonel North testified, the goal from the beginning was to keep the Congress in the dark, and the reasons were obvious and obviously undemocratic. If the Congress and the American people had known what was going on, they might have put a stop to it. Not telling them effectively guarded against the exercise of this democratic principle.

The president and the Congress must design a mechanism for sharing the power to decide what should and should not be kept secret. One possibility is the creation of a committee composed of representatives of the president and a group of legislators from both parties. If the president wished to withhold information, he would have to convince this group that there were legitimate national security reasons to do so. It is clear that reasonable people could be convinced by arguments that were strong enough. If the president failed to convince them, the information would become public. The burden would be on the president to demonstrate why the information should be withheld, and the presumption of the group would be that information should be made public. However, in order for such a system to work, the president must share everything with this group, and there are no safeguards that could guarantee that.

Again, the Iran-Contra affair provides an instructive illustration. In 1980, legislation was passed requiring the executive branch to keep the

House and Senate Intelligence committees "fully and currently informed" of all intelligence activities. If the president determined that because of "extraordinary circumstances" prior notice to these committees of a covert operation was not a good idea, he could restrict such notification to a group of eight legislators, including the party leaders of both chambers and the chairs and ranking minority members of both intelligence committees. Even then, he would be required to report these actions in "a timely fashion" to the full committees.[21] However, as the Iran-Contra hearings revealed, President Reagan decided to ignore these procedures when he undertook the various covert operations associated with this affair. This case suggests that no matter what arrangements on information the Congress makes with the president, there is no guarantee, other than the good will of those involved, that the process will work.

THE ROLE OF GOVERNMENT

There is one final set of expectations and reforms that are, in a certain sense, prerequisite to those that we have discussed. Before considering reforming the institutions that make public policy in this country, we need to explore a prior question: What role should government assume?

Expectations

The constitution against government reflects the Founders' ambivalent view of government, their sense of both its promise and its dangers. This ambivalence did not disappear with the men who gathered in Philadelphia two hundred years ago. Rather, uncertainty and debate about the appropriate role of government has been a constant theme of U.S. history.

At the heart of the debate has been the concept of individualism, a concept deeply rooted in the colonial experience and U.S. political ideology. Cut off from the established and hierarchical societies of Europe and very much alone on the frontier, the new Americans came to believe that they could accomplish much on their own. The democratic character of American society also played a role, as Alexis de Tocqueville observed. In democracies, he said, people feel that they "owe nothing to any man, they expect nothing from any man; they acquire the habit of always considering themselves as standing alone; and they are apt to imagine that their destiny is in their own hands."[22] This individualistic ideology carries with it, of course, a natural antipathy toward collective action— in a word, government.

The circumstances of the American Revolution did little to elevate the reputation of government. In Tocqueville's memorable phrase, the Americans "arrived at a state of democracy without having to endure a democratic revolution . . . they are born equal instead of becoming so."[23] Because they did not need to organize a revolutionary movement to overthrow a feudal system of government, as the French were required to do, the Americans came to nationhood with no driving sense of ideology, no need to create a new society, and no agenda for collective governmental action. Quite the reverse, in fact. For the Americans, government itself, in the form of the British king and the surrogates through whom he ruled the colonies, was the enemy. If there was a political ideology in the American Revolution, it was embodied in Jefferson's Declaration of Independence, in its glittering introductory phrases identifying natural rights that were outside the purview of government, and in the lengthy and legalistic indictment of the abuses of government power by the Crown, which constitutes the bulk of the document.

The constitutional design of a national government with carefully enumerated powers that it would have a great deal of difficulty exercising was a response to this guarded attitude toward government, an attitude rooted on the one hand in the Founders' fear that anarchy would result from too little government and on the other in the individualistic political culture and the legalistic and ultimately antigovernmental revolution. Moreover, with the rise of capitalism, these latter forces were buttressed by a compatible economic ideology. Throughout the nineteenth century, while governments in Europe were expanding their social services to the working class in the face of rising demands from left-wing political parties, similar demands for a larger economic and social role for the U.S. government were resisted with the argument that in an economic system committed to free enterprise, these matters were not appropriate for public policymaking. In the same manner, the view that government should stand on the side of the public interest as against private interests, though really at one with the noblest hopes of the Founders, was not easily accepted. Not until the Populist Era of the late nineteenth century and the Progressive Era of the early twentieth century did the notion of government as a source of collective action in the public interest begin to take hold in the United States. Not until then did it become accepted that the government should foster business competition through antitrust policies, conserve forests against the profit-motivated claims of industry, and protect children from early enslavement in factories and mills. And it was not until the New Deal that an even broader governmental role in such diverse matters as income security, agriculture, securities trading, labor negotiations, and industrial practices came to be accepted.

Thus, the role of the federal government increased slowly and in a piecemeal manner, unencumbered, but also unsupported, by a carefully thought-out ideology. The most dramatic expansion of government's role came in response to the crisis of the Great Depression, but even then there was no new philosophy of what the proper role of the government should be. Historian Richard Hofstadter summarized the New Deal as "a series of improvisations, many adopted very suddenly, many contradictory. Such unity as it had was in political strategy, not in economics."[24] Thus, government expanded but did so without an ideology to legitimize that expansion and with most Americans still committed, in principle at least, to the notions of limited government and free enterprise.

In the 1960s, Lloyd Free and Hadley Cantril presented survey data that showed the effect of this peculiar course of political development on the attitudes of Americans. Free and Cantril found that antigovernment conservatism and progovernment liberalism coexist in the U.S. political psyche. Americans manifest what Free and Cantril called "ideological conservatism" by their support for "individual initiative" rather than "governmental welfare programs," by their skepticism about the idea that social problems can be solved by the government, and by their belief that the federal government wrongly interferes with state and local governments. However, they manifest their "operational liberalism" by their support for federal aid to education, national health insurance, public housing, and federal job and antipoverty programs.[25] Similarly, during the 1980s many Americans, while agreeing with Ronald Reagan's strong condemnation of federal government activism, also indicated strong support for a broad federal role in a whole range of domestic policy areas.[26] But the ideological base for big government remains quite narrow, and therefore when the legitimacy of government actions comes under attack, as it did during the Reagan years, proponents of national government policies are at a loss to defend themselves. The cultural, ideological, and historical high ground in the debate continues to be occupied by those who believe that when all is said and done, government is ultimately the enemy.

Therefore, before proposals for reforming the constitutional system can receive serious consideration, the American people have to become clearer about what they expect from government. A constitution against government makes sense if the people believe that government action should always be suspect. If, however, they believe that government is legitimate, that government has important functions that need to be carried out, that it is better for government to act, even if it must risk acting unwisely, than not to act at all, then it is necessary to rethink U.S. constitutional arrangements and the stalemated political processes toward which they are disposed.

Barriers to Change

Such a reconsideration and redefinition of the public's view of government will not be easy to undertake. Cultural imperatives die hard. As we observed in Chapter 5, trust and confidence in national political institutions and their leaders is as low as it has ever been. Ironically, although much of this distrust seems to have been engendered by the failure of government to act effectively,[27] reforms aimed at enhancing the capacity of government to act are likely to be resisted by those who, because of its failures, have come to distrust government the most. Also, the heterogeneity of the American people, the great geographical expanse of the nation, the multiple and broadly disparate individual interests, all support a bias against the federal government. Until some broadly accepted notion of a general public interest emerges, it will be difficult to assuage the fears of those whose concerns about public policy extend only as far as their immediate self-interest. A renewed concept of a public interest is, in turn, a prerequisite to the development of a new set of expectations about what the proper role of government should be.

Capitalism remains part of the problem. At the cultural level, there is a tension between the self-interested behavior promoted by advocates of the free enterprise system and the concept of community or collective action in the public interest. Politically, business interests, allowed to do essentially as they please in a system where government acts reluctantly, if at all, have been especially advantaged by the current arrangement of institutional power sharing. The fact that so many independent actors need to agree before action can be taken increases the likelihood that those who benefit from current public policy, or the lack thereof, can stop actions that could curtail their benefits. New arrangements designed to facilitate government action would threaten this strategic position and would therefore be resisted by established groups. Although the moneyed interests represented at the Constitutional Convention viewed a stronger national government as advantageous to them, today those interests often find that their resources are even more effective when deployed against relatively weaker local and state governments.

Change

Given the historical, cultural, and economic forces supporting the current conception of government, there is no easy or obvious path to change. As a first step, however, it is important that candidates for public office cease their own antigovernment campaigns. A key message of Jimmy Carter's 1976 presidential campaign and both of Ronald Reagan's successful campaigns was that the government in Washington was what was wrong with the nation and that they, as outsiders, would be best equipped to clean things up. In taking this approach, presidential candidates have followed the lead of members of Congress, many of whom when in their constituencies, deflect criticism from themselves personally by being extraordinarily critical of the Congress as an institution.[28] And of course, criticism of the "pointy headed bureaucrats in Washington" is a staple of virtually every campaign, congressional and presidential alike. Added to all of this is the special contribution of the Reagan years—campaigns that do little more than pander to the electorate's antipathy toward taxes. Candidates now fall over each other in their mad rush to see who can make the most iron-clad pledge to avoid raising taxes. Of course, although this approach often makes good sense electorally, it often makes poor sense economically, and from the perspective of community and government, it is absolutely disastrous because it reinforces the notion that government is the enemy, this time because it takes away your hard-earned money.

If candidates were exclusively antigovernment in their approach, it would be bad enough. But what is worse is that candidates mix antigovernment and antitax rhetoric with promises to support to the hilt the government programs and expenditures that are close to the hearts of those to whom they happen to be speaking at the time. The notion, simply conveyed, is that people in the audience are entitled to the particular services and protections that they value, which should be paid for with someone else's money, and that when these services do not arrive, it is because someone in Washington (never the speaker in question) is doing a lousy job. No wonder public cynicism about government is at record levels and the public view that government is the enemy persists and even thrives.

The remedy, easier stated than implemented, is that the ideals of citizenship need to be retaught—to the American people and to their leaders as well. The latter need to learn what the Founders knew instinctively—that there is virtue to the notion that people should convert a portion of their individual resources to public resources so that the collective good can be achieved. Political leaders need to summon the courage to tell citizens that government does more good than bad, perhaps by describing what life would be like without government: elderly people with no income or medical care, rapacious industries polluting the environment, workers without the right to organize trade unions, farmers left to the vagaries of weather and foreign markets, the hard-earned savings of average Americans deposited in uninsured banks, and the rights of private citizens left to the tender mercies of local police forces. The exact form that this picture takes is not important. It only needs to be vivid enough to counter the phony images evoked by Ronald Reagan and his cohorts of an idyllic America before big government. Once that picture is painted, political leaders need to break the news, as directly as they can, that the good things that government does have a price that must be paid. If all of this succeeds—a big if— then political leaders face another crucial challenge. They need to make good public policies so that citizens will recognize, with Oliver Wendell Holmes, that with their taxes they do indeed buy civilization. And to do that, U.S. policy-making arrangements, as I have argued, need to be changed.

CONCLUDING THOUGHTS

What I am proposing for the U.S. political system is a representational system in which the executive, because of its capacity to generate managerially sound public policy, has a disproportionate say about the shape of public policy while the legislature, because of its capacity to guarantee good public policy judged by democratic standards, has the responsibility of articulating public concerns, overseeing the executive, and holding it to account for its actions. In order for the presidency to take this leading policy-making role, it must develop a more collective nature, drawing upon the administrative resources of the bureaucracy and the political resources of a reinvigorated national political party. In order for the Congress to play its representational role, it must sever its ties with moneyed interest groups and undertake internal reforms that are aimed at creating a greater degree of order and coherence in its procedures and a more intense focus on its representational and executive oversight functions. Finally, for the system to work, the institutional separation between the president and the Congress must be abandoned in favor of a relationship based on continuing dialogue and mutual accountability.

There are substantial barriers to institutional changes of the sort that I have advocated. Americans are not a people given to changing their political institutions; those changes that have taken place throughout U.S. history have been largely the products of a long-term evolutionary process. The policy problems that we have discussed in this book, while serious, are for the most part invisible to mass publics. A variety of political, cultural, and historical factors lead most Americans to conclude that although they might have certain specific political grievances or they might see particular failings in the society at large, basically, things seem to be going along fairly well. With no immediate and visible crisis, Americans will continue to be reluctant, and understandably so, to endorse fundamental changes in the way the political system operates, especially changes that might require amending the Constitution. And even if they were persuaded that constitutional change was a good idea, the process for achieving it would be extraordinarily cumbersome. So delicate were the compromises that the men of Philadelphia entered into, so complex were their arrangements, and so great were the stakes for the individual states that once they completed their work, they built into the Constitution an amending procedure that would be very difficult to use. Moreover, on those occasions when it has been used, none of the changes, save the Twenty-second Amendment, had any effect on the power of either the president or the Congress.

Given the procedural difficulties of securing amendments to the Constitution, those interested in constitutional change would probably be best advised to direct their efforts toward changing the amending process itself. As James Sundquist pointed out, under the current procedures a constitutional amendment can be defeated by the negative votes of as few as thirteen of the ninety-nine state legislative chambers. In addition, seven states require extraordinary state legislative majorities for the ratification of constitutional amendments, thereby making it possible for an even smaller minority of individual state legislators to block a proposed amendment. No other country in the world and, indeed, no state in the United States has such a difficult process for amending its constitution.[29] The ultimate component, then, of the constitution against government is the virtual impossibility of altering it.

Whereas many of the reforms that I have suggested raise no constitutional questions, others, particularly the accountability procedures, will. It is not clear that requiring the president to appear in the Congress and to participate in its debates would be contrary to the words of the Constitution, but it is likely that contemporary constitutional law would view such a procedure as unacceptable. Other reforms discussed would require more easily achieved statutory changes. For example, steps that would more closely integrate the presidency with the federal bureaucracy could be accomplished in part by executive order and in part by acts of Congress. Although the results would not be so dramatic as they might if constitutional changes such as electing the president and the Congress on the same ticket were enacted, strengthening the role of political parties in the process of presidential selection could be accomplished simply by changing party rules and certain state laws. Congressional campaign reforms that would restrict the role of interest groups and establish a system of public financing, as well as other steps that would reduce the impact of interest groups on the legislative process, also are, for the most part, matters of legal rather than constitutional change.

Many of the proposals that I have suggested require neither statutory nor constitutional changes. Reducing the degree to which power in the Congress is fragmented, as well as strengthening the structure and procedures for overseeing the executive, can be accomplished simply by changing the internal rules of the Congress. The major changes in the relative powers of the Congress and the presidency that I have advocated can take place if political leaders and the public are willing to alter their expectations about how these institutions should operate. No constitutional or statutory changes are required for the Congress to defer to the policy leadership of the president or for the Congress to alter the way in which its members view their responsibilities. It certainly will not be easy for the Congress and the president to arrive at this new understanding about their mutual policy-making responsibilities. For this to happen, legislators and presidents alike would have to be willing to discuss and negotiate some of their most cherished institutional prerogatives.

James Sundquist suggested that a prerequisite to such a discussion is a renewed sense of "comity within the system,"[30] of mutual trust derived from a mutual commitment to a larger national purpose. As trite as that might sound, without such comity, institutional change simply will not go forward. Instead, stalemate between the president and the Congress or confrontations that result simply in the enactment of the policy preferences of the winning side regardless of the quality of the resulting public policy will continue to characterize the U.S. political system. Without change, the system, with all of its weaknesses, will struggle along, lurching from one crisis to the next, muddling through, probably avoiding collapse, but certainly failing to be as good as it can be.

Notes

CHAPTER 1

1. Jones 1988:37.
2. Jones 1988:viii.
3. See Finer 1949 and Riggs 1975.
4. Locke 1955:125.
5. Locke 1955:136.
6. Pitkin 1967:209–210.
7. See Mezey 1986 for an earlier discussion of these criteria.
8. Much of this section appeared originally in Mezey 1986.
9. Maass, 1983:12.
10. Although named and defined somewhat differently here, these categories are similar to the ones introduced in Mezey 1979:36ff.

CHAPTER 2

1. This and all subsequent quotes from *The Federalist Papers* carry the number of the paper quoted and the page in the New American Library edition where the quotation can be found. Hamilton's statement is from the first *Federalist Paper* and is on page 33, i.e., *Federalist No. 1*, p. 33.
2. The leading statement of this Lockean position is Hartz 1955.
3. Quoted in Wood 1969:49.
4. Quoted in McDonald 1985:72.
5. Wood 1969:53.
6. McDonald 1985:71.
7. Quoted in Thach 1923:27.
8. Pole 1966:74.
9. Wood 1969:162–163. The major exception was the situation in New York, where the Constitution had vested significant power in the governor. See Thach 1923:chap. 2.
10. Locke 1955:127.
11. Quoted in Thach 1923:42–43.
12. Fisher 1972:254.
13. Wood 1969:404.
14. Quoted in Wood 1969:411.
15. Quoted in Wood 1969:510; *Federalist No. 10*, p. 77.

16. Quoted in Wood 1969:432.

17. This and all subsequent quotes from the proceedings of the Constitutional Convention come from Madison's notes, as presented in Farrand. Each citation carries a volume number and a page number. Gerry's opinion on the "excess of democracy" is found on page 48 of volume 1, i.e., Farrand 1966:1, 48.

18. Farrand 1966:1, 132.

19. *Federalist No. 48*, p. 309.

20. Wood 1969:409.

21. McDonald 1985:144. Also see Hofstadter 1948:chap. 1.

22. Farrand 1966:1, 112.

23. Farrand 1966:1, 51.

24. Farrand 1966:2, 101. Also see Robinson 1983 for a discussion of the different views of the presidency at large at the convention.

25. *Federalist No. 9*, pp. 72–73.

26. *Federalist No. 51*, p. 322.

27. Farrand 1966:1, 48.

28. Farrand 1966:1, 48, 359.

29. Farrand 1966:1, 49.

30. Farrand 1966:1, 134.

31. Farrand 1966:1, 362.

32. Farrand 1966:1, 360.

33. Farrand 1966:1. 362.

34. Farrand 1966:1, 361.

35. Farrand 1966:1, 359.

36. Farrand 1966:2, 279.

37. Farrand 1966:2, 174.

38. *Federalist No. 70*, p. 423.

39. Farrand 1966:1, 65. Throughout the convention, James Wilson was a key advocate of a strong presidency. See DiClerico 1987.

40. Quoted in Hermens 1981:21.

41. Wood 1969:449.

42. See Ceaser 1979:64ff. and Tulis 1987:27ff.

43. Farrand 1966:2, 29.

44. Farrand 1966:2, 31.

45. Farrand 1966:2, 29.

46. Farrand 1966:2, 110.

47. Farrand 1966:2, 31.

48. Farrand 1966:2, 500.

49. See Jillson 1979.

50. See Vile 1967:33.

51. *Federalist No. 47*, p. 301.

52. *Federalist No. 37*, p. 228.

53. *Federalist No. 47*, p. 304.

54. *Federalist No. 48*, p. 308.

55. *Federalist No. 49*, p. 316.

56. *Federalist No. 51*, pp. 321–322.

57. Diggins 1984:59.
58. Diggins 1984:59–60.
59. Vile 1967:62.
60. Farrand 1966:1, 139.
61. Farrand 1966:2, 78.
62. Farrand 1966:2, 76.
63. Wood 1969:435.
64. Farrand 1966:1, 120.
65. Farrand 1966:1, 233.
66. Farrand 1966:2, 389.
67. Farrand 1966:2, 539.
68. Farrand 1966:2, 318.
69. *Federalist No. 69*, p. 418.
70. Farrand 1966:2, 319.
71. Farrand 1966:2, 297.
72. Farrand 1966:2, 392.
73. Farrand 1966:2, 393.
74. Farrand 1966:2, 522.
75. Farrand 1966:2. 538.
76. See Warren 1937:653–654.
77. Farrand 1966:2, 548.
78. Farrand 1966:2, 540.
79. Farrand 1966:2, 541.
80. Farrand 1966:2. 541.
81. Corwin 1984:237; also see Adler 1988.
82. *Federalist No. 64*, p. 393.
83. Quoted in Wood 1969:559.
84. *Federalist No. 51*, p. 322.
85. Quoted in Wood 1969:216.
86. Farrand 1966:1, 51.
87. Farrand 1966:1, 511–512.
88. Farrand 1966:1, 428.
89. Farrand 1966:1, 512.
90. *Federalist No. 62*, p. 380.
91. *Federalist No. 62*, pp. 378–379.
92. See Warren 1937: 527–531.
93. *Federalist No. 39*, pp. 240–241. Emphasis is in the original.
94. *Federalist No. 37*, pp. 226–227.
95. *Federalist No. 37*, p. 227. On the importance of *Federalist No. 37*, see Epstein, 1984:chap. 4.
96. *Federalist No. 55*, p. 342.
97. Quoted in Wood 1969:604.
98. *Federalist No. 51*, p. 322.
99. Quoted in Loss 1982:10.
100. *Federalist No. 26*, p. 168.
101. Tulis 1987:42–45.

102. Quoted in Diggens 1984:57–58.
103. The "Newtonian" term is from Wilson 1908:56.
104. Corwin 1984:201.

CHAPTER 3

1. *Federalist No. 34*, p. 207.
2. See White 1948 and Nachmias and Rosenbloom 1980:39.
3. See Bailey 1964:4.
4. Wayne 1982b:191.
5. See Riker 1955.
6. Binkley 1962a:132.
7. See Riker 1955:466 and Ceaser 1979:222–223.
8. Cronin 1980:chap. 3.
9. Miroff 1982:219.
10. Lowi 1985:20.
11. Robinson 1981:62–63.
12. See Fisher 1978:194–195.
13. 299 U.S. at 320.
14. For discussions of the *Curtiss-Wright* case, see Lofgren 1973 and Adler 1988:30ff.
15. On the ABM treaty controversy, see *Congressional Quarterly Weekly Report,* September 9, 1987, pp. 2229–2232.
16. For an overview of the South African sanctions issue, see *Congressional Quarterly Weekly Report,* October 4, 1986, pp. 2338–2342.
17. See Hirschfield 1982:53–65 for the relevant sections of the Pacificus (Hamilton)–Helvidius (Madison) debate.
18. See Binkley 1962b:155.
19. Nixon made the statement in an interview with David Frost telecast on May 18, 1977. An edited text of the interview is found in Hirschfield 1982:179.
20. See Anderson 1986:148.
21. Corwin 1984:319.
22. See Thomson 1978: 27–31.
23. *Congressional Quarterly Weekly Report,* January 7, 1989, p. 7.
24. On the item veto, see Sundquist 1986:209–215.
25. The pocket veto controversy is discussed by Fisher 1987:17–18.
26. *Federalist No. 77*, p. 459.
27. Corwin 1984:102.
28. See Fisher 1975:51–55.
29. Vile 1967:66
30. Greenstein 1978:45–46.
31. Hargrove 1974:232.
32. Lowi 1985:52.
33. Corwin 1984:147–148.
34. Wayne 1978:30, 220.
35. Schlesinger 1973:331.

36. Chambers 1971:91, 95.

37. Abraham Lincoln, "First Inaugural Address," March 4, 1861, in Brasher 1946:583.

38. Quoted in Bailey 1980:35.

39. Young 1966:28

40. Goodwin 1970:4–5.

41. Galloway 1961:79.

42. Wilson 1956:69.

43. See Harlow 1913:157–158 and Galloway 1961:78.

44. Ornstein et al. 1987:146.

45. Sundquist 1981:160ff.

46. Price 1975:7.

47. Polsby 1968:146.

48. See Cooper and West 1981.

49. Galloway 1961:180–182.

50. See Galloway 1951 and Dodd and Schott 1979:168ff.

51. Fisher 1975: 257–258.

52. See Sundquist 1981:332–340 and Dodd and Schott 1979:chaps. 5 and 6.

53. See Mayhew 1974.

54. See Dodd and Schott 1979:85. The concept of the "policy entrepreneur" is developed in Price 1972.

55. See Sundquist 1981:161.

56. Edwards 1983: 226–236.

57. See Kingdon 1977.

58. See Jacobson 1987: 97–139.

59. Davidson and Oleszek 1981:125.

60. Ornstein et al. 1987:144.

61. Davidson and Oleszek 1981:108.

62. See Parker and Davidson 1979:53–61.

63. Dodd and Schott 1979:76.

CHAPTER 4

1. Burns 1956:186.

2. Light 1983:66.

3. Quoted in Goldman 1968:307.

4. Burns 1973:18.

5. Jones 1982:6–7.

6. Quoted in Bailey 1980:35.

7. Schlesinger 1973:377.

8. Quoted in Bailey 1980:37.

9. Jones 1982:8.

10. Burns 1973:111.

11. Davidson et al. 1966:31–34.

12. Sundquist 1981:19.

13. Neustadt 1980:44.

14. Barber 1977; Tulis 1987; Malbin 1983; Nathan 1983; Light 1983:224–225; Pfiffner 1988.

15. Koenig 1986:6–8.

16. Hargrove 1974:186–187.

17. Skowronek 1984:118.

18. Light 1983:36–40.

19. Light 1983:86.

20. See Neustadt 1954.

21. Wayne 1978:78–79; also see Berman 1979; Gilmour 1971.

22. Quoted in Hess 1976:131; also see Kessel 1975.

23. For a discussion of the Reagan administration's Cabinet Council structure, see Benda and Levine 1988:108–112. On the transition, see Pfiffner 1988:58ff.

24. Wayne 1984:176.

25. On the subgovernment phenomenon, see Hamm 1985.

26. Ornstein et al. 1984:139, 147.

27. Wayne 1978:15. For other discussions of presidential-congressional liaison, see Holtzman 1970; Pika 1978; Davis 1983.

28. See O'Brien 1974.

29. Davis 1979; 1983; Jones 1983.

30. See Wayne 1982a; Jones 1988.

31. See Jones 1983; 1984b.

32. Barber 1977:382. Also see Mazlisch 1973:54–55.

33. See Goldman 1968:340–341; O'Brien 1974:172.

34. Edwards 1980:127.

35. Wayne 1977:97.

36. Wayne 1978:141.

37. Greenstein 1982:59.

38. Schlesinger 1965:652.

39. Edwards 1980:126–127.

40. Schlesinger 1965:652–653.

41. Greenstein 1983:167.

42. Edwards 1980:127, 175.

43. Jones 1984a:2. For another comparison of Carter and Reagan, see Kellerman 1984.

44. Wayne 1978:106.

45. Johnson 1971:446–447.

46. Carter 1982:71.

47. Johnson 1971:459.

48. On the water projects episode, see Jones 1984b.

49. Quoted in Davis 1979:294.

50. Jones 1984a:4; Edwards 1980:175; Davis 1979:294.

51. Greenstein 1983:167.

52. Wayne 1982a:51–52.

53. Neustadt 1980:46.

54. Edwards 1980:141.

55. Carter 1982:78.

56. See Ceaser 1988:185.
57. Quoted in Goldman 1968:308.
58. Schlesinger 1965:652.
59. Heineman and Hessler 1980:xix.
60. Carter 1982:87.
61. See Wayne 1982a.
62. Light 1983:45.
63. Wilson 1908:70–71.
64. See Page and Shapiro 1985; Edwards 1980:167–173.
65. Kernell 1984; 1986.
66. Ornstein 1982:95. For a more complete discussion of the erratic track that Reagan's job approval ratings followed, see Ceaser 1988; and also see Ostrom and Simon 1987.
67. Quoted in Malbin 1983:219.
68. Quoted in Johnson 1980:22.
69. Ornstein 1982:94.
70. Berman 1987:329

CHAPTER 5

1. *Congressional Quarterly Weekly Report,* January 16, 1988, p. 91.
2. See Edwards 1980:14–15, 50–53.
3. Wayne 1978:171.
4. See Peterson 1985 and Edwards 1980:14–15.
5. See Covington 1987.
6. Peterson 1985:19.
7. Edwards 1980:202.
8. Sabato 1988:56.
9. Goldman 1968:308.
10. Neustadt 1980:114.
11. Quoted in Campbell 1986:61, 62.
12. Quoted in Berman 1987:316.
13. Campbell 1986:67, 69.
14. Cronin 1980:15.
15. See Wayne 1982b:196. Also see Barger 1984.
16. See Mueller 1973.
17. It has been suggested that Ronald Reagan's presidency did not follow the traditional pattern of decaying public support. See Ostrom and Simon 1987 and Ceaser 1988.
18. Kernell 1986:210.
19. Schlesinger 1965:195.
20. *Congressional Quarterly Weekly Report,* April 4, 1987, p. 604.
21. *Congressional Quarterly Weekly Report,* March 26, 1988, pp. 821–822.
22. Light 1983:42.
23. Wayne 1978:130.
24. Sabato 1988:49.

25. Galloway 1961:104.
26. Sabato 1988:52.
27. See Ornstein et al. 1987:208–209. Also see Schlesinger 1985.
28. Smith 1985:208–209, 215, 216.
29. Ornstein 1983:204.
30. Jones 1984c:276.
31. Sabato 1988:170.
32. See Walker 1983.
33. Ornstein et al. 1987:72, 77, 92–93, 103.
34. Drew 1982:147.
35. On the conservative nature of the interest group system, see Lowi 1979.
36. Ladd 1984:248.
37. *General Social Surveys,* 1980:75.
38. Hill and Luttbeg 1983:116.
39. Lipset and Schneider 1983:48–49.
40. See Sundquist 1983:chap. 17.
41. Shuman 1987:446.
42. Shuman 1988:62.
43. Ornstein et al. 1987:142, 146, 149.
44. Sundquist 1981:407–408.
45. Reischauer 1983:59.
46. Nadel 1983:246.
47. Campbell 1986:259.
48. Heclo 1977:1.
49. Salamon and Abramson 1984:63; also see Moe 1985.
50. Newland 1984:163, 167.
51. Greider 1982:33.
52. Quoted in Campbell 1986:185.
53. Oppenheimer 1981.
54. Sundquist 1981:454.
55. Caiden 1983:105.
56. Maass 1983:146.
57. Jones 1981:131.
58. Davidson and Oleszek 1981:438.
59. See Ellwood 1983.
60. Campbell 1986:264–265.
61. Cleveland 1986.
62. Greider 1982:37.
63. Heclo and Penner 1983:39.
64. Rudder 1983:206.
65. Rudder 1977:124–126.
66. Maass 1983:169; also see Ferejohn 1983:152.
67. Arnold 1981:285.
68. Greider 1982:58–59.
69. Mayhew 1974.
70. Sundquist 1981:451, 456.

71. Sundquist 1981:451.
72. Moe 1985:238.
73. Ferguson and Rogers 1986:chap. 1.
74. See Jacobson 1987:chap. 5.
75. Dye and Zeigler 1981:193; see also Wahlke 1971.
76. Jacobson 1987:130.
77. Miller and Stokes 1963.
78. See Parker and Davidson 1979.

CHAPTER 6

1. This discussion of the Social Security rescue plan depends heavily upon Light 1985 and De Bella 1986.

2. *New York Times,* February 18, 1981.

3. For details of the final bill, see *Congressional Quarterly Weekly Report,* March 26, 1983, pp. 596–600.

4. Light 1985:195.

5. Light 1985:232.

6. See Weaver 1988.

7. Shuman 1988:152, 269, 277.

8. See *Congressional Quarterly Almanac* 1985:462–466.

9. Quoted in *Congressional Quarterly Almanac* 1984:459.

10. *Bowsher v. Synar,* 478 U.S. 714 (1986). Also see *Congressional Quarterly Weekly Report,* July 12, 1986.

11. Shuman 1988:290.

12. *Congressional Quarterly Weekly Report,* September 26, 1987, pp. 2309–2311.

13. Quoted in *Congressional Quarterly Weekly Report,* October 24, 1987, p. 2571.

14. See *Congressional Quarterly Weekly Report,* December 26, 1987, pp. 3187–3192, and *Congressional Quarterly Weekly Report,* January 2, 1988, p. 14.

15. Quoted in Rauch and Cohen 1985:2318.

16. Quoted in Shuman 1988:281.

17. See *Congressional Quarterly Almanac* 1973:905–917.

18. For a helpful chronology of the events in Lebanon, see *Congressional Quarterly Weekly Report,* February 11, 1984, p. 241.

19. *Weekly Compilation of Presidential Documents,* vol. 18, September 29, 1982, p. 1232.

20. Quoted in *Congressional Quarterly Weekly Report,* October 2, 1982, p. 2469.

21. See *Congressional Quarterly Weekly Report,* October 8, 1983, pp. 2101–2102.

22. Quoted in *Congressional Quarterly Weekly Report,* October 1, 1983, p. 2017.

23. *Congressional Quarterly Weekly Report,* October 8, 1983, p. 2095.

24. These incidents are recounted in *Congressional Quarterly Weekly Report,* October 1, 1983, p. 2019.

25. Rubner 1987:197

26. See Craig 1983; also see Sundquist 1981:chap. 12.

27. Sundquist 1981:345.

28. *Weekly Compilation of Presidential Documents,* vol. 14, June 21, 1978, p. 1147.

29. 462 U.S. 919 (1983). Also see Craig 1988.

30. 462 U.S. at 967.

31. Fisher 1985.

32. See Fisher 1985. For a list of the new post-*Chadha* provisions, see *Congressional Quarterly Almanac* 1986:49–53.

33. See Nathan 1983.

34. Lynn 1984:340.

35. *New York Times,* July 3, 1981.

36. Salamon and Abramson 1984:46.

37. Portney 1984:146.

38. Nathan 1983:78.

39. Nathan 1983:78–80.

40. Fuchs 1988:101.

41. Salamon and Abramson 1984:47.

42. Moe 1985:262.

43. Newland 1984:162–163; also see Benda and Levine 1988:114–120 and Fuchs 1988:90ff.

44. Quoted in *Congressional Quarterly Almanac* 1985:70.

45. On this point, see Kornbluh 1987:23.

46. Sharpe 1987-1988:569.

47. *Congressional Quarterly Almanac* 1985:76.

48. *Congressional Quarterly Almanac* 1985:83.

49. *Congressional Quarterly Almanac* 1984:88–89.

50. *Congressional Quarterly Almanac* 1985:68.

51. Sharpe 1987-1988:559.

52. Sharpe 1987-1988:560–563.

53. North's congressional testimony is excerpted in *Congressional Quarterly Weekly Report,* July 11, 1987, pp. 1519–1539.

54. *Congressional Quarterly Weekly Report,* July 18, 1987, pp. 1556–1558.

55. *Congressional Quarterly Weekly Report,* July 11, 1987, p. 1527.

56. *Congressional Quarterly Weekly Report,* July 25, 1987, p. 1645.

57. See Mezey 1988; Newland 1984:163.

58. Lowi 1985:174.

CHAPTER 7

1. On children's attitudes toward the presidency, see Hess and Easton 1960 and Jaros 1967. On attitudes toward the presidency among adults, see Greenstein 1965; Kernell et al. 1975; Wayne 1982b.

2. See Cronin 1980:chap. 1.

3. The literature on the reform of the presidency is vast. Some of the classics are Corwin and Koenig 1956; Burns 1973; 1984; Hardin 1974. Two excellent

discussions of political reform with special relevance to presidential-congressional relations are Sundquist 1986 and Robinson 1985.

4. See Sundquist 1981 for a full discussion of these reforms.

5. See Polsby 1983:89ff and Ceaser 1982:91–96.

6. See Polsby 1983:173–185 and Ceaser 1982:chap. 5.

7. See Robinson 1985:167–174; also see Buchanan 1987:chap. 7.

8. For some assessments of the problem and suggestions for solutions, see Nathan 1983; Heclo 1977; Campbell 1986; Rourke 1984.

9. See Parker and Davidson 1979 and Parker 1977.

10. See Davidson and Oleszek 1981:106ff.

11. For a complete inventory of recent proposals for congressional reform, see Rieselbach 1986:155–158.

12. See Mezey 1979:chap. 9.

13. See Sorauf 1988:369–374; also see Jacobson 1985.

14. Smith 1985:228.

15. See Sundquist 1981:335.

16. Reported in Ignatius 1988:23.

17. See Cutler 1986:2.

18. See Schattschneider 1942; Committee on Political Parties 1950; Burns 1963.

19. See Strum 1977.

20. Berger 1974, especially chap. 9. Also see Maass 1983:216–253.

21. See *Congressional Quarterly Almanac* 1980:66–67.

22. Tocqueville 1966:99.

23. Tocqueville 1966:101.

24. Hofstadter 1948:332.

25. Free and Cantril 1968:13–32.

26. See Ferguson and Rogers 1986:chap. 1.

27. See Miller 1974; Citrin 1974; Lipset and Schneider 1983.

28. Fenno 1978:162–168.

29. Sundquist 1986:242.

30. Sundquist 1981:479.

References

Adler, David Gray (1988). "The Constitution and Presidential Warmaking: The Enduring Debate." *Political Science Quarterly* 103:1 (Spring):1–36.

Anderson, Ann Stuart (1986). "A 1787 Perspective on Separation of Powers." In Robert A. Goldwin and Art Kaufman, *Separation of Powers: Does It Still Work?* Washington, D.C.: American Enterprise Institute.

Arnold, R. Douglas (1981). "The Local Roots of Domestic Policy." In Thomas E. Mann and Norman J. Ornstein, eds. *The New Congress.* Washington, D.C.: American Enterprise Institute.

Bailey, Harry A., Jr., ed. (1980). *Classics of the American Presidency.* Oak Park, Ill.: Moore Publishing.

Bailey, Thomas A. (1964). *A Diplomatic History of the American People.* New York: Appleton-Century-Crofts.

Barber, James David (1977). *The Presidential Character: Predicting Performance in the White House,* 2nd ed. Englewood Cliffs, N.J.: Prentice-Hall.

Barger, Harold M. (1984). *The Impossible Presidency: Illusions and Realities of Executive Power.* Glenview, Ill.: Scott, Foresman.

Benda, Peter M., and Charles H. Levine (1988). "Reagan and the Bureaucracy: The Bequest, the Promise, and the Legacy." In Charles O. Jones, ed. *The Reagan Legacy: Promise and Performance.* Chatham, N.J.: Chatham House.

Berger, Raoul (1974). *Executive Privilege: A Constitutional Myth.* Cambridge, Mass: Harvard University Press.

Berman, Larry (1979). *The Office of Management and Budget and the Presidency.* Princeton: Princeton University Press.

———— (1987). *The New American Presidency.* Boston: Little, Brown.

Binkley, Wilfred E. (1962a). *American Political Parties: Their Natural History,* 4th ed. New York: Alfred A. Knopf.

———— (1962b). *President and Congress,* 3rd rev. ed. New York: Vintage Books.

Brasher, Roy P., ed. (1946). *Abraham Lincoln: His Speeches and Writings.* Cleveland: World Publishing.

Buchanan, Bruce (1987). *The Citizen's Presidency.* Washington, D.C.: Congressional Quarterly Press.

Burns, James MacGregor (1956). *The Lion and the Fox.* New York: Harcourt Brace.

———— (1963). *The Deadlock of Democracy.* Englewood Cliffs, N.J.: Prentice-Hall.

———— (1973). *Presidential Government: The Crucible of Leadership.* Boston: Houghton Mifflin.

———— (1984). *The Power to Lead.* New York: Simon and Schuster.

Caiden, Naomi (1983). "The Politics of Subtraction." In Allan Schick, ed. *Making Economic Policy in Congress*. Washington, D.C.: American Enterprise Institute.

Campbell, Colin S.J. (1986). *Managing the Presidency: Carter, Reagan,and the Search for Executive Harmony*. Pittsburgh: University of Pittsburgh Press.

Carter, Jimmy (1982). *Keeping Faith: Memoirs of a President*. New York: Bantam Books.

Ceaser, James W. (1979). *Presidential Selection: Theory and Development*. Princeton: Princeton University Press.

––––– (1982). *Reforming the Reforms: A Critical Analysis of the Presidential Selection Process*. Cambridge, Mass: Ballinger Publishing.

––––– (1988). "The Reagan Presidency and American Public Opinion." In Charles O. Jones, ed. *The Reagan Legacy: Promise and Performance*. Chatham, N.J.: Chatham House.

Chambers, William N. (1971). "Andrew Jackson." In Morton Borden, ed. *America's Eleven Greatest Presidents*, 2nd ed. Chicago: Rand McNally.

Citrin, Jack (1974). "Comment: The Political Relevance of Trust in Government." *American Political Science Review* 68:3 (September):973–988.

Cleveland, Harlan (1986). "Coherence and Consultation: The President as Manager of American Foreign Policy." *Public Administration Review* 46:(March/April):97–104.

Committee on Political Parties of the American Political Science Association (1950). "Toward a More Responsible Party System." *The American Politica, Science Review* 44:3 (September):15–99.

Cooper, Joseph, and William West (1981). "The Congressional Career in the 1970s." In Lawrence Dodd and Bruce Oppenheimer, eds. *Congress Reconsidered*, 2nd ed. Washington, D.C.: Congressional Quarterly Press.

Corwin, Edward S. (1984). *The President: Office and Powers, 1787–1984*. New York: New York University Press.

Corwin, Edward S., and Louis W. Koenig (1956). *The Presidency Today*. New York: New York University Press.

Covington, Cary (1987). "Staying Private: Gaining Congressional Support for Unpublicized Presidential Preferences on Roll Call Votes." *Journal of Politics* 49:3 (August):737–755.

Craig, Barbara (1983). *The Legislative Veto: Congressional Control of Administration*. Boulder, Colo.: Westview Press.

––––– (1988). *Chadha: The Story of an Epic Constitutional Struggle*. New York: Oxford University Press.

Cronin, Thomas E. (1980). *The State of the Presidency*, 2nd ed. Boston: Little, Brown.

Cutler, Lloyd N. (1986). "To Form a Government." In Robert A. Goldwin and Art Kaufman, eds. *Separation of Powers: Does It Still Work?* Washington, D.C.: American Enterprise Institute.

Davidson, Roger H., David M. Kovenock, and Michael K. O'Leary (1966). *Congress in Crisis*. Monterey, Calif.: Brooks, Cole.

Davidson, Roger H., and Walter J. Oleszek (1981). *Congress and Its Members*. Washington, D.C.: Congressional Quarterly Press.

Davis, Eric L. (1979). "Legislative Liaison in the Carter Administration." *Political Science Quarterly* 94:2 (Summer):287–302.

———— (1983). "Congressional Liaison: The People and the Institutions." In Anthony King, ed. *Both Ends of the Avenue: The Presidency, the Executive Branch, and Congress in the 1980s.* Washington, D.C.: The American Enterprise Institute.

De Bella, Paul M. (1986). "Social Security Reform and Political Linkage Mechanisms: A Case Study." Senior Honors Thesis, DePaul University, Chicago, Ill.

DiClerico, Robert E. (1987). "James Wilson's Presidency." *Presidential Studies Quarterly* 17:2 (Spring):301–317.

Diggins, John P. (1984). *The Lost Soul of American Politics: Virtue, Self-Interest and the Foundations of Liberalism.* Chicago: University of Chicago Press.

Dodd, Lawrence C., and Richard L. Schott (1979). *Congress and the Administrative State.* New York: John Wiley.

Drew, Elizabeth (1982). "Politics and Money, I." *New Yorker,* December 6, 1982.

Dye, Thomas R., and L. Harmon Zeigler (1981). *The Irony of Democracy: An Uncommon Introduction to American Politics,* 5th ed. Monterey, Calif.: Duxbury Press.

Edwards, George C., III (1980). *Presidential Influence in Congress.* San Francisco: W. H. Freeman.

———— (1983). *The Public Presidency.* New York: St. Martin's Press.

Ellwood, John W. (1983). "Budget Control in a Redistributive Environment." In Allan Schick, ed. *Making Economic Policy in Congress.* Washington, D.C.: American Enterprise Institute.

Epstein, David F. (1984). *The Political Theory of The Federalist.* Chicago: University of Chicago Press.

Farrand, Max, ed. (1966). *The Records of the Federal Convention of 1787.* Vols. 1 and 2. New Haven: Yale University Press.

Fenno, Richard F., Jr. (1978). *Home Style: House Members in Their Districts.* Boston: Little, Brown.

Ferejohn, John (1983). "Congress and Redistribution." In Allan Schick, ed. *Making Economic Policy in Congress.* Washington, D.C.: American Enterprise Institute.

Ferguson, Thomas, and Joel Rogers (1986). *Right Turn.* New York: Hill and Wang.

Finer, Herman (1949). *The Theory and Practice of Modern Government.* New York: Holt.

Fisher, Louis (1972). *President and Congress: Power and Policy.* New York: The Free Press.

———— (1975). *Presidential Spending Power.* Princeton: Princeton University Press.

———— (1978). *The Constitution Between Friends: Congress, the President and the Law.* New York: St. Martin's Press.

———— (1985). "Judicial Misjudgments About the Lawmaking Process: The Legislative Veto Case." *Public Administration Review,* 45:Special Issue (November):705–711.

———— (1987). *The Politics of Shared Power: Congress and the Executive* 2nd ed. Washington. D.C.: Congressional Quarterly Press.

Free, Lloyd A., and Hadley Cantril (1968). *The Political Beliefs of Americans: A Study of Public Opinion.* New York: Simon and Schuster.

Fuchs, Edward Paul (1988). *Presidents, Management, and Regulation.* Englewood Cliffs, N.J.: Prentice-Hall.

Galloway, George (1951). "The Operation of the Legislative Reorganization Act of 1946." *American Political Science Review* 45:1 (March):41–68.

———— (1961). *History of the House of Representatives.* New York: Thomas Y. Crowell.

General Social Surveys, 1972–1980: Cumulative Codebook (1980). Chicago: National Opinion Research Center.

Gilmour, Robert S. (1971). "Central Legislative Clearance: A Revised Perspective." *Public Administration Review* 31:2 (March/April):150–158.

Goldman, Eric (1968). *The Tragedy of Lyndon Johnson.* New York: Alfred A. Knopf.

Goodwin, George, Jr. (1970). *The Little Legislatures: Committees of Congress.* Amherst: University of Massachusetts Press.

Greenstein, Fred I. (1965). "Popular Images of the President." *American Journal of Psychiatry* 122:5 (November):523–529.

———— (1978). "Change and Continuity in the Modern Presidency." In Anthony King, ed. *The New American Political System.* Washington, D.C.: American Enterprise Institute.

———— (1982). *The Hidden-Hand Presidency: Eisenhower as Leader.* New York: Basic Books.

———— (1983). "Reagan and the Lore of the Modern Presidency: What Have We Learned?" In Fred I. Greenstein, ed. *The Reagan Presidency: An Early Assessment.* Baltimore: The Johns Hopkins University Press.

Greider, William (1982). *The Education of David Stockman and Other Americans.* New York: E. P. Dutton.

Hamm, Keith E. (1985). "Legislative Committees, Executive Agencies, and Interest Groups." In Gerhard Loewenberg, Samuel C. Patterson, and Malcolm Jewell, eds. *Handbook of Legislative Research.* Cambridge, Mass.: Harvard University Press.

Hardin, Charles M. (1974). *Presidential Power and Accountability.* Chicago: University of Chicago Press.

Hargrove, Erwin C. (1974). *The Power of the Modern Presidency.* New York: Alfred A. Knopf.

Harlow, Ralph V. (1913). *The History of Legislative Methods in the Period Before 1825.* New Haven: Yale University Press.

Hartz, Louis (1955). *The Liberal Tradition in America: An Interpretation of American Political Thought Since the Revolution.* New York: Harcourt Brace.

Heclo, Hugh (1977). *A Government of Strangers: Executive Politics in Washington.* Washington, D.C.: The Brookings Institution.

Heclo, Hugh, and Rudolph G. Penner (1983). "Fiscal and Political Strategy in the Reagan Administration." In Fred I. Greenstein, ed. *The Reagan Presidency: An Early Assessment.* Baltimore: The Johns Hopkins University Press.

Heineman, Ben, Jr., and Curtis Hessler (1980). *Memorandum for the President.* New York: Random House.

Hermens, Ferdinand A. (1981). "The Choice of the Framers." *Presidential Studies Quarterly* 11:1 (Winter):9–27.

Hess, Robert, and David Easton (1960). "The Child's Changing Image of the President." *Public Opinion Quarterly* 24:632–644.

Hess, Stephen (1976). *Organizing the Presidency*. Washington, D.C.: The Brookings Institution.

Hill, David B., and Norman R. Luttbeg (1983). *Trends in American Electoral Behavior*, 2nd ed. Itasca, Ill.: F. E. Peacock.

Hirschfield, Robert S., ed. (1982). *The Power of the Presidency*. New York: Aldine Publishing.

Hofstadter, Richard (1948). *The American Political Tradition*. New York: Vintage Books.

Holtzman, Abraham (1970). *Legislative Liaison: Executive Leadership in Congress*. Chicago: Rand McNally.

Ignatius, David (1988). "Is This Any Way for a Country to Buy Weapons?" *Washington Post National Weekly Edition*, July 4–10, 1988.

Jacobson, Gary (1985). "Parties and PACs in Congressional Elections." In Lawrence C. Dodd and Bruce I. Oppenheimer, eds. *Congress Reconsidered*, 3rd ed. Washington, D.C.: Congressional Quarterly Press.

———— (1987). *The Politics of Congressional Elections*, 2nd ed. Boston: Little, Brown.

Jaros, Dean (1967). "Children's Orientation Toward the President: Some Additional Theoretical Considerations and Data." *Journal of Politics* 29:2 (May):368–387.

Jillson, Calvin C. (1979). "The Executive in Republican Government: The Case of the American Founding." *Presidential Studies Quarterly* 9:4 (Fall):386–402.

Johnson, Haynes (1980). *In the Absence of Power*. New York: Viking.

Johnson, Lyndon Baines (1971). *The Vantage Point: Perspectives of the Presidency, 1963–1969*. New York: Popular Library.

Jones, Charles O. (1981). "House Leadership in an Age of Reform." In Frank Mackaman, ed. *Understanding Congressional Leadership*. Washington, D.C.: Congressional Quarterly Press.

———— (1982). *The United States Congress: People, Place, and Policy*. Homewood, Ill.: Dorsey Press.

———— (1983). "Presidential Negotiations With Congress." In Anthony King, ed. *Both Ends of the Avenue: The Presidency, the Executive Branch, and Congress in the 1980s*. Washington, D.C.: American Enterprise Institute.

———— (1984a). "Carter and Congress: From the Outside In." Paper presented at the Annual Meeting of the American Political Science Association, Washington, D.C., August 30–September 2, 1984.

———— (1984b). "Keeping Faith and Losing Congress: The Carter Experience in Washington." *Presidential Studies Quarterly*, 14:3 (Summer):437–445.

———— (1984c). "A New President, A Different Congress, A Maturing Agenda." In Lester M. Salamon and Michael S. Lund. *The Reagan Presidency and the Governing of America*. Washington, D.C.: The Urban Institute Press.

———— (1988). "Ronald Reagan and the U.S. Congress: Visible-Hand Politics." In Charles O. Jones, ed. *The Reagan Legacy: Promise and Performance*. Chatham, N.J.: Chatham House.

Kellerman, Barbara (1984). *The Political Presidency: Practice of Leadership.* New York: Oxford University Press.

Kernell, Samuel (1984). "The Presidency and the People." In Michael Nelson, ed. *The Presidency and the Political System.* Washington, D.C.: Congressional Quarterly Press.

———— (1986). *Going Public: New Strategies of Presidential Leadership.* Washington, D.C.: Congressional Quarterly Press.

Kernell, Samuel, Peter W. Sperlich, and Aaron Wildavsky (1975). "Public Support for Presidents." In Aaron Wildavsky, ed. *Perspectives on the Presidency.* Boston: Little, Brown.

Kessel, John H. (1975). *The Domestic Presidency: Decision-Making in the White House.* North Scituate, Mass.: Duxbury Press.

King, Gary, and Lyn Ragsdale (1988). *The Elusive Executive.* Washington, D.C.: Congressional Quarterly Press.

Kingdon, John (1977). "Models of Legislative Voting." *Journal of Politics* 39:3 (August):563–595.

Koenig, Louis (1986). *The Chief Executive,* 5th ed. New York: Harcourt Brace Jovanovich.

Kornbluh, Peter (1987). "The Covert War." In Thomas W. Walker, ed. *Reagan Versus the Sandinistas.* Boulder, Colo.: Westview Press.

Ladd, Everett Carll (1984). "The Reagan Phenomenon and Public Attitudes Toward Government." In Lester M. Salamon and Michael S. Lund. *The Reagan Presidency and the Governing of America.* Washington, D.C.: The Urban Institute Press.

Light, Paul (1983). *The President's Agenda: Domestic Policy Choice From Kennedy to Carter.* Baltimore: The Johns Hopkins University Press.

———— (1985). *Artful Work: The Politics of Social Security Reform.* New York: Random House.

Lipset, Seymour Martin, and William Schneider (1983). *The Confidence Gap.* New York: The Free Press.

Locke, John (1955). *Of Civil Government: Second Treatise.* Chicago: Henry Regnery. (Originally published in 1689).

Lofgren, Charles (1973). "*United States v. Curtiss-Wright Export Corporation:* An Historical Reassessment." *Yale Law Journal* 83:1 (November):1–32.

Loss, Richard (1982). "Alexander Hamilton and the Modern Presidency: Continuity or Discontinuity." *Presidential Studies Quarterly* 12:1 (Winter):6–25.

Lowi, Theodore J. (1979). *The End of Liberalism: The Second Republic of the United States,* 2nd ed. New York: W. W. Norton.

———— (1985). *The Personal President.* Ithaca, N.Y.: Cornell University Press.

Lynn, Laurence E., Jr. (1984). "The Reagan Administration and the Renitent Bureaucracy." In Lester M. Salamon and Michael S. Lund. *The Reagan Presidency and the Governing of America.* Washington, D.C.: The Urban Institute Press.

Maass, Arthur (1983). *Congress and the Common Good.* New York: Basic Books.

McDonald, Forrest (1985). *Novus Ordo Seclorum: The Intellectual Origins of the Constitution.* Lawrence, Kans.: University Press of Kansas.

Madison, James, Alexander Hamilton, John Jay (1961). *The Federalist Papers.* Ed. Clinton Rossiter. New York: New American Library. (Originally published 1787–1788).

Malbin, Michael J. (1983). "Rhetoric and Leadership: A Look Backward at the Carter National Energy Plan." In Anthony King, ed. *Both Ends of the Avenue: The Presidency, the Executive Branch, and Congress in the 1980s.* Washington, D.C.: American Enterprise Institute.

Mayhew, David R. (1974). *Congress: The Electoral Connection.* New Haven: Yale University Press.

Mazlisch, Bruce (1973). *In Search of Nixon: A Psychohistorical Inquiry.* Baltimore: Penguin Books.

Mezey, Michael L. (1979). *Comparative Legislatures.* Durham, N.C.: Duke University Press.

――― (1986). "The Legislature, The Executive, and Public Policy: The Futile Quest for Congressional Power." *Congress and the Presidency* 13:1 (Spring):1–20.

Mezey, Susan Gluck (1988). *No Longer Disabled: The Federal Courts and the Politics of Social Security Disability.* Westport, Conn.: Greenwood Press.

Miller, Arthur H. (1974). "Political Issues and Trust in Government." *American Political Science Review* 68:3 (September):951–972.

Miller, Warren E., and Donald F. Stokes (1963). "Constituency Influence in Congress." *American Political Science Review* 57:1 (March):45–57.

Miroff, Bruce (1982). "Monopolizing the Public Space: The President as a Problem for Democratic Politics." In Thomas E. Cronin, ed. *Rethinking the Presidency.* Boston: Little, Brown.

Moe, Terry M. (1985). "The Politicized Presidency." In John E. Chubb and Paul E. Peterson, eds. *The New Direction in American Politics.* Washington, D.C.: The Brookings Institution.

Mueller, John (1973). *War, Presidents, and Public Opinion.* New York: John Wiley.

Nachmias, David, and David H. Rosenbloom (1980). *Bureaucratic Government USA.* New York: St. Martin's Press.

Nadel, Mark V. (1983). "Making Regulatory Policy." In Allan Schick, ed. *Making Economic Policy in Congress.* Washington, D.C.: American Enterprise Institute.

Nathan, Richard P. (1983). *The Administrative Presidency.* New York: John Wiley.

Neustadt, Richard E. (1954). "Presidency and Legislation: The Growth of Central Clearance." *American Political Science Review* 48:3 (September):641–671.

――― (1980). *Presidential Power,* 2nd ed. New York: John Wiley.

Newland, Chester A. (1984). "Executive Office Policy Apparatus: Enforcing the Reagan Agenda." In Lester M. Salamon and Michael S. Lund. *The Reagan Presidency and the Governing of America.* Washington, D.C.: The Urban Institute Press.

O'Brien, Lawrence F. (1974). *No Final Victories.* Garden City, N.Y.: Doubleday.

Oppenheimer, Bruce I. (1981). "Congress and the New Obstructionism: Developing an Energy Policy." In Lawrence C. Dodd and Bruce I. Oppenheimer, eds. *Congress Reconsidered,* 2nd ed. Washington, D.C.: Congressional Quarterly Press.

Ornstein, Norman J. (1982). "Assessing Reagan's First Year," in Norman J. Ornstein, ed. *President and Congress: Assessing Reagan's First Year.* Washington, D.C.: American Enterprise Institute.

————— (1983). "The Open Congress Meets the President." In Anthony King, ed. *Both Ends of the Avenue: The Presidency, the Executive Branch, and Congress in the 1980s.* Washington, D.C.: American Enterprise Institute.

Ornstein, Norman J., Thomas E. Mann, and Michael J. Malbin (1987). *Vital Statistics on Congress, 1987–1988.* Washington, D.C.: Congressional Quarterly Press.

Ornstein, Norman J., Thomas E. Mann, Michael J. Malbin, Allan Schick, and John F. Bibby (1984). *Vital Statistics on Congress, 1984–1985.* Washington, D.C.: American Enterprise Institute.

Ostrom, Charles W., Jr., and Dennis M. Simon (1987). "The Environmental Connection, Political Drama, and Popular Support in the Reagan Administration." Paper presented at the Annual Meeting of the Southern Political Science Association, Charlotte, N.C., November 1987.

Page, Benjamin I., and Robert Y. Shapiro (1985). "Presidential Leadership Through Public Opinion." In George C. Edwards III, Steven A. Shull, and Norman C. Thomas, eds. *The Presidency and Public Policy-Making.* Pittsburgh: University of Pittsburgh Press.

Parker, Glenn R. (1977). "Some Themes on Congressional Unpopularity." *American Journal of Political Science* 21:1 (February):93–109.

Parker, Glenn R., and Roger H. Davidson (1979). "Why Do Americans Love Their Congressmen So Much More Than Their Congress." *Legislative Studies Quarterly* 4:1 (February):53–61.

Peterson, Mark A. (1985). "Domestic Policy and Legislative Decision-Making: Congressional Responses to Presidential Initiatives, 1953–1981." Paper presented at the Annual Meeting of the Midwest Political Science Association, Chicago, Ill., April 1985.

Pfiffner, James P. (1988). *The Strategic Presidency: Hitting the Ground Running.* Chicago: Dorsey Press.

Pika, Joseph A. (1978). "White House Office of Congressional Relations: A Longitudinal Analysis." Paper presented at the Annual Meeting of the Midwest Political Science Association, Chicago, Ill., April 1978.

Pitkin, Hanna F. (1967). *The Concept of Representation.* Berkeley: University of California Press.

Pole, J. R. (1966). *Political Representation in England and the Origins of the American Republic.* Berkeley: University of California Press.

Polsby, Nelson W. (1968). "The Institutionalization of the U.S. House of Representatives." *American Political Science Review* 62:1 (March):144–168.

————— (1983). *Consequences of Party Reform.* New York: Oxford University Press.

Portney, Paul R. (1984). "Natural Resources and the Environment: More Controversy Than Change." In John L. Palmer and Isabel V. Sawhill, eds. *The Reagan Record.* Cambridge, Mass.: Ballinger Publishing.

Price, David (1972). *Who Makes the Laws?* Cambridge, Mass.: Schenkman Publishing.

Price, H. Douglas (1975). "Congress and the Evolution of Legislative 'Professionalism.'" In Norman J. Ornstein, ed. *Congress in Change: Evolution and Reform*. New York: Praeger.

Rauch, Jonathan, and Richard E. Cohen (1985). "Budget Frustration Boiling Over." *National Journal*, October 12, 1985.

Reischauer, Robert D. (1983). "Getting, Using, and Misusing Economic Information." In Allan Schick, ed. *Making Economic Policy in Congress*. Washington, D.C.: American Enterprise Institute.

Rieselbach, Leroy N. (1986). *Congressional Reform*. Washington, D.C.: Congressional Quarterly Press.

Riggs, Fred W. (1975). *Legislative Origins: A Comparative and Contextual Approach*. International Studies Association, Occasional Papers No. 7. Pittsburgh: International Studies Association.

Riker, William H. (1955). "The Senate and American Federalism." *American Political Science Review* 49:2 (June):452–469.

Robinson, Donald L. (1983). "The Inventors of the Presidency." *Presidential Studies Quarterly* 13:1 (Winter):8–25.

———, ed. (1985). *Reforming American Government: The Bicentennial Papers of the Committee on the Constitutional System*. Boulder, Colo.: Westview Press.

Robinson, Michael J. (1981). "Three Faces of Congressional Media." In Thomas E. Mann and Norman J. Ornstein, eds. *The New Congress*. Washington, D.C.: American Enterprise Institute.

Rourke, Francis E. (1984). "The Presidency and the Bureaucracy: Strategic Alternatives." In Michael Nelson, ed. *The Presidency and the Political System*. Washington, D.C.: Congressional Quarterly Press.

Rubner, Michael (1987). "Antiterrorism and the Withering of the 1973 War Powers Resolution." *Political Science Quarterly* 102:2 (Summer):193–215.

Rudder, Catherine E. (1977). "Committee Reform and the Revenue Process." In Lawrence C. Dodd and Bruce I. Oppenheimer, eds. *Congress Reconsidered*. New York: Praeger.

——— (1983). "Tax Policy: Structure and Choice." In Allan Schick, ed. *Making Economic Policy in Congress*. Washington, D.C.: American Enterprise Institute.

Sabato, Larry J. (1988). *The Party's Just Begun: Shaping Political Parties for America's Future*. Glenview, Ill.: Scott, Foresman.

Salamon, Lester M., and Alan J. Abramson (1984). "Governance: The Politics of Retrenchment." In John L. Palmer and Isabel V. Sawhill, eds. *The Reagan Record*. Cambridge, Mass.: Ballinger Publishing.

Schattschneider, E. E. (1942). *Party Government*. New York: Rinehart.

Schlesinger, Arthur M., Jr. (1965). *A Thousand Days: John F. Kennedy in the White House*. Greenwich, Conn.: Fawcett Publications.

——— (1973). *The Imperial Presidency*. Boston: Houghton Mifflin.

Schlesinger, Joseph A. (1985). "The New American Political Party." *American Political Science Review* 79:4 (December):1152–1169.

Sharpe, Kenneth E. (1987-1988). "The Post-Vietnam Formula Under Seige: The Imperial Presidency and Central America." *Political Science Quarterly* 102:4 (Winter):549–569.

Shuman, Howard (1987). "Congress and Budgeting." In David C. Kozak and John D. Macartney, *Congress and Public Policy: A Source Book of Documents and Readings*, 2nd ed. Chicago: Dorsey Press.

———— (1988). *Politics and the Budget: The Struggle Between the President and the Congress*, 2nd ed. Englewood Cliffs, N.J.: Prentice-Hall.

Skowronek, Stephen (1984). "Presidential Leadership in Political Time." In Michael Nelson, ed. *The Presidency and the Political System*. Washington, D.C.: Congressional Quarterly Press.

Smith, Steven S. (1985). "New Patterns of Decisionmaking in Congress." In John E. Chubb and Paul E. Peterson, eds. *The New Direction in American Politics*. Washington, D.C.: The Brookings Institution.

Sorauf, Frank J. (1988). *Money in American Elections*. Glenview, Ill.: Scott, Foresman.

Strum, Philippa (1977). "A Symbolic Attack on the Imperial Presidency: An American Question Time." In Thomas E. Cronin and Rexford G. Tugwell, eds. *The Presidency Reappraised*, 2nd ed. New York: Praeger.

Sundquist, James (1981). *The Decline and Resurgence of Congress*. Washington, D.C.: The Brookings Institution.

———— (1983). *Dynamics of the Party System: Alignment and Realignment of Political Parties in the United States*, revised ed. Washington, D.C.: The Brookings Institution.

———— (1986). *Constitutional Reform and Effective Government*. Washington, D.C.: The Brookings Institution.

Thach, Charles C., Jr. (1923). *The Creation of the Presidency, 1775–1789*. Baltimore: The Johns Hopkins University Press.

Thomson, Harry C. (1978). "The First Presidential Vetoes." *Presidential Studies Quarterly* 8:1 (Winter):27–31.

Tocqueville, Alexis de (1966). *Democracy in America*, vol. 2. New York: Alfred A. Knopf. (Originally published in 1840).

Tulis, Jeffrey K. (1987). *The Rhetorical Presidency*. Princeton: Princeton University Press.

Vile, M.J.C. (1967). *Constitutionalism and the Separation of Powers*. Oxford: Clarendon Press.

Wahlke, John C. (1971). "Policy Demands and System Support: The Role of the Represented." *British Journal of Political Science* 1 (July):271–290.

Walker, Jack L. (1983). "The Origins and Maintenance of Interest Groups in America." *American Political Science Review* 77:2 (June):390–406

Warren, Charles (1937). *The Making of the Constitution*. Boston: Little, Brown.

Wayne, Stephen J. (1977). "Running the White House: The Ford Experience." *Presidential Studies Quarterly* 7:2-3 (Spring/Summer):95–100.

———— (1978). *The Legislative Presidency*. New York: Harper and Row.

———— (1982a). "Congressional Liaison in the Reagan White House: A Preliminary Assessment of the First Year." In Norman J. Ornstein, ed. *President and Congress: Assessing Reagan's First Year*. Washington, D.C.: American Enterprise Institute.

———— (1982b). "Great Expectations: What People Want from Presidents." In Thomas E. Cronin, ed. *Rethinking the Presidency*. Boston: Little, Brown.

_____ (1984). "Comments: Politics Instead of Policy." In Lester M. Salamon and Michael S. Lund. *The Reagan Presidency and the Governing of America.* Washington, D.C.: The Urban Institute Press.

Weaver, R. Kent (1988). *Automatic Government: The Politics of Indexation.* Washington, D.C.: The Brookings Institution.

White, Leonard D. (1948). *The Federalists: A Study in Administrative History, 1789–1801.* New York: The Free Press.

Wilson, Woodrow (1908). *Constitutional Government: A Study in American Politics.* Houghton Mifflin.

_____ (1956). *Congressional Government.* Cleveland: World Publishing. (Originally published in 1885).

Wood, Gordon (1969). *The Creation of the American Republic, 1776–1787.* Chapel Hill: University of North Carolina Press.

Young, James Sterling (1966). *The Washington Community: 1800–1828.* New York: Harcourt Brace.

Index